WORLD WAR II
IN SECRET

WORLD WAR II IN SECRET
By Gavin Mortimer

First published in North America in 2015 by Zenith Press, an imprint of
Quarto Publishing Group USA Inc, 400 First Avenue North, Suite 400,
Minneapolis, MN 55401 USA, by arrangement with Quid Publishing
© Quid Publishing 2015

Zenith Press titles are also available at discounts in bulk quantity for
industrial or sales-promotional use. For details write to Special Sales
Manager at Quarto Publishing Group USA Inc., 400 First Avenue North,
Suite 400, Minneapolis, MN 55401 USA.

To find out more about our books, visit us online at www.zenithpress.com.

ISBN: 978-0-7603-4764-5

Set in Akzidenz Grotesk and New Century Schoolbook

Printed and bound in China

Conceived, designed and produced by
Quid Publishing
Level 4 Sheridan House
Hove BN3 1DD
England

Design and illustration: Simon Daley

WORLD WAR II IN SECRET

The Hidden Conflict 1939 to 1945

Gavin Mortimer

ZENITH
PRESS

CONTENTS

◀ A patrol of the Special Air Service pose with some joyous French people in the late summer of 1944 shortly after the British had liberated their village from four years of Nazi Occupation.

TIMELINE

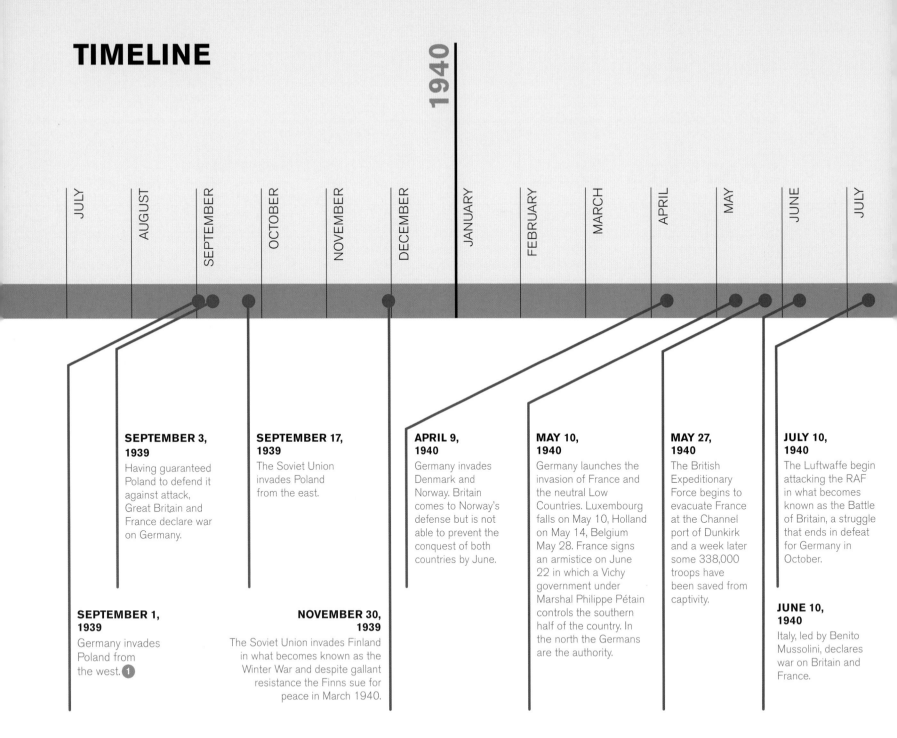

1940

JULY · AUGUST · SEPTEMBER · OCTOBER · NOVEMBER · DECEMBER · JANUARY · FEBRUARY · MARCH · APRIL · MAY · JUNE · JULY

SEPTEMBER 3, 1939

Having guaranteed Poland to defend it against attack, Great Britain and France declare war on Germany.

SEPTEMBER 17, 1939

The Soviet Union invades Poland from the east.

APRIL 9, 1940

Germany invades Denmark and Norway. Britain comes to Norway's defense but is not able to prevent the conquest of both countries by June.

MAY 10, 1940

Germany launches the invasion of France and the neutral Low Countries. Luxembourg falls on May 10, Holland on May 14, Belgium May 28. France signs an armistice on June 22 in which a Vichy government under Marshal Philippe Pétain controls the southern half of the country. In the north the Germans are the authority.

MAY 27, 1940

The British Expeditionary Force begins to evacuate France at the Channel port of Dunkirk and a week later some 338,000 troops have been saved from captivity.

JULY 10, 1940

The Luftwaffe begin attacking the RAF in what becomes known as the Battle of Britain, a struggle that ends in defeat for Germany in October.

SEPTEMBER 1, 1939

Germany invades Poland from the west. ①

NOVEMBER 30, 1939

The Soviet Union invades Finland in what becomes known as the Winter War and despite gallant resistance the Finns sue for peace in March 1940.

JUNE 10, 1940

Italy, led by Benito Mussolini, declares war on Britain and France.

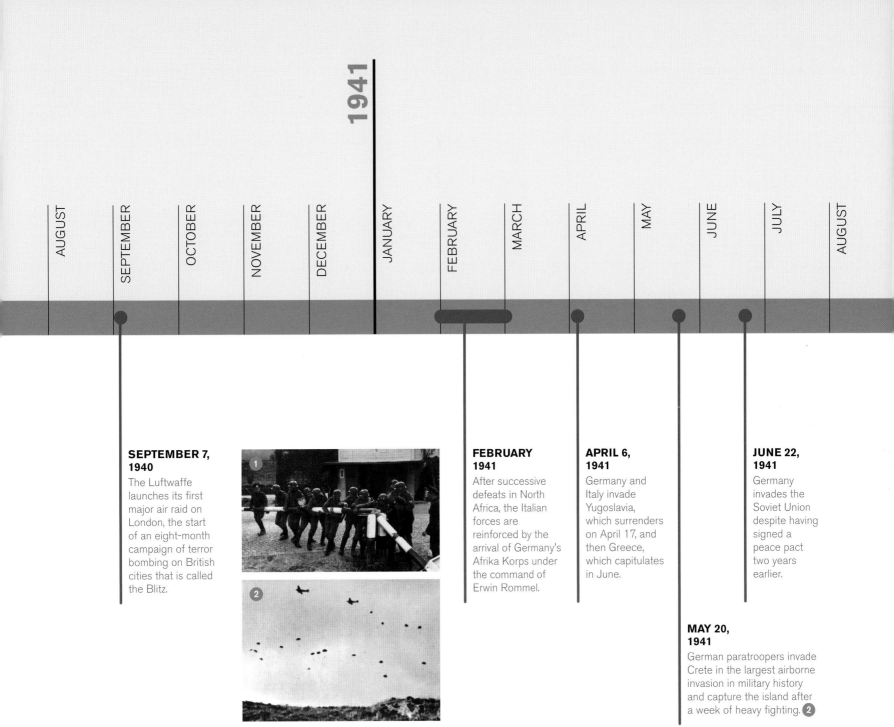

1941

AUGUST

SEPTEMBER

OCTOBER

NOVEMBER

DECEMBER

JANUARY

FEBRUARY

MARCH

APRIL

MAY

JUNE

JULY

AUGUST

SEPTEMBER 7, 1940
The Luftwaffe launches its first major air raid on London, the start of an eight-month campaign of terror bombing on British cities that is called the Blitz.

FEBRUARY 1941
After successive defeats in North Africa, the Italian forces are reinforced by the arrival of Germany's Afrika Korps under the command of Erwin Rommel.

APRIL 6, 1941
Germany and Italy invade Yugoslavia, which surrenders on April 17, and then Greece, which capitulates in June.

JUNE 22, 1941
Germany invades the Soviet Union despite having signed a peace pact two years earlier.

MAY 20, 1941
German paratroopers invade Crete in the largest airborne invasion in military history and capture the island after a week of heavy fighting.

SEPTEMBER

OCTOBER

NOVEMBER

DECEMBER

1942

JANUARY

FEBRUARY

MARCH

APRIL

MAY

JUNE

JULY

AUGUST

SEPTEMBER

**DECEMBER 8,
1941**
The United States
and Britain declare
war on Japan
on the same day
Japanese troops
begin an invasion
of south-east Asia.

**DECEMBER 11,
1941**
Germany and Italy
declare war on the
United States.

**JUNE
1942**
The US defeats
the Japanese
navy at the
Battle of Midway. **4**

**DECEMBER 7,
1941**
Japan launches a surprise
attack on the US Pacific Fleet
at Pearl Harbor in Hawaii. **3**

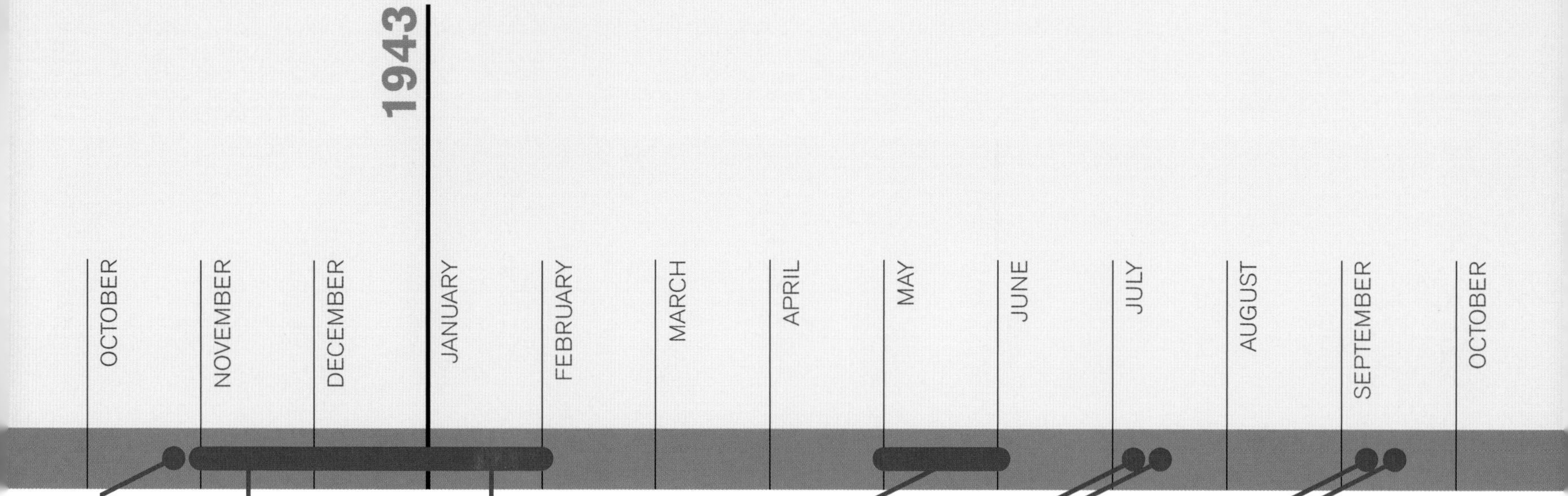

1943

OCTOBER | NOVEMBER | DECEMBER | JANUARY | FEBRUARY | MARCH | APRIL | MAY | JUNE | JULY | AUGUST | SEPTEMBER | OCTOBER

NOVEMBER 8, 1942

American and British forces invade Algeria and Morocco in French North Africa against Vichy French forces, who offer little resistance.

NOVEMBER 1942 TO FEBRUARY 1943

A Soviet counter-offensive traps the remnants of the German Sixth Army in the city of Stalingrad.

MAY 1943

Axis forces in Tunisia surrender to the Allies, marking the end of the war in North Africa.

JULY 10, 1943

US and British troops begin the invasion of Sicily and within a month the island has fallen.

SEPTEMBER 8, 1943

The Italian government surrenders unconditionally to the Allies, and Germany responds by seizing control of Rome and northern Italy, establishing a puppet fascist regime under Mussolini, who is sprung from captivity by German commandos on September 12.

OCTOBER 23, 1942

The British Eighth Army launches an offensive at El Alamein in North Africa.

JULY 5, 1943

The biggest tank battle in history begins near Kursk in the Soviet Union and ends with defeat for Germany.

SEPTEMBER 3, 1943

The Allies launch the invasion of Italy six weeks after Pietro Badoglio replaced Benito Mussolini as leader.

1944

NOVEMBER

DECEMBER

JANUARY

FEBRUARY

MARCH

APRIL

MAY

JUNE

JULY

AUGUST

SEPTEMBER

OCTOBER

NOVEMBER

JUNE 6, 1944
British, Canadian, and American troops land on five Normandy beaches as the invasion of France begins with Operation Overlord.

JUNE 13, 1944
The first V-1 flying rocket is launched at London.

JUNE 22, 1944
Soviet troops launch a massive offensive in Belarus and drive the Germans east across the Vistula River into central Poland.

AUGUST 25, 1944
Having broken out of the Normandy beachhead, the Allies liberate Paris with the help of Free French forces. **5**

1945

DECEMBER | JANUARY | FEBRUARY | MARCH | APRIL | MAY | JUNE | JULY | AUGUST | SEPTEMBER | OCTOBER | NOVEMBER | DECEMBER

MARCH 24, 1945
Some 16,000 British and American airborne troops drop onto the eastern bank of the Rhine in the biggest single airborne operation in history, known as Operation Varsity.

APRIL 30, 1945
Hitler commits suicide in his Berlin bunker.

AUGUST 6, 1945
The United States drops an atomic bomb on the southern Japanese city of Hiroshima. 6

AUGUST 9, 1945
The United States drops an atomic bomb on the city of Nagasaki on the island of Kyushu in Japan.

AUGUST 15, 1945
Emperor Hirohito orders the surrender of Japanese forces and World War II is over.

DECEMBER 1944
The Germans launch a final desperate counterattack in the Ardennes in what becomes known as the Battle of the Bulge and are eventually repulsed by the Americans.

APRIL 16, 1945
The Soviet army launch their final offensive and encircle Berlin.

MAY 7, 1945
Admiral Karl Dönitz signs the Germans surrender and the war in Europe officially ends the following day in what is known as VE (Victory in Europe) Day.

AUGUST 8, 1945
The Soviet Union declares war on Japan.

INTRODUCTION

One of the ironies of war is that history has shown over and over that the victor is often not the one who has the biggest army or the most powerful weapons or the fastest ships but the one who fights with most intelligence. Brain is a more potent weapon in war than brawn, as the Greeks demonstrated in around 1200 BC when they gained entry to the city of Troy, hidden inside a giant wooden horse. As Homer wrote in his *Odyssey*:

"What a thing was this, too, which that mighty man wrought and endured in the carven horse, wherein all we chiefs of the Argives were sitting, bearing to the Trojans death and fate!

"But come now, change thy theme, and sing of the building of the horse of wood, which Epeius made with Athena's help, the horse which once Odysseus led up into the citadel as a thing of guile, when he had filled it with the men who sacked Ilion."

The "guile" of which Homer talked has proved critical in wars ever since, developing in line with technology and evolving as wars have also evolved. In the Middle Ages this guile came to be known as "espionage," from the French word meaning to spy. One of the greatest spies was Francis Walsingham, the spymaster of Queen Elizabeth I in the late 16th century, whose job it was to protect his sovereign from Catholics wishing to overthrow Protestant England. This he did through an elaborate spy network that ranged across Europe. Walsingham was also one of the earliest codebreakers, deciphering the secret messages used by plotters in the letters they wrote to one another.

Subterfuge has always been a vital part of warfare, going back to ancient times when the Greek army sought a way to break their ten-year siege of the city of Troy. Leaving the horse outside the city gates, the Greeks pretended to sail away, to the delight of the Trojans, who believed it was a gift for having endured the siege. But once the horse was brought inside the city, out climbed several Greek soldiers, who then opened the gates for their returning comrades.

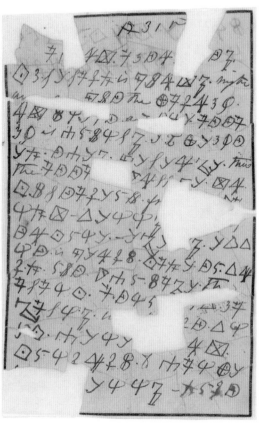

Espionage continued to play a key role in warfare over the next 300 years, growing more sophisticated with the dawning of the Industrial Revolution. The American Civil War of 1861 to 1865 was more advanced than any conflict that had gone before, featuring as it did photography, heavy artillery, aerial warfare (hot-air balloons used for reconnaissance), the rapid-fire Gatling gun, and "ironclad" ships. Espionage also became more erudite. One of the most famous Confederate spies was the beautiful Rose Greenhow, a society woman trained by the Rebels to use cipher. In the summer of 1861 she smuggled a coded message out of Washington DC to the Confederate camp at Manassas Junction, 30 miles (48km) south of the capital, concealed in the chignon hair of 16-year-old Bettie Duval, one of Greenhow's maids. Decoded, the message read: "McDowell has certainly been ordered to advance on the sixteenth. ROG." It was confirmation that Brigadier General Irvin McDowell planned to lead his Union troops south in one week's time. When the offensive was launched and the two armies clashed at Bull Run, the first major battle of the war, it was the Confederates who triumphed.

The North's spy network was controlled by a Scot, Allan Pinkerton, a private detective before the war, who had among his operatives a Welshman called Pryce Lewis. In June 1861 he obtained invaluable intelligence on Confederate intentions in West Virginia by virtue of pretending to be a sympathetic English aristocrat (Britain was officially neutral in the war but many sided intellectually with the South). Traveling in a vehicle, dressed in the finest London-made clothes, and with a trunk full of port, Lewis wined and dined a succession of high-ranking southern officers, loosening their tongues with alcohol and reporting back to Washington.

The clichéd view of World War I is one of two great armies facing each other over a few hundred yards of no-man's land but that is to belie the many ingenious ruses deployed by all combatants in an attempt to gain the smallest of advantages in the first truly global conflict.

In February 1915 France established its *section de camouflage*, a unit of professional artists and painters whose job was to disguise gun batteries from the view of German aircraft. Germany and Britain followed suit, and all three combatants also excelled in digging secret tunnels under the battlefield. The most famous was the one that was used by the British to detonate mines on the Messines Ridge in June 1917, resulting in the death of thousands of German soldiers.

There were other equally terrible secret weapons introduced on the Western Front. In 1915 the Germans and French used poison gas and the following year the British gave warfare the tank. Naval warfare also saw some extraordinary innovations during World War I,

notably the British Q Ships, merchant weapons to the periscopes of German U-boat commanders but which behind the innocent façade concealed a vast array of firepower. The Royal Navy also formed a "dazzle section," a camouflage unit who by painting vessels with the "razzle-dazzle" of vivid stripes, curves, and zigzags broke up the outline of the ship's hull and made it harder to detect on the ocean.

Though World War I is best remembered for its wanton slaughter, many hundreds of thousands men survived and many junior officers of 1914–1918—such as Winston Churchill, Erwin Rommel, George Patton, and Bernard Montgomery—were in positions of power when the world erupted in conflict a quarter of a century later. Not only had they seen the efficacy of battlefield deception, but the huge advancements in technology, particularly communications and air power, opened up myriad new opportunities for clandestine warfare. In 1939 the world was about to witness the first real Secret War.

▲ World War I also threw up secret innovations at sea. The Royal Navy formed a "dazzle section" in which vessels were painted with the "razzle-dazzle" of vivid stripes, curves, and zigzags. These broke up the outline of the ship's hull and made it harder to detect on the ocean. The ship in this photo is the minelayer, HMS *London*, seen here in 1918.

The traditional image of World War I was of murderous trench warfare and little military strategy but in fact there was much ingenuity displayed in the "secret war." As well as camouflage units composed of professional artists and painters, snipers sometimes carried out their deadly work from fake tree stumps, while others burrowed under the ground and laid mines.

THE AXIS ATTACKS

Even before war erupted in September 1939 Germany was secretly plotting its conquest of Europe by removing the threat of Russia with the Molotov–Ribbentrop Pact. With Stalin, Hitler planned to carve up Eastern Europe before turning his rage on the west. The invasion of the Low Countries and France involved the first use of airborne troops in warfare, an innovation that helped the German war machine overrun western Europe in a matter of weeks. By the summer of 1940 Hitler had only the British to beat, but they proved to be an implacable enemy who would engage in secret wars with Germany at sea, in the air and on the ground in the months and years that followed.

SECRET PACTS AND POOR POLAND

In 1938 the German chancellor, Adolf Hitler, demanded "changes in Europe," changes that would of course be to the betterment of the Third Reich. Having already altered the map of Europe by marching German troops into Austria in March and declaring an *Anschluss* (connection), Hitler turned his attention next to Czechoslovakia. Britain and France had initially vowed to defend Czechoslovakia from Nazi annexation though the two powers rebuffed an offer of help from the Soviet Union, whose leader, Josef Stalin, felt threatened by Hitler's aggressive ambition.

In September 1938 the Soviet Union was excluded from the Munich conference at which the future of Czechoslovakia was discussed by Europe's major western powers. The outcome, what was known as the "Munich Agreement," ceded to Germany the Sudetenland, the areas in the northern, southwest, and western areas of Czechoslovakia populated predominantly by German speakers.

British Prime Minister Neville Chamberlain returned home a hero to most, confidently declaring he had secured "Peace in Our Time," although a minority —including Conservative MP Winston Churchill— accused Chamberlain of appeasing the Nazi leader, saying: "You were given the choice between war and dishonor. You chose dishonor, and you will have war."

Less than six months after the Munich Agreement, Hitler broke his promises by invading the rest of Czechoslovakia, German troops entering the capital Prague on March 15, 1939. Humiliated by Hitler's action, Chamberlain abandoned his policy of appeasement and on March 29 sent a message to Poland, guaranteeing British support against "any action which threatened Polish independence, and which the Polish Government accordingly considered it vital to resist."

It was a rash commitment by Chamberlain, a challenge to Hitler, who felt emboldened, having already exposed the timidity of the British and French governments. It was particularly ill-judged in light of the snub to the Soviet Union the previous September as Britain was in no position to defend Poland if the Soviet Union didn't also lend its support.

Chamberlain viewed Stalin and communism with distaste (a result of the widescale Purges in the 1930s that caused the executions of thousands of people seen by Stalin as potential opponents) and his approaches to the Soviet Union were weak and ineffectual.

Not so Hitler. Though he too harbored a vehement dislike for what he termed Bolshevism, he decided to seek an agreement with Stalin so he could achieve his objective of occupying Poland.

The first tentative advances were well-received by the Soviet leader, still bitter at his treatment by Chamberlain at the Munich Conference and a man who consequently distrusted Britain.

On May 3, 1939 Stalin replaced Maxim Litvinov as his foreign commissar with Vyacheslav Molotov, a man who preferred "dealing with dictators to dealing with liberal democracies." Germany, meanwhile, sensing Britain's reluctance to engage with the Soviet Union, exploited the situation by dispatching Joachim von Ribbentrop, Hitler's foreign minister, to Moscow in late August to discuss the conditions for a pact between the two countries.

Though Ribbentrop's trip to Russia was no secret, much of what was agreed in Moscow was as Germany and the Soviet Union signed the nonaggression pact, better known as the Molotov–Ribbentrop Treaty, on August 23. When the text of the Treaty was promulgated it was couched in the anodyne language of diplomacy, the two nations agreeing to "desist from any act of violence, any aggressive action, and any attack on each other, either individually or jointly with other Powers." Article II of the Treaty stated that should either Germany or the Soviet Union be attacked by a third Power, "the other High Contracting Party shall in no manner lend its support to this third Power."

Nazi leader Adolf Hitler, seen here inspecting the ranks of the Hitler Youth at the Nuremberg Rally in 1935, outmaneuvered the western powers by negotiating a secret pact with the Soviet Union in the summer of 1939.

What wasn't published, however, was the "Secret Additional Protocol," which comprised four articles:

Article I. *In the event of a territorial and political rearrangement in the areas belonging to the Baltic States (Finland, Estonia, Latvia, Lithuania), the northern boundary of Lithuania shall represent the boundary of the spheres of influence of Germany and U.S.S.R. In this connection the interest of Lithuania in the Vilna area is recognized by each party.*

Article II. *In the event of a territorial and political rearrangement of the areas belonging to the Polish state, the spheres of influence of Germany and the U.S.S.R. shall be bounded approximately by the line of the rivers Narev, Vistula, and San.*

Article III. *With regard to Southeastern Europe attention is called by the Soviet side to its interest in Bessarabia. The German side declares its complete political disinterestedness in these areas.*

Article IV. *This protocol shall be treated by both parties as strictly secret.*

With the stroke of a pen, Molotov and Ribbentrop had eliminated Poland as a buffer between their two countries and in doing so sealed the country's fate. When Germany invaded Poland, the Soviet Union would turn the eastern portion into a barrier against which to guard against any possible German expansion in the coming years. To Stalin that seemed the wiser course of action than the existence of an independent Poland, and it would also allow him to expand his own empire by occupying the Baltic States of Estonia, Latvia, Lithuania, and Finland (he attacked on November 30, 1939). For Britain, France, and the rest of Western Europe the nonaggression pact presaged disaster, although owing to the four articles kept secret by Germany and the Soviet Union none of them knew it at the time.

WINSTON CHURCHILL ON POLAND

In his *History of the Second World War,* Winston Churchill described Britain's guarantee to defend Poland thus: "History, which, we are told, is mainly the record of the crimes, follies, and miseries of mankind, may be scoured and ransacked to find a parallel to this sudden and complete reversal of five or six years' policy of easygoing placatory appeasement, and its transformation almost overnight into a readiness to accept an obviously imminent war on far worse conditions and on the greatest scale."

Yet as the preeminent historian Basil Liddell Hart pointed out in his own history of the conflict, Churchill was writing with the benefit of hindsight. In fact, in the spring of 1939 he had supported the guarantee given to Poland, telling Chamberlain he was in "complete agreement." The only notable dissenter was the former Prime Minister David Lloyd-George, who warned against the impracticability of such a guarantee. Like all lone voices who shout in the face of popular opinion, he was ridiculed for his stance, *The Times of London* writing that it was an "outburst of inconsolable pessimism from Mr Lloyd George who now seems to inhabit an odd and remote world of his own."

The first nation after Poland to suffer as a consequence of the nonaggression pact was Finland. In November 1939 they were attacked by Soviet forces in what Stalin believed would be a short war. Not only was the Finnish army tiny compared to Russia's, but for years the Soviets had been running a secret surveillance network in the country. The Finnish communist party had provided their Soviet counterparts with detailed intelligence on Finland's armed forces as well as information on defensive fortifications, notably the Mannerheim Line, the defensive line constructed on the Karelian Isthmus by Finland in the interwar years. Such was the extent of Soviet intelligence on the Mannerheim Line, and other defensive positions in Finland, that in 1938 the Soviet secret service published a secret book containing maps, photographs and descriptions of all the fortifications. Then, following the Molotov–Ribbentrop Pact, a German military attaché in Helsinki handed to the Russians in September 1939 a detailed map of the defenses situated on the Karelian Isthmus.

Yet despite all this secret intelligence the Soviets were initially repulsed by the Finns when they launched their invasion at the end of November 1939. Outnumbering their enemy three to one (with as many as 30 times the number of aircraft), the Soviet troops suffered from a lack of decisive leadership, a result of all the experienced officers executed on Stalin's orders during the Purges of the 1930s. Eventually, in March 1940, the Soviets' overwhelming superiority proved decisive and the "Winter War" ended with the subjugation of Finland. But the months of tough fighting had been a painful reality check for Stalin and the Soviet High Command; the campaign had also been a revelation for Hitler, who no longer regarded the Red Army with such apprehension.

Soviet leader Josef Stalin ordered his forces to invade Finland in November 1939. He believed it would be a short war because his intelligence services had been running a secret surveillance network in Finland for years. But the ferocity of the Finnish resistance shook the Soviet ground troops.

BLITZKRIEG

On the first day of September 1939, less than six months after Neville Chamberlain had sent Poland his guarantee, German troops invaded the country, the act of aggression that led to the outbreak of World War II. Despite brave Polish resistance their armed forces were hopelessly ill equipped to resist the Nazi war machine. On September 17, Soviet troops invaded Poland from the east and two days later German and Soviet soldiers met near Brest Litovsk.

There then followed what came to be known as the "Phony War," a six-month hiatus in which there was no land fighting in Western Europe, although a British Expeditionary Force numbering more than 150,000 soldiers was shipped to France. The calm ended in April 1940 when German forces invaded Norway and Denmark, quickly overrunning the two Scandinavian countries.

Now Holland, Belgium and France braced themselves for an attack, as did Britain, whose Expeditionary Force had been deployed along the French–Belgian border for months in readiness for the German invasion. Between them the Allies had the equivalent of 156 divisions and more than 4,000 tanks, greater numbers than their enemy, whose numerical advantage lay only in aircraft.

It was this inferiority that, in the winter of 1939–40, prompted the German High Command to secretly alter its plans for an invasion of the Low Countries. Originally, the Nazis intended to concentrate the bulk of their attack on the right wing, with Army Group B driving through the plains of Belgium to the Somme river in France, a similar route to that taken by German troops in 1914. Hitler—a veteran of World War I—already

Despite the rapid advance of the German forces through the Low Countries, there were some pockets of resistance. Here a Nazi tank is held up at a bridge destroyed by the Belgians on June 11, 1940.

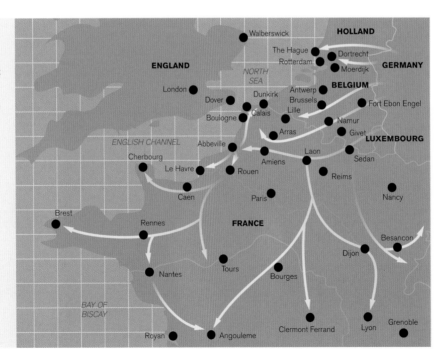

INVASION OF THE LOW COUNTRIES, 1940

The six months after the outbreak of war in September 1939 were known as the Phony War. Then the Germans shattered the peace with the invasion of Denmark and Norway in April 1940. The following month the Nazi war machine swept west across the Low Countries, conquering Holland, Belgium, and France in a matter of weeks.

Walberswick
HOLLAND
The Hague
Dortrecht
Rotterdam
Moerdijk
GERMANY
ENGLAND
NORTH SEA
London
Antwerp
BELGIUM
Dunkirk
Brussels
Dover
Fort Ebon Engel
Calais
Lille
Boulogne
Namur
Arras
Givet
LUXEMBOURG
ENGLISH CHANNEL
Abbeville
Laon
Sedan
Cherbourg
Amiens
Le Havre
Rouen
Reims
Caen
Paris
Nancy
Brest
Rennes
FRANCE
Besancon
Dijon
Tours
Nantes
Bourges
BAY OF BISCAY
Clermont Ferrand
Lyon
Grenoble
Royan
Angouleme

harbored reservations about the strategy and these deepened when, on January 10, 1940, the plans of this offensive fell into Belgium hands after a German aircraft crash-landed near Vucht.

Now Hitler had no doubt that the best course of action was to adopt the invasion plan formulated by General Erich von Manstein, chief of staff of Army Group A, the previous October. This called for a thrust through the countryside of the Ardennes in Belgian Luxembourg, a move that would be both audacious and unexpected, and spearheaded by seven armored divisions under the command of General Heinz Guderian.

Guderian was a military visionary, a dynamic tank commander whose intention was not only to smash through the Low Countries but then advance through France all the way to the English Channel "to cut the main arteries of the opposing army far behind its front."

But Guderian and his armored divisions would only be able to advance with lightning speed across the Low Countries if the bridges over the Meuse and the Albert Canal were not destroyed by the Belgians, allowing them time to withdraw and extend their defensive line that began at Fort Eben-Emael all the way to the coast, as they did a quarter of a century earlier.

It was imperative, therefore, to capture Fort Eben in an operation of clinical precision before the Belgians had time to blow up the bridges. Hitler summoned General Kurt Student, Commander of 7 Fliger Division, to Berlin in late October 1939 and told him, "I have a job for you and I want to know if you can do it." The Nazi leader then explained what he wanted, the capture of the fort by a small force of airborne troops. "The top is like a grassy meadow," explained Hitler. "They have heavy artillery in cupolas and casemates. I think some of our silent gliders could land on top of the fort and your men storm the works. Is that possible?"

Student was skeptical, and rightly so. The fort had been built in the early 1930s and was half a mile (800m) from north to south with its revolving gun emplacements positioned in such a way that each provided covering fire for the other in the event of an assault. Its sheer walls were over 130ft (40m) high and impossible to scale, while the fort also boasted a man-made ditch, an elaborate trench system, and a series of outer walls. Approximately 1,200 soldiers lived inside the fort and were able to move around through the series of sophisticated tunnels with a filtered ventilation system that was immune to a gas attack.

Despite his skepticism Student said an assault might indeed be possible. A daylight—or at the very worst, a twilight—operation might pull it off but what worried him most was "the amount and type of explosives needed to be used against the fortifications."

Here, Hitler let Student into a secret: a team of munitions experts had invented a new explosive charge, called the "Hohlladung" (Hollow Charge), powerful enough to blow a hole in any fortification, be it constructed of steel or concrete. Its only drawback was that its power came from its 110lb (50kg) weight and was too big for the barrel of an artillery gun. Rather it had to be exploded by a demolition team.

The disclosure of the new explosive put a new complexion on the operation and Student was now imbued with confidence. In that case, remarked Hitler: "I order you to take Fort Eben-Emael. All aspects of the operation must remain absolutely secret. The code name for this operation will be GRANIT [Granite]."

HOLLOW CHARGE BOMB

The Germans' secret weapon during the capture of Fort Eben-Emael was the Hollow Charge or "Hohlladung" (below). Weighing 110lb (50kg), it was powerful enough to blow a hole in steel and concrete fortifications but required a specially trained demolition team to prime. The charge successfully destroyed the fort's 14 guns during an operation that cost the lives of only six German soldiers.

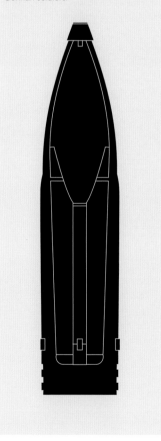

Student selected his GRANIT force from the Engineer Detachment of his airborne division, under the command of Lieutenant Rudolf Witzig. Over the winter of 1939–40 the force trained in the utmost secrecy in the Rhineland on a plateau similar to the one they would encounter at Eben-Emael, even on occasion concealing their gliders in furniture vans for fear the enemy might get wind of their intention. The men selected for the operation weren't allowed leave or to write to their families and anyone found discussing their training with outsiders was liable to be court-martialled.

When the attack was launched in the early morning of May 10, 1940, all 85 soldiers knew exactly their role in the assault. The nine gliders (one was shot down and the other aborted because of a tow-rope problem—in which was Witzig) were released 12 miles (19km) from the fort at a height of 650ft (2,000m) while at the same time a number of dummy gliders were released to confuse the Belgian defenders. They landed right on top of the fort at 0525 hours, five minutes before the start of the main invasion, having achieved the surprise they'd intended. Now the demolitions teams set about laying the hollow charges in the 14 gun positions, relying not just on their secret weapon but also on smaller, more conventional charges placed near the barrels of the guns.

Having disabled the guns GRANIT force next attacked the fort itself, using the hollow charges to destroy the blast doors so they could gain entry to the complex tunnel system. Scores of Belgians panicked and fled, others were captured, and though there were attempts to retake the fort the counterattacks were unsuccessful and a day later the German ground forces arrived. The impregnable Fort Eben-Emael had proved to be anything but and the Germans had pulled off a stunning surprise attack for the loss of just six men.

As a result of the elimination of Fort Eben-Emael, and the capture by airborne troops of other key defensive points in Belgium and Holland, the Allies believed that the Germans' main attack was being directed solely through the right flank as originally intended. But then on May 13, Guderian's three panzer corps crossed the Meuse at Sedan, beyond the western limits of another defensive fortification believed to be inviolate—the Maginot Line.

In fact it wasn't so much their faith in the Maginot Line that proved fatal to the French, more their belief that the main German attack would follow a similar pattern to that of 1914. Consequently they pushed too far into Belgium, leaving themselves exposed further south through the supposedly impenetrable terrain of the Ardennes. They had also failed to appreciate the belligerent brilliance of Guderian, who was in the van of the panzer thrust on May 13 over a narrow one and a half mile (2.4km) stretch of the Meuse. So successful was the attack that Hitler ordered Guderian to halt for two days to allow time for the infantry to catch up and provide cover on the panzers' flank along the Aisne.

Within three weeks of the invasion of the Low Countries, the British Expeditionary Force was forced into a humiliating retreat across the Channel from Dunkirk, while Holland, Belgium, and France all surrendered. The conquest of continental Western Europe was complete thanks to the top-secret operation of the GRANIT Force, and the surprise thrust of Guderian. Though the two complemented one another it was the latter that proved conclusive. "The Battle of France is one of history's most striking examples of the decisive effect of a new idea, carried out by a dynamic executant," he wrote in *The History of the Second World War*. "The effect proved as decisive as other new ideas had been in earlier history—the use of the horse, the long spear, the phalanx, the flexible legion, the 'oblique order', the horse archer, the longbow, the musket, the gun, the organization of armies in separate and maneuvrable divisions. Indeed, it proved more immediately decisive."

LIEUTENANT RUDOLF WITZIG

Lieutenant Rudolf Witzig's glider landed in a meadow east of the Rhine, whereupon he flagged down a passing car within minutes and hitched a lift back to Cologne-Ostheim airfield. Commandeering a Junkers 52, Witzig guided the pilot to the downed glider where it was hooked up and took off towards the target. At 0830 hours the glider swooped down close to the paratroopers' command post and Witzig emerged to resume command of the operation. He was subsequently promoted and awarded the Knight's Cross of the Iron Cross, Nazi Germany's highest honor for bravery on the battlefield. The citation described how: "The fort was already rendered defenseless and the garrison pinned down on May 10 by a specially selected unit of the Luftwaffe under the leadership of Oberleutnant Witzig and deploying new combat means. The garrison dropped their arms when an attacking unit of the Army, after heavy combat, established contact with the detachment Witzig." Witzig took part in the invasion of Crete the following year and was wounded, though he recovered to assume command of the 18th Parachute Regiment. He died in 2001.

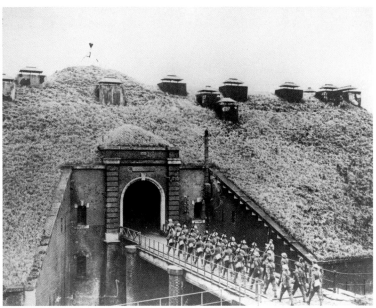

THE MAGINOT LINE

Contrary to popular belief the Maginot Line was not a continuous line of forts running the length of France's border with Germany. In some areas there was no need for artificial defenses because of natural barriers such as the River Rhine. But where the terrain was flatter and more open to attack from the east, the French constructed 50 large forts ("ouvrages" in French), each one approximately 9 miles (15km) apart. Smaller defensive outposts were built between the forts, consisting of anything from 200 to 500 soldiers. The big forts contained as many as 1,000 men and were protected by reinforced steel that the French believed impregnable.

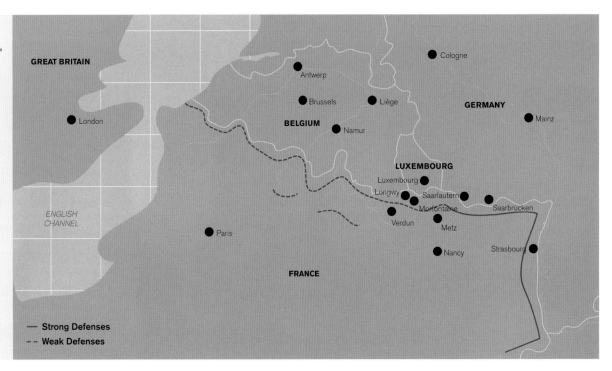

GREAT BRITAIN

London

ENGLISH CHANNEL

Antwerp

Brussels

Liège

Namur

BELGIUM

Cologne

GERMANY

Mainz

LUXEMBOURG

Luxembourg

Longwy

Saarlautern

Montfontaine

Saarbrücken

Verdun

Metz

Paris

Nancy

Strasbourg

FRANCE

— Strong Defenses

-- Weak Defenses

GREAT BRITAIN'S GUERRILLA FIGHTERS

With Poland, Norway, Denmark, the Low Countries, and France all under the Nazi jackboot by the end of June 1940, Great Britain knew that it was inevitable that Adolf Hitler would look to extend his domination of Europe by sending a large-scale invasion force over the Channel. Although 338,000 British and Allied troops had been evacuated from the beaches of Dunkirk in late May and early June, tens of thousands of weapons, vehicles and nearly all Britain's 450 tanks had been lost. Prime Minister Winston Churchill was aware that the country was ill-prepared to repel an invasion. In fact Hitler was initially against invading Britain, believing he could persuade their government to accept his peace terms, but when it became apparent Churchill would not enter into negotiations, the Nazi leader ordered his chiefs of staff on July 2, 1940 to start formulating an invasion plan, codenamed Operation Sealion. On the same day Churchill and his War Cabinet agreed that: "The regular defenses require supplementing with guerrilla-type troops, who will allow themselves to be overrun and who thereafter will be responsible for hitting the enemy in the comparatively soft spots behind zones of concentrated attack."

By deploying guerrilla troops Churchill had in mind the tactics of the South African Boers during their war with Britain at the turn of the century. So effective had these small number of commandos been in launching hit and run raids against the far bigger and better armed British army—and then melting into the veldt—that the British resorted to setting up concentration camps, in which they detained the men's families, in an attempt to flush out their enemy.

The War Cabinet had studied the ease with which the Nazis had swept across Europe and believed they had spotted a chink in the armor. The German armored corps had thrust rapidly through enemy territory with their supply lines unimpaired despite the speed of their advance. The British, acknowledging that they had not the resources to resist a large-scale landing on the coast, planned to attack their enemy from behind, using pockets of saboteurs to blow up bridges, mine roads, and attack supply convoys, seriously slowing up any German advance across Britain.

Colonel Colin Gubbins was the man selected to lead the guerrilla force. A veteran of World War I, Gubbins had experience of guerrilla warfare from time spent in Russia in 1919/20 when the Bolsheviks were fighting Tsarist White Russian forces, and also in Ireland in the 1920s, as the Irish Republican Army stepped up its armed struggle against British rule in the north of the country. Gubbins had actually been in Warsaw in September 1939 when the Nazis invaded Poland and he spent several months working with Polish and Czech underground networks.

Back in Britain in the spring of 1940, Gubbins was put in charge of the Independent Companies, the forerunners of the commandos, and led them to Norway where they unsuccessfully tried to beat back the German invasion. That failure hadn't dampened his enthusiasm for taking on the might of the German army when he was appointed commander of the guerrilla force that was to be called the Auxiliary Units. "It was decided to call this secret army Auxiliary Units —a name which seemed harmless and meaningless—in order to keep secret the true nature of our intended work," recalled Gubbins. "These underground forces must have some general title for daily military purposes but it must be such as to give no indication whatever of their role and of such uninteresting and general nature as to excite no interest."

AUXILIARY WEAPONRY

In formulating the role of the Auxiliary Units, Gubbins wrote in July 1940 that their primary role would be to "harry and embarrass the enemy by all means in their power from the first day he lands, their particular targets being tanks and lorries in lager, ammunition dumps, HQs, small straggling parties and posts etc." To this end the recruits were trained rigorously at Coleshill, learning how to fire machine guns, rifles, and revolvers, as well as being schooled in the use of commando knives, knuckledusters, rubber truncheons, and clubs called knobkerries that were designed to silently eliminate sentries. The Auxiliary Units were also taught how to use explosives, conventional and otherwise. Major Nigel Oxenden, a cousin of Colin Gubbins, who was one of the Unit's training officers recalled that they were "… assisted by introductions to one or two men who had already been chosen by MI5 and equipped with bottles of sulphuric acid and little capsules of potassium chlorate and sugar, with which to make a crude and unreliable delay incendiary out of a bottle of petrol."

Winston Churchill was a war correspondent during the South African War of 1899–1902 and was impressed with what he saw and heard of the Boer irregulars who called themselves "Kommandos." They would provide the inspiration for the British special forces forty years later. Here a group of Kommandos pose with a Krupp Howitzer gun, circa 1900.

Gubbins was informed that "the highest possible degree of secrecy must be maintained" when recruiting men to his Auxiliary Units, a formidable challenge as he was allowed only six weeks to raise his force, the time the British government believed the Nazis needed to prepare an invasion fleet.

Dividing the country into 20 sectors, Gubbins allotted to each an underground headquarters of two officers and 10 regular soldiers. The officers and men who formed the "combat units" were recruited primarily from the defunct Independent Companies, soldiers already conversant with guerrilla warfare. "Then I set out to establish around the sectors cells of suitable civilians who knew the country well," recalled Gubbins. He called these cells Operational Patrols and found hundreds of willing recruits from the ranks of the Home Guard, the volunteer defense force established in May 1940 that contained many veterans of World War I who didn't require much in the way of a refresher course to recall their time in the army a quarter of a century earlier. In total approximately 3,500 men were recruited to the Operational Patrols (which varied in strength from four to eight men per patrol) from around the country, with particular emphasis in Kent and Sussex where it was believed the German invasion force would land.

Additionally Gubbins staffed his Operational Patrols with farmers, landowners or even poachers, men who, whichever side of the law they lived on, were skilled in moving stealthily through the countryside.

Gubbins also formed The Special Duties Branch, in effect the "eyes and ears" for the Operational Patrols, although to maintain the maximum secrecy neither section was aware of the other's existence. The Branch were civilians, men and women, young and old, who lived in the area and knew every back street and every short cut. Numbering an estimated 4,000 in total, they were sent on weekend training courses where they were schooled in surveillance techniques, vehicle and

regiment identification and how to drop messages without arousing suspicion. There was also a signal section, the heart of the Auxiliary Units, which by means of radio would coordinate the sectors all across the country. The radio operators were female, members of the Auxiliary Territorial Service, known colloquially as "Secret Sweeties."

No matter into what branch of the Auxiliary Units they had been recruited, no one was allowed to mention their existence to outsiders, with each recruit signing the Official Secrets Act. Many of the Operational Patrols masqueraded as the Home Guard.

While the Operational Patrols were billeted in the stable block of Coleshill House in Wiltshire and while they trained with some of the latest weapons, Royal Engineers constructed underground more than 650 operational bases for patrols in the countryside. These were well concealed in woods with a camouflaged

▲ Appearances were deceptive at Coleshill House in Wiltshire in the southwest of England. The resplendent Coleshill House was home to the Auxiliary Units' Operational Patrols and it was here the recruits learned the arts of sabotage and hand-to-hand combat.

Major General Colin Gubbins during an investiture at Buckingham Palace in 1944 in which he was awarded the Order of St Michael and St George. Gubbins was a brilliant military innovator and the man responsible for forming the very secret Auxiliary Units in 1940.

entrance and an emergency escape exit, and inside was stockpiled enough food for a fortnight. It wasn't believed that the Auxiliary Units would survive much longer in their guerrilla war against the Germans.

By the end of July Gubbins reported to the War Cabinet on the progress of his force, stating: "These Auxiliary Units are equipped with special Molotov bombs, delay action fuses and plastic H.E., incendiary bombs and devices of various kinds from non-military stocks, as well as the rifle and grenade. Their task is to harry and embarrass the enemy by all means in their power from the first day he lands, their particular targets being tanks and lorries in larger ammunition dumps, headquarters, small straggling parties, and posts etc. Their object is, in cooperation with the regular forces, to prevent the invader establishing a secure foothold, and thus to facilitate his defeat."

August came and went but the Germans never appeared off the English coast. Instead the invasion was fought in the skies above southern England, ending in September with defeat for the German Luftwaffe in the Battle of Britain. Fall arrived and Hitler postponed Operation Sealion until the following spring, but by then the Nazi leader had cast his eyes east, to the invasion of Russia. Nonetheless the Auxiliary Units weren't stood down until the spring of

1944, and by then it was the Germans preparing to meet an invasion force in northern France. Ironically, when the Allies launched D-Day, scores of veterans from the Auxiliary Units were involved, many putting the skills they had learned four years earlier to good use in the Special Air Service (SAS). Parachuting deep behind enemy lines on SAS operations, these soldiers spent weeks living off the land in central France, attacking German convoys heading north to Normandy and blowing up railway lines.

It wasn't until April 1945, with the war in Europe all but won, that the British public learned of the Auxiliary Units. The *Times*, in an article headlined "BRITAIN'S SECRET 'UNDERGROUND' INVASION SPY FORCE STOOD DOWN," informed its astonished readers of the Auxiliary Units that nearly five years earlier had been trained for "a hazardous role which required both skill and courage." The *Times* added with glee that the unit's countryside hideouts were "so perfectly camouflaged that many people have walked over some of them without discovering their existence … [and] the movement was so secretly organized that even today many of its members do not know the identity of others."

An Auxiliary Patrol in Spetisbury, Dorset, circa 1940. Note the array of headgear worn by the men, including what appears to be a woolen deer stalker by the patrol leader (center, middle). He also seems to the only one among them who is armed, with a Tommy Gun.

THE BLITZ AND THE RADAR RACE

The British had been expecting the Blitz, what they called the "Knockout Blow," ever since the German air force laid waste to Guernica during the Spanish Civil War in 1937. As tens of thousands of volunteers flocked to join the part-time Air Raid Precaution (ARP), they were put to work digging trench shelters in parks, building brick street shelters and sandbagging important buildings. Flocks of barrage balloons were winched above London and 38 million gas masks were handed out, and when Britain declared war on Germany on September 3 the country was prepared for what was expected to be an immediate onslaught from the skies above.

But the Luftwaffe didn't show. Not in September or in October, or into the winter of 1939–40. To some civilians it became known as "the Bore War," to others "Sitzkrieg," but the most popular name given to this eerily quiet period was "The Phony War."

Yet as far as the British were concerned this was anything but a Phony War. Within weeks of the outbreak of war, the Directorate of Air Ministry Intelligence appointed Dr Reginald Jones to its ranks. Jones was a brilliant young physicist from Oxford University whose task was to examine what technology the Nazi military machine might unleash on Great Britain.

Hardly had Jones got his feet under the table when a mysterious package was delivered to the British embassy in Oslo, Norway. The accompanying note said it was "from a well-wishing German scientist" and inside were page after page of handwritten notes (in German) about a number of the Nazis' secret weapons.

The package—what the British called the "Oslo Report"—was considered by many a plant but the more Jones read of it, the more he suspected it was genuine. In particular, he was intrigued by the description of a radio beam device that could direct German aircraft to targets by use of transmission pulses. This had potentially catastrophic consequences for Britain. Imagine fleets German bombers navigating their way

FREYA RADAR

The Germans stole a march on Britain in the development of early warning radar when they introduced the Freya system —named after the Norse Goddess Freyja—in 1937. The Freya radar was more technically advanced than anything the British had in the late 1930s, operating as it did on a 3.9ft (1.2m) wavelength compared to Britain's 39ft (12m). Consequently Freya used a smaller and more maneuvrable antenna system. The British defense system, called the Chain Home radar, had a glaring deficiency—namely its inability to detect hostile aircraft flying at under 5,000ft (1,524m). this led to the introduction of the Chain Home Low (CHL) radar, a more advanced system that could detect aircraft flying as low as 500ft (152m). Erected on towers as high as 190ft (60m), the CHL radar set could pick up German aircraft at ranges of up to 18 miles (30km).

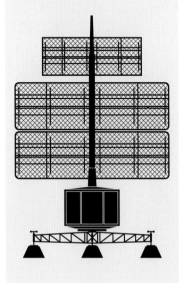

to British cities at night, or in poor weather, to drop their loads with deadly accuracy!

All Britain had by way of defense was a chain of coastal radar stations with their fixed high steel masts, at 328ft (100m) high and capable of detecting hostile aircraft in a 120 degree arc out to sea, but unable to track them once they headed inland.

The British knew that the Germans had a superb long-range mobile radar, the Freya, able to track aircraft through 360 degrees and to a range of 75 miles (121km), while their short-range Wurzburg was also superior to anything Britain possessed. But now Jones feared the Nazis had developed a secret radar far more sophisticated than anything previously seen.

Yet despite his concerns, the young Jones made little headway in convincing his superiors that the Germans had a secret weapon in their hands. Then a slice of luck. In March 1940 a Heinkel 111 bomber was shot down over England, and in the wreckage was a scrap of paper on which was written: "Beacon Plan A … Knickebein from 0600 hours on 315°." "Knickebein" was German for "crooked leg," but other than that the words baffled investigators.

Jones was told to solve the riddle, and soon he received more assistance from a captured German airman who told his interrogators that Knickebein was "something like the *X-Gerat* [X-equipment]." The prisoner assumed the British knew all about the X-Gerat, but they didn't, though it didn't take Jones long to deduce it was a system that worked on the same principle, first developed by Germany in the 1930s for use in civil aviation, of using radio beams for aircraft directional guidance.

An RAF Beaufighter night fighter fitted with the Mark IV AI (Airborne Interception) radar. The Beaufighters, with their maximum speed of 323mph and armed with four 20mm cannon and six .303in machine guns, were a formidable foe for the Luftwaffe bombers. With the AI radar they became a deadly menace in the night skies over Britain.

But the British were now in a race against time. In June 1940 one of the Luftwaffe's elite squadrons, *Kampfgruppe* 100 (KGr100), had returned to Germany to train on the X-Gerat, while in the meantime German engineers spent the summer constructing a chain of radio transmitters on the northern French coast that would guide the bombers to their targets.

On August 14, 21 aircraft from KGr100 took off from their base in Brittany for their inaugural attack using the X-Gerat system. As the bombing force took off from their base, radio beams from two of the radio transmitters intersected over the targets—some factories in the Midlands—and once in air the radio operators inside the Heinkels switched on their Lorenz receivers and tuned into the frequency between 30.0 and 33.3kHz. The steady monotone signal in their headsets told them they were following the radio beam. If the operator heard dots or dashes he knew his pilot

RIGHT A woman polishes the cockpit glazing of a Heinkel 111, the Luftwaffe bomber that was at the forefront of the "Blitz" on British cities from September 1940 to May 1941.

BELOW RIGHT The Airborne Interception (AI) radar was a high-powered transmitter and a receiver which enabled the Beaufighter's operator to track enemy aircraft to a minimum range of 328ft (100m). Fitted halfway along the fuselage, the AI radar box looked like a small television screen and was suspended from the low roof just behind the dome. The operator sat beneath on a swivel seat from where he could look through a Perspex dome.

FAR RIGHT An RAF Beaufighter fitted with the AI radar.

THE KNICKEBEIN

The Knickebein worked on the principle, first developed by Germany in the 1930s for use in civil aviation, of using radio beams for aircraft directional guidance. Shortly before a Luftwaffe bombing mission two "Knickebein" transmitters on the Channel coast began emitting radio beam that intersected directly over the target. Once the aircraft were airborne the radio operators switched on their receivers and tuned into the frequency between 30.0 and 33.3 kilohertz. The steady monotone signal in their headsets broadcast on this frequency indicated they were following the radio beam while dots and dashes indicated they had strayed off course. Meanwhile the radio operator waited for the signal for the second beam laid across the first beam. When he heard the signal he knew they were approximately 12 miles (19km) from the target and the operator pressed a key on a clock that activated a pointer. Now it was the task of the pilot to hold his course steady until the target was reached.

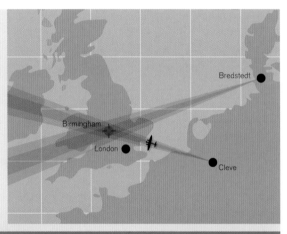

Bredstedt

Birmingham

London

Cleve

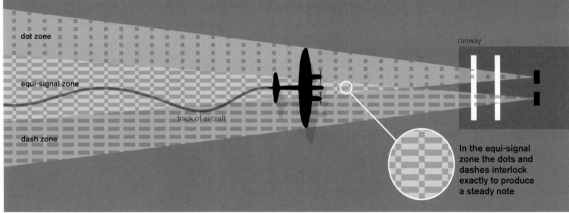

dot zone

equi-signal zone

dash zone

track of aircraft

runway

In the equi-signal zone the dots and dashes interlock exactly to produce a steady note

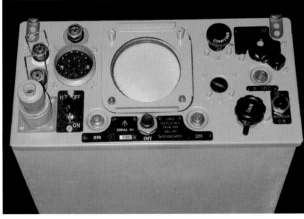

had veered away from the beam and was off course. The bombers flew down the beam until the radio operator heard the "advance signal" on a second receiver. This was another beam laid across the main one they were following. The advance signal told the crew they were 12 miles (19km) from the target, and 6 miles (9.7km) further on they crossed a second beam and the radio operator pressed a button that started the time clock. When they cut across a third beam the operator pressed the time clock again. One of the clock hands stopped. The second hand continued until it reached the first and the electric contact released the bombs over the target.

By now, however, Jones had discovered the full extent of the Luftwaffe's secret weapon, and revealed all to Churchill, who marveled at the German ingenuity, saying the system "was never surpassed by tales of Sherlock Holmes or Monsieur Lecoq."

Describing Britain as being engaged in "a wizard war," Churchill ordered the RAF to waste no time in coming up with countermeasures to block the Knickebein. A new unit, 80 Wing, was formed and various methods experimented with in the hope of blocking the German radio beams. Under the direction of Wing Commander Edward Addison, a phony beam using diathermy sets from hospitals was produced that imitated the dots and dashes of the German beam. Its drawback? It only worked at short range. Addison turned to Dr Robert Cockburn at the Telecommunications Research Establishment in Swanage and, in a top-secret program codenamed "Aspirin," they began constructing sophisticated long-range radio jammers.

But the "Aspirin" program was not yet finished when, on Saturday, September 7, the Luftwaffe launched its first major air assault on London with 950 bombers. The damage to life and property was huge and the raids continued with KGr100 using the Knickebein in their role as Beleuchtergruppe ("Firelighters"), dropping incendiaries with pin-point precision so the

MARK IV AIRBORNE INTERCEPTION

Britain's Ministry of Information produced a successful propaganda campaign to help dissemble the introduction of the Mark IV Airborne Interception (AI). The reason Flight-lieutenant John Cunningham could see in the dark to shoot down so many enemy aircraft, so the propaganda went, was because he ate so many carrots rich in vitamin A. The campaign was also intended to inspire civilians to grow and eat their own vegetables at a time of strict rationing. The Ministry of Agriculture did its best for the humble carrot, too, producing pamphlets on how the vegetable could be used as a substitute for fruit and other vegetables that had become scarce because of rationing. Among the recipes promoted were carrot jam and curried carrot. The campaign paid off with the Ministry reporting in December 1941 that the production of carrots in Britain had risen from its prewar level of 289,000 tons to 469,000 tons in 1941. Flight-lieutenant Cunningham bore his nickname with good grace, reflecting after the war: "By May 1941 I had 12 successful combats in my Beaufighter," he reflected after the war. "I was given the nickname, 'Cat's Eyes' by the Air Ministry to cover up the fact that we were flying aircraft with radar because there was never any mention of radar at that period. So by the time I had had two or three successes, the Air Ministry felt they would have to explain that I had very good vision by night … it would have been easier had the carrots worked. In fact, it was a long, hard grind and very frustrating."

target was illuminated for the waves of bombers that followed.

Fortunately for the British, the "Aspirin" radio jammers were introduced in the same month and soon, in the words of one RAF fighter pilot, Peter Townsend, their "dots and dashes, disagreeing with those of *Knickebein*, put confusion among the German bombers, sending some of them literally flying around in circles or ending up lost in the pitch-dark."

Yet despite the introduction of "Aspirin," the Luftwaffe still managed to inflict appalling casualties on the British people, never more so than the night of November 14, 1940, when the Midlands city of Coventry was firebombed and approximately 550 civilians lost their lives.

But just five days later the RAF scored a success of their own when Flight-lieutenant John Cunningham shot down a Junkers 88 bomber flying a Bristol Beaufighter. It was the first of 20 aerial victories for the man the British press soon dubbed "Cat's Eyes" Cunningham.

By the fall of 1940 the Mark IV AI was being installed in Beaufighters, a powerful aircraft with a maximum speed of 323mph and armed with four 20mm cannon and six .303in machine guns. As well as the pilot, Beaufighters carried a radar operator who sat inside a Perspex dome halfway along the fuselage. Suspended from the low roof just behind the dome was the AI radar box, complete with a rubber visor and a set of control knobs. Once airborne, the radar operator switched on the box and slipped on the vizor. Visible were two luminous green lines, one horizontal and the other vertical, and in his headset the operator listened to a series of radio blips. If an aircraft came within range an echo bounced back and it appeared on the green lines as a cluster of sparkling lights, known as blips. If the enemy aircraft climbed higher the blip (on the vertical tube) grew bigger so the radar operator told the pilot to climb. From the blip on the vertical tube it

was possible see if the aircraft was port or starboard. The radio operator gave instructions to the pilot—increase throttle, decrease speed—until the blips sat squarely across the tubes. Then the aircraft was visible to the pilot, and he chose the moment to attack.

AI radar enjoyed a moderate success initially, its potency hindered by the lack of ground radar stations able to track enemy aircraft inland. Instead the RAF had to rely largely on searchlights or just good luck in locating the enemy in the night skies. But by early 1941 advances in British ground radar meant they could complement AI with Ground-Controlled Interception (GCI). Now a controller on the ground could spot hostile aircraft as they crossed the British coastline, alerting the nearest night fighter to their location. Over the radio the ground controller would guide the RAF

fighter to within AI range of the enemy aircraft, at which point the radar operator would take over.

The Luftwaffe's complacency evaporated as the RAF night fighters started inflicting heavier casualties on their bombers. In March 1941 the Luftwaffe lost 100 men, in April 190 air crew were killed or captured, and then in May 1941 the Blitz ended. Hitler had given up on Britain; instead he turned his eyes east to Russia and the following month launched what would prove to be his ill-fated invasion. The "Wizard War" over British skies was over—for the time being. It would return, however, three years later with a terrifying new secret weapon that had also been revealed in the notes delivered to the British embassy in Oslo in November 1940. Something to do with flying rockets.

▲ The London Blitz began on Saturday September 7, 1940 and continued unabated for the next 57 days and nights. The Luftwaffe came mostly at night but gradually the RAF fighters—thanks to the secret radar war—began developing the technology to shoot down the Nazi aircraft in the dark.

THE ABWEHR SPYING GAME

Spies. The very word conjures an image of glamour and guile, like Mata Hari, the exotic dancer executed by the French in 1917 for passing secrets to Germany, or Pryce Lewis, the Welshman who posed as a British nobleman during the American Civil War to spy on the Confederacy. In reality wartime espionage is usually a sordid and tedious business, at least for those doing the actual spying.

The World War II espionage battle between Britain and Germany began as early as 1937 when Hitler ordered the Abwehr, the German army's military intelligence branch, to establish a spy ring in Britain. In fact two "rings" were planted: one comprising relatively inexperienced spies (around 400 agents in total) who were found work in low-paid and menial occupations, and the other "Ring 2," composed of approximately 35 more experienced operators able to pass themselves off as respectable members of British society.

It didn't take the British long to become aware of the German espionage plot. They were insinuating their own agents into Germany and one of them, a Welshman called Arthur Owens, had been passing information to British intelligence as early as 1936. Running a company that manufactured marine batteries, Owen's work took him often to Germany and he reported back on what he had seen in their shipyards.

Owens' frequent trips to Germany didn't go unnoticed by the Abwehr and in 1938 one of their agents in Britain, Nikolaus Ritter, contacted him and Owens agreed to work for them in return for money and sexual favors from attractive young women. His duplicity was shortlived, however, and in September 1938 Owens told the British authorities of his new role and of the radio receiver he had been given. Owens now became a double agent.

Also in 1938 the British apprehended Joseph Kelly, an Irish bricklayer who had volunteered to work for the Abwehr. Kelly "talked," telling MI5 all he knew, including the name and location of his "handler"— Walther Reinhardt, whose cover was of a German diplomat.

Gradually the British began to identify many of the German agents working in Britain but when war broke out in September 1939 they knew more would arrive, after the occupation of Norway, Denmark, and the Low Countries. Most would be non-Germans or—as a British report later put it—"Germans who are held to their work by blackmail or perhaps because they have a trace of Jewish blood or some stain in their escutcheon."

The complexion of the spying game changed in May 1940, not just with the German invasion of Belgium, Holland and France, but with the appointment of Winston Churchill as British prime minister. One of his early acts was to reorganize the country's intelligence agencies to meet the increased threat posed from spies (and a particular fear in the British press, "Fifth Columnists").

JOHN BINGHAM

In 2014 Britain's National Archives released declassified files that revealed another triumph for MI5 over the German Abwehr. John Bingham, whose cover name was "Jack King," had originally been instructed to infiltrate the British premises of Siemens, the German industrial company. In the course of this covert operation Bingham encountered a "crafty and dangerous woman" called Marita Perigoe. Of mixed Swedish and German origin, Perigoe was married to a member of Mosley's British Union of Fascists and harbored a deep hatred of Britain. Bingham fooled her into believing he was a Gestapo agent looking for people who could be relied on to help in the event of an invasion. Through Perigoe, Bingham was introduced to a dozen Nazi sympathizers whom he similarly duped into believing he was a German agent. He exploited their liking for the cloak-and-dagger side of espionage work, "offering to supply them with invisible ink for secret communications and meeting them in the basement of an antique shop." In return the sympathizer passed on intelligence about secret research on the development of jet aircraft and a new amphibious German tank. MI5 decided not to arrest the sympathizers, fearing that to do so would disrupt an important mine of intelligence.

Mata Hari was the stage name of Dutch-born Margaretha Zelle. In the years before the outbreak of World War I, Hari was an exotic dancer in Paris. When war broke out she became a German spy and was subsequently caught and executed by the French in 1917.

Churchill sacked the incumbent MI5 chief, and appointed as his successor David Petrie, a Scot whose courteous exterior concealed a tough and tenacious character.

Churchill's concerns appeared justified when, a few weeks later, two Norwegian spies parachuted into Britain. One was shot trying to evade arrest but the other, Nicolai Hansen, cooperated and told the British of his instructions to set up a spy ring.

Alarmed by the prospect of dozens of spies parachuting into Britain, MI5 established an official detention centre in south London, Camp 020, under the command of the fearsome Major Robin Stephens, nicknamed "Tin Eye" on account of the monocle he wore over his right eye.

Stephens was an intimidating interrogator and in the months and years following the establishment of Camp 020 he had plenty of hapless Abwehr agents to question. Unwittingly, the Germans had helped the British crack their spy rings with their conquest of most of Europe. Now "agents" such as Arthur Owens (who the British suspected was genuinely sympathetic to the Nazi cause) couldn't travel overseas to meet their handlers in person; instead all messages had to be passed by radio, allowing MI5 to control everything Owens said. It also enabled MI5 to feed the Abwehr information that would ensure the apprehension of all future German agents: for example, when making false identity papers put the person's Christian name before their surname, and date the cards prior to May 1, 1940. Both were errors that would alert the authorities to false documents.

In the next 12 months around two dozen German agents arrived in Britain, either by boat or by parachute, and all wound up at Camp 020. There they were given a stark choice by Stephens: start working for the British, or be shot. Although Britain executed 13 German spies during the war, a captured secret agent was of far more use as a double agent than swinging at the end of a hangman's noose.

At the start of 1941 the success of British intelligence was reflected in the formation of the Twenty Committee (20 in Roman Numerals being XX, or a double cross), under the chairmanship of an Oxford don, Sir John Masterman. One of his early success came in April 1941 when two Norwegian-born German secret agents, John Moe and Tor Glad, landed by seaplane off the northeastern tip of Scotland. Within hours of their arrival the pair had turned themselves in, claiming to be pro-British and eager to become double agents. They were taken to Camp 020 and interrogated by Stephens, who concluded that Moe, who had a Norwegian father and English mother, was sincere. He was less convinced by Glad, however, and Stephens suspected his real mission "is one of penetration with [Moe] as the unwitting cover." In other words, Glad was a genuine German agent who had duped Moe into believing they were going to work as double agents. Nonetheless MI5 decided that "the risk in employing [Glad] is no more than is normally contingent to doublecross work."

The pair were given codenames (characters in a popular American comic strip) with Moe as "Mutt" and Glad as "Jeff," and installed in a suburban house in north London, unaware that their telephone was tapped and the house observed. On April 29 they made contact with the Germans via wireless, relaying the cover story that had been provided by MI5, and to the delight of the British the Abwehr believed every word. Ensnared by the web of deceit, the Germans were fed false information over the ensuing months, so that they believed a highly organized escape network was in operation in Norway. The pair told the Abwehr that the network's code symbol was a small red triangle (the reason for this isn't known but appeared to signify nothing in particular), and that any Norwegian whose identity papers bore this symbol was a member of the organization. It was all fictitious, but later reports indicated that the German secret service expended much time in trying to smash the escape network.

To make sure the Germans continued to trust "Mutt and Jeff," the British intelligence services had one of its men firebomb a flour store in north London (having first removed the flour) and the sabotage was reported in the press—to the delight of the Germans, who believed it was the work of the two Norwegians. Further deceptions followed to maintain the ruse (including the bombing of an electricity station) and in return the Germans dropped a second wireless transmitter and codebook, two lengths of fuses for sabotage, and £200 in cash. By 1944 Mutt and Jeff had outlived their usefulness as spies; Glad was imprisoned (the British still unconvinced of his fidelity) and Moe was allowed to join the Norwegian army. The pair's espionage career had hardly been remarkable; no great secrets revealed that thwarted an invasion or smashed a spy ring, but in their own small way Moe and Glad played their part in helping MI5 defeat the Abwehr in the Intelligence War. They been used by the British as a small cog in a large wheel of deception that began turning in early 1941 and continued to do so until 1944 when, thanks to the elaborate Double Cross system, the Germans were fooled into believing D-Day would be on the beaches of Calais and not Normandy. No wonder that by the end of 1941 Sir John Masterman was able to boast of MI5's success: "We actively ran and controlled the German espionage system in this country."

FALLSCHIRMJÄGER CONQUER CRETE

As we saw in Chapter one, German paratroopers—Fallschirmjäger—had taken part with great success in the invasion of the Low Countries in May 1940, seizing during the assault on Holland the road and railway viaducts over the Diep, the bridges over the Old Maas at Dordrecht and Waalhaven airfield at Rotterdam. Hitler was ecstatic. As Cajus Bekker wrote in his 1964 book *The Luftwaffe War Diaries*, Hitler "had deliberately not used the paratroops in Poland in order not to expose the secret of this new weapon unnecessarily."

In fact the Nazis' secret airborne weapon was first deployed a few weeks before the assault on Holland during Germany's invasion of Norway and Denmark. So it was in April 1940 that the world witnessed for the first time the use of paratroopers in war when in the early morning of April 9, 12 Junkers 52s appeared out of the gray dawn light over the small Danish island of Masnedo. The paratroopers achieved total surprise, seizing their target, which was the 2-mile (3km) bridge

connecting the islands of Falster and Seeland, and which was the sole land link between the nearby ferry terminal in the south to Copenhagen. A few hours later paratroopers dropped into Norway and by the evening of the 9th had achieved another landmark for airborne troops—the capture the first capital city, Oslo.

Some voices within both the Allied and the German military expressed surprise that Hitler had revealed his secret aerial weapon in Scandinavia; wouldn't he have been better advised to have kept his paratroopers hidden until the greater logistical challenge presented by France and the Low Countries? But Denmark and Norway were trial runs, an opportunity to see how effective airborne troops were. The emphatic results gave Hitler the confidence to deploy them in the audacious seizure of the Dutch bridges, and the following year the Fuhrer decided to use them en masse in the biggest airborne operation ever staged. The problem was that no longer were paratroopers a secret, so if they were to be used it would have to be a surprise in order to catch the enemy off-guard.

The target was the Mediterranean island of Crete, measuring approximately 160 miles × 20 miles (258km × 32km), which had been occupied by the British in October 1940 following Italy's attack on Greece. Situated in the Mediterranean, equidistant between Athens and the Egyptian coast, Crete's air strip allowed British bombers to attack the Romanian oil fields that were vital to the German war effort, while its harbors were a haven for the Royal Navy, whence they could attack German supply ships.

Hitler had been determined to seize Crete within days of the British occupation and events in the spring of 1941 strengthened his resolve. On April 6, Germany attacked Greece and Yugoslavia and both countries were soon overrun with German troops reaching up to the Aegean and Mediterranean coasts. Now only Crete barred the Nazi way to the outer Mediterranean but the island's defenders, some 28,600, including British,

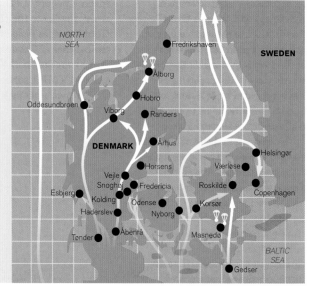

OPERATION WESERUBUNG

On April 9 ,1940, Germany launched the first airborne invasion of a country when 12 Junkers 52s appeared over the small Danish island of Masnedo. The paratroopers achieved total surprise, seizing their target, which was the 3km bridge connecting the islands of Falster and Seeland. A few hours later paratroopers jumped into Norway and by the evening of the 9th had captured the capital, Oslo, having stunned the city's defenders with their landings.

■ Danish mines

■ German mines

⍟ Parachute landings

Australians and New Zealanders—were well dug in on the island under the command of General Freyberg, a New Zealander—who had won the Victoria Cross in World War I. (German intelligence estimated the island garrison at around 9,000 men, a serious miscalculation.)

But much as Hitler wanted Crete as his "crowning glory" in the Balkans campaign, he faced a problem. He had recently dispatched General Erwin Rommel and his Afrika Korps to North Africa to aid the Italians who had been thrown out of Libya a few months earlier, and he was in the throes of finalizing plans to invade Russia. In short, he didn't have the troops to spare for what could be a bloody battle for Crete. So once again he turned to General Kurt Student and his Fallschirmjäger, giving them 20 days to plan for "Operation Mercury."

All the planning for the first airborne invasion in military history was done in the utmost secrecy and in the beginning of May the Airborne Corps received instructions to entrain for an unknown destination. Traveling through Hungary, Romania, and Bulgaria until they reached the Mediterranean Sea at Salonika, the paratroopers established a camp to the east of an airfield near the village of Topolia, and the next day, May 16, the officers were told their mission by Student at the Hotel Grande Bretagne in Athens.

The island would be attacked at four different locations with the Assault Regiment, commanded by Brigadier General Meindl, dropping to the west and securing the airfield at Malemes. The second regiment, led by Captain Wiedemann was tasked with occupying the town of Rethymnon and its adjoining airfield, and the first regiment under major Walther would jump into Gourmes in the north and capture Heraklion.

The third regiment, under the command of Colonel Richard Heidrich, and reinforced by a parachute-engineer battalion, was tasked with seizing the town of Chania on the northwest coast of Crete.

The invasion began at eight o'clock in the morning of May 20 with 3,000 paratroopers jumping from 400ft (122m) onto a rocky and uneven terrain. The British and Dominion troops had been expecting an airborne attack—despite the secrecy of the Germans, Greek agents in Athens couldn't but notice the arrival of thousands of fit young men—but they were shocked by the numbers of parachutes filling the clear blue sky. There was inadequate air support for the ground defenders and a lack of anti-aircraft guns so that, while the soldiers in Crete fought fiercely, by dusk on the first day of the invasion the number of paratroopers had doubled.

▲ The success of the German airborne troops inspired Britain to form its own equivalent—the Parachute Regiment. Here waves of British paratroopers jump into Holland in September 1944 as part of the ill-fated Operation Market Garden—better known as the Battle for Arnhem.

Hitler **(BELOW)** poses with a group of airborne troops after decorating them with the Iron Cross for bravery during the invasion of Denmark and Norway **(OPPOSITE BELOW LEFT)**. Meanwhile a detachment of mountain troops prepare to embark the cruiser *Admiral Hipper* **(RIGHT)** to reinforce the airborne troops in Denmark. Germany had little difficulty overcoming Denmark's small army, despite their courage **(OPPOSITE BELOW RIGHT)**. With Denmark in German hands, the local population listened to the Terms of the Occupation **(OPPOSITE ABOVE)**.

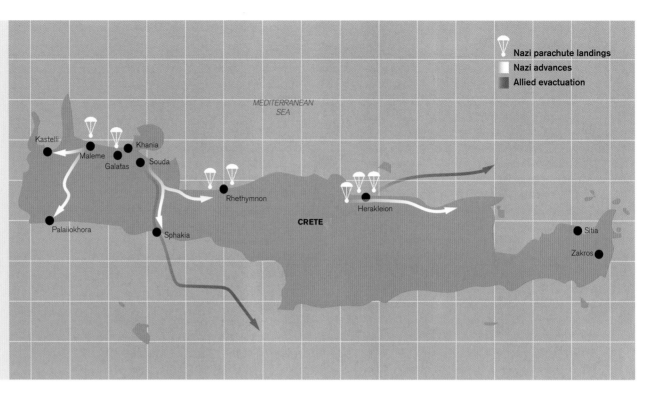

OPERATION MERCURY

The battle of Crete began on May 20 and at the end of the first day's fighting the German airborne forces had suffered heavy casualties. But reinforcements on May 21, and the failure of Allied commanders to seize the initiative, allowed the Germans to seize the strategically important Maleme airfield. In the days that followed, reinforcements were flown in and the Allies were forced into a humiliating evacuation of the island at the end of May.

Nazi parachute landings
Nazi advances
Allied evacuation

MEDITERRANEAN SEA

Kastelli
Maleme
Khania
Galatas
Souda
Palaiiokhora
Sphakia
Rhethymnon
Herakleion
CRETE
Sitia
Zakros

On May 21 Malemes airfield fell to the Germans, enabling them to use it to reinforce the Airborne Corps with Alpine troops from the 5th Mountain Division arriving by transport planes. Together the paratroopers and the mountain troops repulsed a New Zealand counterattack the following day, an action that proved to be turning point in the battle for Crete. With the airstrip gone, and growing ever more fearful of a major seaborne landing, the British began withdrawing to the eastern tip of the island to prepare for an evacuation. This operation began on May 28 and continued until the last day of the month, by which time the Royal Navy had lost three cruisers and six destroyers to the Luftwaffe, with 13 more vessels damaged. In all, 16,500 of Crete's defenders were rescued but more than 12,000 soldiers were killed or captured. The psychological effect was also grievous, yet another humiliation for the British and her Allies following the loss of Greece and Yugoslavia and reverses in North Africa at the hands of the dashing General Rommel.

Of the 22,000 Fallschirmjäger that jumped into Crete, 4,000 were killed, with approximately half that number wounded. "The Fuhrer was very upset by the heavy losses suffered by the parachute units," recalled General Kurt Student after the war. "And came to the conclusion that their surprise value had passed. After that he often said to me: 'The day of parachute troops is over.'"

Although the Germans deployed Fallschirmjäger again in the war—notably during the successful capture of the Aegean island of Leros, 248 miles

BARON VON DER HEYDTE

One of the officers involved in the Crete operation was Baron von der Heydte, later promoted to Lieutenant-Colonel. In December 1944 he led the first and only German night drop as part of their offensive in the Ardennes. Ordered by Field Marshal Model on December 9 to prepare for a top-secret special mission," Heydte was given a week to train his men—many of whom had never parachuted in a daylight drop, let alone a night operation. On December 15 Heydte received details of the mission, codenamed "Stösser." His task was to seize and hold a number of roads and bridges, identified as bottlenecks, to facilitate the rapid advance of the 6th SS Panzer Army. Less than 48 hours later, just after midnight on December 17, Heydte and 1,200 paratroopers took off in more than 100 transport planes but they encountered snow and high winds, and only 250 men assembled on the drop zone 75 miles (120km) behind American lines. Though he rounded up a further 150 paratroopers in the next few hours, Heydte's force was too small to complete its mission and he surrendered to the Americans.

(400km) northwest of Crete, in November 1943—it was the Allies who put their faith in the efficacy of airborne troops. Winston Churchill, impressed by what the Fallschirmjäger had accomplished in Denmark, Norway, and Holland, ordered the establishment of a British Parachute Regiment, and they first saw action during the invasion of Morocco and Algeria in November 1942. Active also during the invasions of Sicily and Italy in 1943, the Parachute Regiment, along with the American 101 Airborne Division, played decisive roles in the invasion of Normandy in June 1944.

In March 1945, as if to prove to Hitler how wrong he had been in his declaration that "the day of parachute troops is over," the Allies undertook the largest airborne operation in history when 16,000 British and Americans helped secure a foothold across the Rhine in western Germany. Almost five years after Hitler had unleashed the Fallschirmjäger on Denmark, paratroopers were no longer a secret, but they could still be lethally effective.

Though the Allies lost 12,000 men on Crete—either killed or captured—the Germans also suffered heavy casualties. Of the 22,000 Fallschirmjäger that took part in the operation (LEFT), 4,000 were killed and another 2,000 wounded. Hitler was shocked by the extent of the losses and for the rest of the war the Nazi leader was reluctant to sanction large-scale airborne operations, telling General Kurt Student: "The day of parachute troops is over."

THE U-BOAT WOLFPACKS

There was little secret about the U-boat in 1939. The German submarine fleet had been a constant menace throughout World War I and the British knew their number and effectiveness had grown during the 1930s as Hitler re-armed Germany. What Great Britain didn't know was that by the end of August 1939 there were already 17 U-boats prowling the Atlantic and a further 14 in the North Sea.

On the day Britain declared war on Germany, September 3, the U-boat fleet recorded its first "kill," the liner SS *Athenia* sunk in the Atlantic en route from Glasgow to Montreal with the loss of over 100 lives. A fortnight later the Royal Navy aircraft carrier, *Courageous*, was torpedoed west of the British Isles and soon British naval and merchant vessels were being sent to the bottom of the sea with grim regularity.

By the end of 1939 114 ships—and over 420,000 tons—had been lost to the U-boats, and with the fall of France in June 1940 the threat increased, not just from submarines but from German surface vessels and the Luftwaffe, all enjoying the freedom of the seas now that the French navy was no more. Additionally, now that French naval bases were in German hands, more U-boats could be sent out to sea.

In October 1940 U-boats sank 63 ships (more than 350,000 tons), a record tally and the result of a new submarine tactic, drawn up in secret by Admiral Karl Dönitz and labelled "Rudeltaktik." To the British it was the tactics of the "wolfpack," described thus by Basil Liddell Hart in his *History of World War Two*:

"When the existence of a convoy had been approximately established, U-boat Command headquarters ashore would warn the nearest U-boat group, which would send a submarine to find and shadow the convoy and 'home' the others onto it by wireless. When they were assembled on the scene, they

would launch night attacks on the surface, preferably upwind of the convoy, and continue these for several nights. During daylight the U-boats would withdraw well clear if the convoy and its escort."

It was tactic used by the U-boats in World War I and one that proved swiftly and savagely successful. Launching a surface attack meant that the U-boats had an advantage in speed over any British escort vessel and they could easily outrun a pursuer.

The British had anti-submarine measures of course. Ships carried a sonar system known as ASDIC (Anti-Submarine Detection Investigation Committee), but it emitted just one sound impulse which, if it hit a submarine, would return a "ping." In addition the aircraft of Coastal Command carried the ASV (airborne surface vessel) Mk.II radar, which had a maximum range of 36 miles (58km). But what good was radar at night, when the pilots had no chance of spotting an enemy submarine on the black sea? Initially the RAF dropped rocket flares, but all these did was warn the U-boat that an aircraft was in the vicinity. Flares were superseded by the "snowflake illuminator," far more powerful and able to flood a wide area with light.

Then Squadron Leader Humphrey de Verde Leigh of Coastal Command had an idea: why not fit searchlights onto the aircraft themselves? In March 1941 experiments began using a 22-million candlepower, 24in searchlight in a Wellington bomber that had been deployed earlier in the war as a magnetic minesweeper, and so already carried a generator. Fitted in a retractable aperture under the aircraft's fuselage, the "Leigh Light" as it became known was an instant success. On its first operational patrol, a Leigh Light carried by a Wellington of 172 Squadron located an Italian submarine in the Bay of Biscay. Depth charges were dropped and the badly damaged submarine was forced to beach on the Spanish coast.

Yet despite the fact that more U-boats were now being sunk—47 had been lost by September 1941—far

◀ A Leigh Light being cleaned. These were searchlights fitted in a retractable aperture under an aircraft's fuselage that were used by the RAF to help spot U-boats at sea.

more were coming off the production line, and they were also being manufactured to a stronger standard with their welded pressure hulls proving more durable than the earlier versions. By the end of 1941 there were 86 operational U-boats and a further 150 undergoing final trials. Consequently, the first six months of 1942 witnessed a shocking toll on Allied merchant shipping, with over 3 million tons sunk, 90 per cent of which was in the Atlantic. By August 1942 the total strength of the U-boat fleet numbered 300 and the Allies feared they would lose the Battle of the Atlantic. At the Allied Conference at Casablanca, Morocco, in January 1943, the British and Americans discussed how best to defeat the U-boat menace; for until they did a successful invasion of Western Europe was out of the question.

There were changes in command—the most notable being the appointment of Admiral Sir Max Horton as the commander-in-chief of the Western Approaches to the British Isles. Horton was a brilliant submariner and his plan was to be more aggressive in the battle against the U-boats, using more destroyers and frigates to ruthlessly hunt down the German submarines in coordination with increased air support.

Horton also had the advantage of some new secret weapons that had been trialled during 1942. The first was a more sophisticated ASDIC system which instead of emitting just one sound impulse sent out three, and

Admiral Sir Max Horton, the aggressive and innovative submariner, who was appointed commander-in-chief of the Western Approaches to the British Isles in November 1942 and who was ruthless in hunting down and destroying the German wolfpacks that had caused so much damage to Allied shipping in the early years of the war.

The ASDIC was a transmitter-receiver that emitted a directional sound wave (1) through the water. If this transmitted wave collided with a submerged object, such as a U-boat (2), it was reflected back and picked up by the receiver (sound) beneath the ship (3)

ASDIC SONAR SYSTEM

The development in the ASDIC system meant that rather than just emitting one sound impulse, it sent out three and any return "ping" revealed the U-boat's depth and distance, enabling the Royal Navy to pinpoint precisely its location. This sonar system, coupled with the introduction of weapons such as the Hedgehog and Squid, turned the Battle of the Atlantic the way of the Allies. ASDIC didn't stand for "Allied Submarine Detection Investigation Committee," but was a deliberate ploy by the British to throw the Germans off the trail of their secret weapon by using an acronym that made no reference to sound experimentation.

ABOVE RIGHT HMS *Wesctott* was one of many Royal Navy ships to be fitted with one of the new Allied secret weapons in the war against the U-boats. The "Hedgehog" consisted of 24 small depth charges fired from the bow of the vessel that exploded at different depths and locations close to the submarine.

BELOW RIGHT A salvo of 24 Hedgehog bombs in flight, fired from a Royal Navy vessel, with a German U-boat their target.

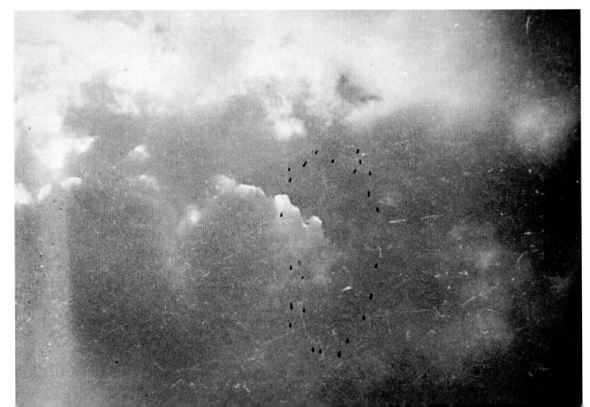

THE HEDGEHOG

Type Anti-submarine Mortar

Shell 65lb (29kg)

Calibre 7in (18cm)

Barrels 24

Effective firing range over 650ft (200m)

Filling 30lb (14kg) TNT or 35lb (16kg) Torpex

The Hedgehog was the brainchild of the Royal Navy's Directorate of Miscellaneous Weapons Development (DMWD). The Royal Navy's High Command was initially skeptical of the Hedgehog's effectiveness but a successful trial run on the destroyer HMS *Westcott* in May 1941 won them over and the Hedgehog was introduced into operational service in 1942. It caused fear among the crews of German U-boats because of its ability to fire 820ft (250m) ahead of the attacking vessel.

any return "ping" would reveal the U-boat's depth and distance, enabling the Royal Navy to pinpoint precisely its location. That wasn't the only the development in anti-submarine warfare; hitherto a problem for all surface vessels seeking to destroy U-boats was that their only weapon was the cumbersome depth charge dropped from the stern of the ship. But when the vessel was directly over the submarine, preparing to fire the depth charge, the U-boat's signal was lost and it in effect disappeared. To close this escape route, the British invented two devices: the "Hedgehog" consisted of 24 small depth charges fired from the bow of the vessel that exploded at different depths and locations close to the target. The "Squid," as the name implies, was more deadly, firing three large depth charges that were so powerful that they could fracture a submarine's hull so that even if the U-boat wasn't sunk, the damage inflicted would force it to the surface.

Meanwhile in the air there had also been innovations, with necessity once again proving the mother of inventions. To counter the RAF's ASV Mk.II radar, the Germans had fitted U-boats with a device called "Metox," a radio receiver that warned them of the approach of an aircraft carrying a Mk.II radar. The Americans therefore developed an advanced 10cm radar set called the DMS-100, which couldn't be detected by the U-boats, and by early 1943 it was being used over the Atlantic to great effect.

These new Allied inventions, coupled with Horton's counteroffensive, turned the Battle of the Atlantic in their favor. In May 1943 Donitz informed Hitler that "we are facing the greatest crisis in submarine warfare, since the enemy, by means of new location devices … makes fighting impossible, and is causing us heavy losses." By the end of that month U-boat losses had doubled, forcing Donitz to withdraw his submarine fleet from the North Atlantic while they tried to devise a method to negate the new technology being used against them.

Donitz ordered German scientists to come up with a method of avoiding radar detection, and a solution was soon found. By coating the submarine with a composite of rubber and carbon, a submarine's echo was markedly reduced thereby making it far less likely that its 'ping' would be detected by Allied radar. The Germans were triumphant but their delight soon turned to dismay when it was discovered that prolonged exposure to seawater eroded the protective coat and exposed the U-boat to radar.

By the late summer of 1943, with the American war effort now nearing its maximum capacity, more Allied ships were being manufactured than were being sunk. The reverse was true for the U-boats, which reluctantly re-entered the Atlantic in the latter half of 1943. In the first three months of 1944 they managed to sink just three merchant ships out of 3,360 that crossed the ocean in 105 convoys. They, on the other hand, had 36 submarines sent to the ocean bed. The Battle of the Atlantic had been won, thanks to astonishing advances in radar and sonar, without forgetting the Squid and the Hedgehog.

ITALIAN INGENUITY AND THE HUMAN TORPEDO

The Royal Navy had a contemptuous view of their Italian counterparts in World War II. Admiral Sir Andrew Cunningham, commander-in-chief of the British Mediterranean Fleet 1939–43, made no secret of his "healthy contempt" for the Italian navy, much of which was badly damaged at Taranto in November 1940 when Swordfish bombers from HMS *Illustrious* launched an aerial attack that secured for the Royal Navy control of the Mediterranean.

Yet it was an error on the part of the British to be so dismissive of their foe, who, after the Taranto attack, thirsted for vengeance with the secret weapon they had been developing since the summer of 1940.

Junio Valerio Borghese was a charismatic submarine commander who, in August 1940, was appointed commander of the *Scire*, a 620-ton submarine with a 50-man crew. The *Scire*, along with the submarine *Gondar*, had been converted to "assault craft transport" with three steel cylinders welded on deck (one forward and two aft), all having the same pressure resistance as the submarine. In these cylinders would be transported the secret weapon of the Italian navy—human torpedoes.

The human torpedo was pioneered at the tail end of World War I by the Italian navy. Sub-lieutenant Raffaele Paolucci and naval engineer Major Raffaele Rossetti sank the prestigious Austro-Hungarian battleship *Viribus Unitis*, at anchor in the Croatian harbor of Pula, on November 1, a symbolic act of sabotage that was a metaphor for the end of the Habsburg Empire.

In the interwar years the Italian navy developed their new weapon, which, in the words of one engineer, Elios Toschi, was "in size and shape very similar to a torpedo but is in reality a miniature submarine with entirely novel features, electrical propulsion, and a steering wheel similar to that of an airplane ... equipped with a long-range underwater breathing gear, the operators will be able, without any connection with the surface, to breathe and navigate under water at any

depths up to thirty meters and carry a powerful explosive charge into an enemy harbor."

When Italy, led by its fascist leader Benito Mussolini, entered the war on Germany's side in June 1940, the 10th Light Flotilla had been formed as a specialist human torpedo unit under the command of Commander Catalano Gonzaga. Its training centre was established at San Leopoldo, near the naval academy at Livorno, and here the select band of men who passed the rigorous selection process were taught how to operate the "pigs" as the torpedoes were christened.

The torpedoes used were similar in dimension to those used nearly a quarter of a century earlier. With a maximum speed of 2.5mph, the torpedoes were 22ft (6.7m) long by 1ft 8in (0.5m) wide. The pilot, always an officer, sat at the front, steering the torpedo using a fly wheel connected to a rheostat, while his No. 2 sat at the rear. Their feet were secured by stirrups and a windscreen provided a breakwater, enabling the pilot to steer using the luminous instrument panel. The pair wore a rubber diving suit and their six-hour oxygen bottles were carried on their backs.

At the front of the torpedo—in the "pig's snout"— which was nearly 6ft (1.8m) long, were over 660lb (300kg) of explosives. A clutch by the pilot allowed him to detach the warhead from the rest of the torpedo. Behind the head was the fore trimming tank, then the accumulator battery, the electric motor, the stern trimming tank and the propeller shaft with the rudders attached to the propeller. The second crew member sat above the electric motor with his back resting against a trunk containing a tool kit, among which were net cutters, scissors, clamps, and a length of rope.

The 10th Light Flotilla scored their first success in September 1941 in Gibraltar, three human torpedoes sinking three British ships at anchor: the naval tanker *Denby Dale*, the motorship *Durham* and the tanker *Fiona Shaw*. Though none of the vessels was particularly illustrious, it was a propaganda coup all the same, and

▲ Junio Valerio Borghese, the ardent fascist and charismatic submarine commander who commanded the 10th Light Flotilla to many successes against British shipping using human torpedoes in 1941 and 1942.

The month before the *Queen Elizabeth* was sunk by the human torpedo attack, another Royal Navy battleship, HMS *Barham* **(ABOVE AND BELOW RIGHT)**, had been spectacularly destroyed by a U-boat in an attack that resulted in the loss of 841 crewmen. The moment of the *Barham*'s explosion was caught on film by a cameraman on board the nearby *Valiant*, itself severely damaged in the raid on Alexandria.

one seized on by Mussolini. The six crew members were awarded the Silver Medal in recognition of their valour and Borghese, who piloted the submarine to Gibraltar, was promoted to commander for his success "in bringing back his submarine and its crew to the base, despite the difficulties due to determined pursuit by the enemy."

Three months later the Italians decided to unleash their secret weapon against a Royal Navy still reeling from the loss of the aircraft carrier *Ark Royal* (sunk by a German U-boat on November 13 off Gibraltar) and the battleship *Barham* (destroyed 12 days later with the loss of 841 crewmen). This time their targets were the remaining two battleships in the British Mediterranean fleet, the *Queen Elizabeth* and the *Valiant*, both of which had been ordered into anchorage in Alexandria following the sinking of the *Barham*.

The operation began in mid-December, the submarine *Scire* slipping away from its base on the Aegean island of Leros and reaching the edge of Alexandria undetected despite the minefields and submarine nets that littered the Mediterranean. On the evening of December 18 three human torpedoes, crewed by Captain Antonio Marceglia and Petty Officer Spartaco Schergat, Captain Vincenzo Martellotta and Petty Officer Mario Marino, and Sub-lieutenant Luigi Durand de la Penne, and Petty officer Emilio Bianchi, departed the submarine, which then turned for home.

Immediately after leaving the *Scire*, the three "Pigs" had a stroke of good fortune when three British destroyers hove into view. The harbor's net gates opened and the guide lights went on, allowing the

LEFT The remains of a British Swordfish bomber brought down during the raid on Taranto.

BELOW LEFT HMS *Illustrious*, the aircraft carrier from which the Royal Navy launched the attack on the Italian fleet.

OPPOSITE A British reconnaissance photograph of the damage caused to the Italian fleet in the Mediterranean at Taranto Harbor in November 1940. Swordfish bombers had launched the ferocious attack from HMS *Illustrious*.

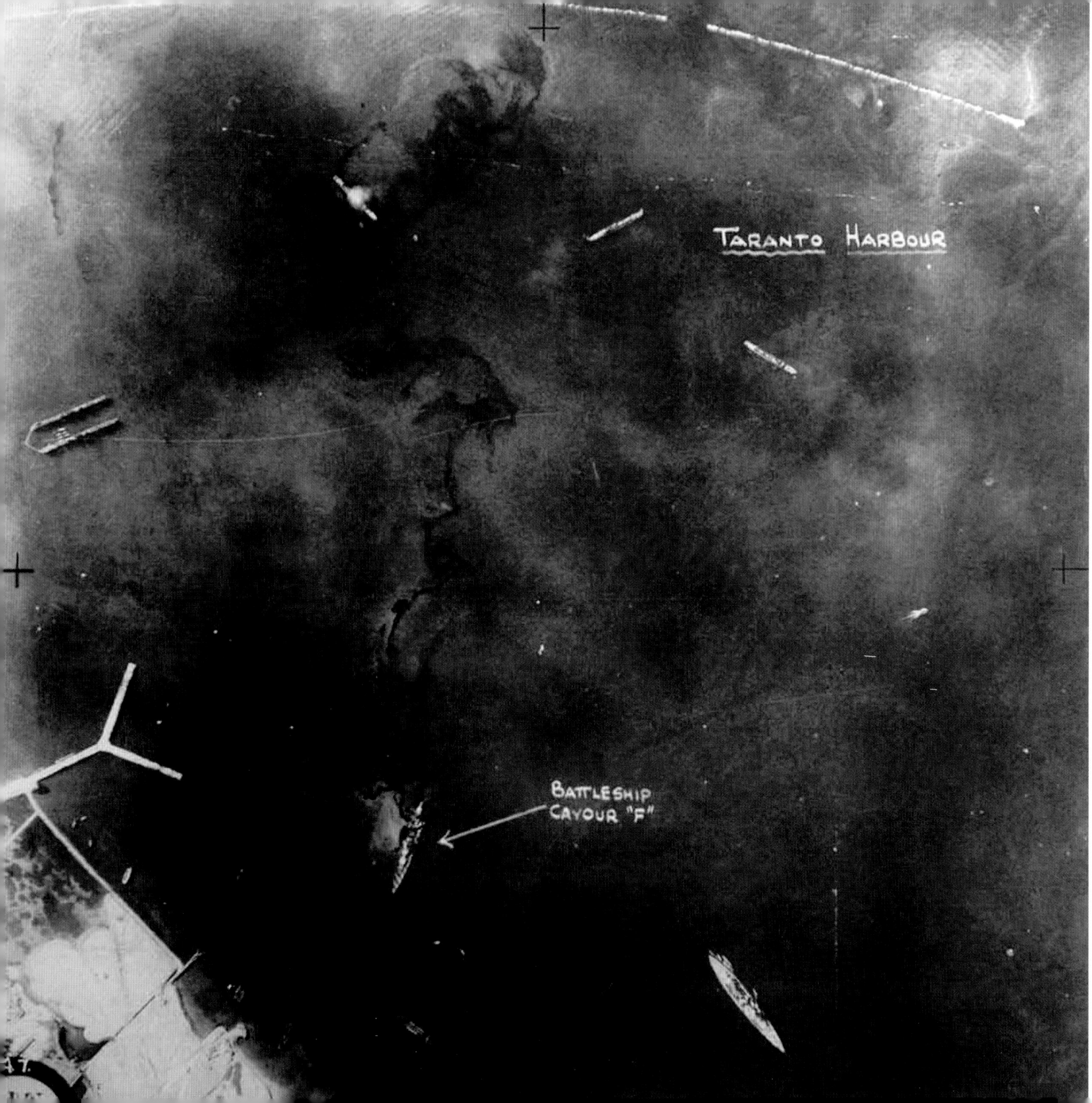

TARANTO HARBOUR

BATTLESHIP
CAVOUR "F"

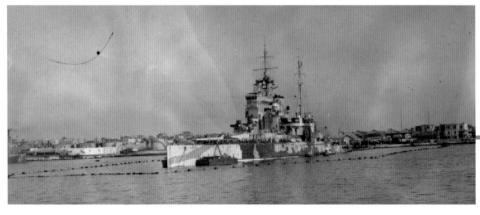

raiders to slip unseen into Alexandria ahead of the enemy vessels. Though the three torpedoes had lost one another in the black water each knew their orders: de la Penne and Bianchi were to attack the *Valiant*, Marceglia and Schergat the *Queen Elizabeth* and Martellotta and Marino a loaded oil tanker.

De la Penne and Bianchi soon saw ahead of them the huge hull of the 32,000-ton battleship. Encountering the anti-torpedo protective netting, Bianchi cut through it and they approached their target. But the exertion of dealing with the netting had exhausted Bianchi to such an extent that he fainted, slipping from the "Pig" and floating to the surface. Regaining consciousness, he clung to a buoy in the water, out of sight of British sentries patrolling the *Valiant* above.

Beneath the waves de la Penne had discovered the disappearance of Bianchi but his most immediate concern was the "Pig," which for an unaccountable reason had dropped like a stone to the seabed. Diving down to investigate, de la Penne discovered that a steel wire had snagged the propeller and despite his best efforts he was unable to restart the motor. De la Penne was faced with a stark choice: either abort the mission or try and drag the "Pig" a few meters so it was directly beneath the hull of the *Valiant*. He decided on the latter, managing with every last ounce of his strength to haul the torpedo until it was underneath the *Valiant*'s port bulge and close to the turret's shell room and magazine. Setting the fuse on the warhead to explode at 0500 hours, two hours hence, de la Penne surfaced and soon found Bianchi clinging to the mooring buoy at the bow of the *Valiant*. The pair were spotted by British sentries above and were taken on

HMS *Queen Elizabeth* **(ABOVE AND BELOW)** was blown up by the Italians as it lay in anchor in Alexandria in December 1941 in one of the most daring sabotage acts of the war. Winston Churchill even described it as an exploit requiring "extraordinary courage and ingenuity."

board the ship for questioning. They said nothing, until, at 0450 hours, de la Penne made a statement to Captain Morgan, subsequently described in the Italian's report on the operation:

"I told him that in a few minutes his ship would blow up, that there was nothing he could do about it and that, if he wished, he could still get his crew into a place of safety. He again asked me where I had placed the charge and as I did not reply he had me escorted back into the hold. As we went along I heard the loudspeakers giving orders to abandon ship, as the vessel had been attacked by Italians, and saw people running aft … a few minutes passed (they were infernal ones for me: would the explosion take place?) and then it came. The vessel reared with extreme violence. All the lights went out and the hold became filled with smoke."

The charge had exploded under the port bulge, holing an area some 60ft by 30ft (18m by 9m) and causing extensive flooding in several compartments and some electrical damage. De la Penne and Bianchi were taken up on deck where they saw the ship begin to list to port some four or five degrees. The two Italians turned their gaze towards the *Queen Elizabeth* just a few hundred yards away. They could see startled sailors standing in her bows, watching the drama on the *Valiant*. Suddenly a great explosion rent the air and the *Queen Elizabeth* "rose a few inches out of the water and fragments of iron and other objects flew out of her funnel, mixed with oil, which even reached the deck of the *Valiant*, splashing every one of us standing on her stern."

The *Queen Elizabeth* had been blown up by Marceglia and Schergat, who, having cut through the antisubmarine net, fixed their warhead 5ft (1.5m) beneath the hull of the battleship so that it exploded under the "B" boiler room, devastating its double bottom structure and inflicting damage over a section of the ship measuring 190ft by 60ft (58m by 18m). Compartment by compartment the vessel began

THE HUMAN TORPEDO

Crew	2
Type	Mini manned torpedo submarine
Length	16.4ft (5m)
Beam	2ft (0.61m)
Surface speed	1 knot
Submerged speed	4.5 knots
Range	15 miles (24km)
Armament	1 x 300kg or 2 x 150kg warhead

The Italian 10th Light Flotilla established their base at San Leopoldo, near the naval academy at Livorno, in September 1940, and Junio Valerio Borghese oversaw the training required to master the human torpedoes. The human torpedoes used by the 10th Light Flotilla were modeled on those invented at the end of World War I by Italian engineers. They were over 21ft (6.7m) in length and 1ft 9in (53cm) in diameter. The pilot, always an officer, sat at the front steering the torpedo, while the other crew member was at the rear. Their feet were secured by stirrups and a windscreen provided a breakwater, enabling the pilot to steer the torpedo using the instrument panel.

flooding up to the main deck level until eventually the *Queen Elizabeth* sank to the bottom of Alexandria harbor.

The third crew, Martellotta and Marino, successfully destroyed a 10,000-ton oil tanker (the name of which they never discovered) to complete a night of devastating triumph for the 10th Light Flotilla.

Yet despite the success of the Alexandria raid it marked the acme of the human torpedo. Other raids followed—including the sinking of three merchant supply ships in Gibraltar in May 1943—but the Royal Navy increased its defenses. Never again would it be humiliated by Italy and her secret underwater weapon, which even won the respect of Winston Churchill. Addressing a secret session of the House of Commons on April 23, 1942, the British prime minister said of the Alexandria raid: "Extreme precautions have been taken for some time past against the varieties of human torpedo or one-man submarine entering our harbors. Not only are nets and other obstructions used but underwater charges are exploded at irregular intervals in the fairway. None the less these men had penetrated the harbor. Four hours later explosions occurred in the bottoms of the *Valiant* and the K, produced by limpet bombs [sic] fixed with extraordinary courage and ingenuity, the effect of which was to blow large holes in the bottoms of both ships and to flood several compartments, thus putting them both out of action for many months."

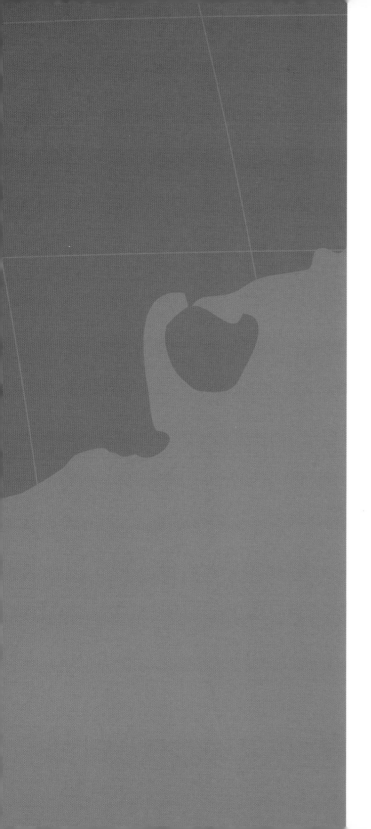

FIGHTING BACK

On the back foot for the first two years of the war, Britain began fighting back with its brains as some of the finest mathematical minds in the world helped crack Germany's Enigma code. With the American decryption teams achieving something similar against Japan, the Allies had the upper hand in the secret war of intelligence. Japan's attack on Pearl Harbor in December 1941 had brought the USA into the war and in between April and June 1942, America struck back with attacks of its own. Britain was no longer alone in its fight to save the free world and in November 1942 the Allies invaded North Africa.

THE ENIGMA CODEBREAKERS

There were few secrets in World War II as closely guarded as the one concerning Bletchley Park, a beautiful old manor house in rural Buckinghamshire that from the outside looked like the setting for a Jane Austen novel. Inside, however, was the operational headquarters of arguably the most secret project of the war—the British decryption project that cracked the German Enigma codes. Yet despite being described by Winston Churchill as "the geese that laid the golden eggs," the 9,000 people employed at Bletchley Park (at the height of the codebreaking) were forbidden by the Official Secrets Act from ever discussing their vital contribution to the war effort for decades after. Not until Frederick Winterbotham, one of the architects of Ultra, published his book, *The Ultra Secret*, in 1974 did the men and women (80 per cent of Bletchley Park employees were female) begin to receive the recognition they deserved.

But the Enigma saga began more than half a century earlier, in the final year of World War I, when a German engineer, Arthur Scherbius, patented a commercial encryption device and then formed a business partnership with Richard Ritter. The Scherbius and Ritter Company struggled to attract interest from the German military in 1918, not surprisingly given the way the war was going, and by the early 1920s the pair had merged their company and were manufacturing commercial Enigma machines as the Cypher Machines Stock Company.

As the 1920s progressed the Enigma machine was modified and improved, with a Model B, C, and finally, in 1927, the Model D. No longer the cumbersome 50kg typewriter mechanism of its early years, the Enigma Model D was sold throughout the world in the late 1920s and 1930s. The British scientist and author Brian Ford described it as a "masterpiece of design," adding: "In use, a key pressed by the operator would connect one of 26 letter circuits, passing a current to one of 26 contacts in the encoding unit. Electrical current was then passed through three rotors, each of them wired so that the letter was changed. The turning of the rotors to make a new set of contacts each time a key was pressed meant that each letter was transposed to a different character every time." Additionally, the Enigma machine solved the problem of the receiving machine needing to feed power from the keys to replicate the original action. It did this by "adding a reflector system that connected each contact to another and routed the circuit back through the three rotors." This allowed the receiver to recover the original text but not a third party attempting to intercept the message en route.

The Italians were the first to recognize the potential of Enigma for military espionage and they were soon followed by the Germans, who improved the device by adding a fourth rotor to make decryption even harder. That wasn't all; the Germans built a plugboard into their Enigma 1 Model so that the operator could exchange letters in pairs, further reducing the chances that any hostile power would be able to crack their codes.

But unbeknown to the Germans, forces were already work against their Enigma machine. In 1928 the German government had sent one of the encryption

Codebreakers hard at work within Bletchley Park. So secret was their role that it was not until the 1970s that their contribution to the war effort was recognized with the publication of a book entitled *The Ultra Secret.*

◄ Bletchley Park Manor in rural Buckinghamshire, the operational headquarters of arguably the most secret project of the war—the British decryption project that cracked the German Enigma codes.

machines to their embassy in Warsaw, but the parcel came to the attention of the Polish intelligence services, who intercepted it, studied the Enigma machine over the weekend, and then carefully repackaged it and sent it onwards to the German embassy.

Armed with this information the Poles' top codebreaker, Marian Rejewski, designed a decoder, which recreated the settings of the German Enigma device that had encoded the initial text, thereby enabling the operator to read the original message. So delighted were the Poles with their decoder that they called it the "Cryptological Bomb" and throughout the 1930s they were able to decode the German Enigma messages. By the end of the decade, as war loomed in Europe, the Poles shared their secret with the British. Amazed at what the Poles had pulled off, the British expanded their Government Code and Cypher School, installing it in Bletchley Park and building new huts to house the additional staff recruited into the school.

In August 1939 one of the Polish "Bombs" arrived at Bletchley Park and it was turned over to the School's star pupil—a 27-year-old Englishman called Alan Turing. One of the most brilliant mathematicians of his generation, whose paper on "computable numbers" was hailed as a work of outstanding foresight, Turing, with the help of other gifted mathematicians and grouped together in what became known as Hut 8, began work on a new and improved version of the Polish device. With each of the three rotors having 26 possible settings, that meant there were 17,756 possible settings in total on the German machine (26 × 26 × 26). The decoding machine that Turing helped design was 6ft 6in (2m) high and 6ft 6in (2m) wide, and capable of trying all 17,756 theoretical settings in just 20 minutes.

Alan Turing, the young mathematics genius who led the decryption work at Bletchley Park in what was known as Hut 8. Although his postwar life was not happy, Turing's efforts in cracking the Nazis' secret code was recognized in 2014 with the release of the film *The Imitation Game*.

ENIGMA ENCRYPTION

The Enigma encrypter used three components that worked independently of each other. The 26 wires (above right) transmitted an electrical signal that passed through a plugboard and then through three rotors (left, middle and right) that altered the direction of the input signal's direction as it passed through the Enigma machine. The rotors rotated independently while enciphering a message so the left, middle and right rotors never worked in tandem. In other words, the message was encrypted 26 times by 26 times by 26 times, meaning that someone seeking to decrypt the Enigma message would have to press 17,576 keys to find the starting point for the original message.

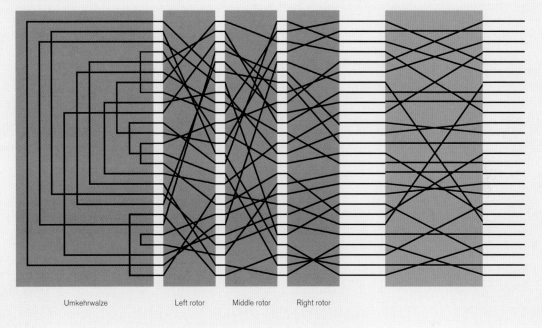

Scrambler

Stecker

Umkehrwalze   Left rotor   Middle rotor   Right rotor

The decoder did this by performing electrically a chain of logical deductions based on a portion of plaintext and rejecting those that produced a contradiction—the majority—leaving just a small number that could be examined more closely.

The first decoder was operational in March 1940 under the codename "Victory," a second was installed in August and more followed as the British began to see the fruits of their endeavors, not just against the U-boats in the Battle of the Atlantic (Bletchley Park cracked German naval codes in June 1941) but more particularly in North Africa where the British were striving to record their first campaign victory of the war.

In September 1941 Ultra decoded the Enigma keys used by General Erwin Rommel's Libyan headquarters in communicating with Rome and Berlin. Together with the reconnaissance carried out by the Long Range Desert Group (see page 98), General Claude Auchinleck was able to check many of Rommel's moves during the "Crusader" Offensive of November and December 1941. Additionally, many Axis ships dispatched across the Mediterranean to bring much-needed supplies to German and Italian forces were sunk because of intercepted Enigma messages. So successful was Ultra in North Africa that occasionally the British were compelled to refrain from acting for fear of alerting Rommel to the fact they had cracked his codes. On one occasion, in May 1942, two German spies were transported across the Libyan desert to Cairo so they could report back on British activity in the Egyptian

BOMBE

The rear view of a British "Bombe" decoding machine plugged up with three menus, in Hut 11 at Bletchley Park, now a museum. The decoding machine that Turing helped design was nearly 6ft 6in (2m) high and to its operators—predominantly women, Hut 11 was known as the "Hellhole" on account of the demanding work.

A four-rotor German Enigma cypher machine with a second operator display made during World War II. This type of machine, devised by the German Navy in 1939, was used to encode wartime messages requiring a particularly high degree of security.

capital. The pair were kept under surveillance for several weeks, allowed to report back to their handlers as if nothing was amiss, before being arrested.

At the end of 1942 Alan Turing was sent to the United States to advise the Americans on their version of the Bombe decrypting machine. Bigger than their British counterparts, the American naval machine decoded 30 times quicker and became operational in May 1943.

Twelve months later Ultra—the name under which all the Allied decoding projects were known—played a crucial role in planning Operation Overlord, the landings in Normandy, furnishing commanders with comprehensive intelligence on 56 of the 58 German divisions in Western Europe. "Decisive" was how Dwight Eisenhower, the Supreme Allied Commander of Operation Overlord, summed up Ultra's contribution to the successful invasion of France in 1944.

Yet at the end of the war the thousands of men and women who had worked so hard in the battle of the codebreakers received scant recognition. Forbidden by the Official Secrets Act to discuss their role (the advent of the Cold War meant that much of Ultra's work was still relevant in the 1950s and 60s) they returned to their civilian jobs. Alan Turing continued his pioneering research into computing machinery and artificial intelligence, but in 1952 pleaded guilty to a charge of gross indecency. His admission of homosexuality, then illegal in Britain, impinged on his professional life, denying him the security clearance required to continue working as a cryptographic consultant for the British government's Communications Headquarters, the successor to the wartime Government Code and Cypher School. Turing committed suicide in 1954 and it is only in recent years that his contribution to Britain's wartime decoding achievements has been belatedly honored. As Hugh Alexander, his successor in charge of Hut 8, commented: "There should be no question in anyone's mind that Turing's work was the biggest factor in Hut 8's success. In the early days he was the only cryptographer who thought the problem worth tackling."

ULTRA INTELLIGENCE

On the Joint Intelligence Committee in Cairo in 1942 was Lieutenant-Colonel Enoch Powell, who recalled: "I remember very vividly the day when I was introduced to uncle Henry, for uncle Henry was the pet name by which Ultra went in the Middle East. … [It] told us the most significant and important things, in particular facts that enabled the German supply position in North Africa to be calculated more accurately than was known to Rommel himself. The cargoes, places of arrival, capacity of ships, ammunition state, the transportation difficulties, these became part of a picture."

THE JAPANESE PURPLE CIPHER

The Japanese had their own encryption machine that was modeled on the rotor technology of the Enigma. They called it "97-shiki Obun Injiki," translated as Alphabetical Typewriter 97, with the digits referring to the Japanese year 2597 (1937 in the West), the year the machine was invented.

The Japanese were proud of their encryption machine, which operated on four rotors like the German Enigma machine. With the arrogance that characterized Japanese attitudes in the 1930s, they believed none of the so-called decadent Western Powers would be able to decrypt their machine. It comprised two Underwood typewriters, one for input and one for output, a feature that had its advantages and disadvantages. On the one hand the presence of two typewriters cut down on errors and manpower but this meant the machine was unwieldy and, because the typewriters were electrical, made it less portable than the Enigma.

More significantly according to the USA's National Security Agency, there was an additional weakness: "The machines split the Japanese syllabary into vowels and consonants, and enciphered each separately. Once this 20/6 split was recognized, the basic attack against Purple was cribbing … furthermore, they enciphered English-language diplomatic texts."

The Americans had been working on breaking the Japanese codes throughout the 1930s, a task made all the more urgent in the summer of 1937 when conflict erupted between Japan and China in what was termed the Second Sino-Japanese War (the first was in 1894–95). Japan's imperialist policy and naked aggression alarmed the USA and its military chiefs were desperate to gain an intelligence advantage over their rival in the Pacific.

William Friedman (see box) had been appointed chief of the army's Signals Intelligence Service (SIS) in 1930

A replica of the Japanese Purple Code. Built by Friedman and his team of cryptologists, the machine copied the actions of the Japanese original and was called the "Purple Analog."

WILLIAN FRIEDMAN

Son of a Russian Jew whose family emigrated to the United States in 1892, William Friedman graduated from Cornell University in 1914. Upon America's entry into World War I in 1917, he was employed as a cryptologist. William continued in this field in the 1920s before being appointed chief of the army Signals Intelligence Service (SIS) in 1930, during which time he wrote numerous papers and articles about scientific cryptography. After the war Friedman, now a colonel, was a key cryptologist of the Department of Defense until his retirement in 1955. Nine years later President Harry Truman awarded him the Medal of Merit, the highest presidential civilian award, and he died in November 1969. William Friedman is buried in Arlington National Cemetery and the epitaph on his gravestone reads: "Knowledge is Power."

and the US Navy also had their own team of codebreakers working on the case, the Code and Signal Section (CSS). The problem was that neither team wanted to cooperate with the other, professional jealously precluding the formation of a crucial alliance.

Eventually it was the SIS who scored the first major triumph, cracking Japan's Red Code—their diplomatic cipher—in March 1939. The success was soured, however, by the revelation that the Japanese had now developed a Purple Code, named "after the color of the folders that held the decryptions, to distinguish it from other Japanese ciphers."

Friedman and his team of cryptologists strove to break this new code but it took them a further 18 months before they succeeded. One September afternoon in 1940 codebreaker Frank Rowlett achieved the vital breakthrough, yelling "That's it!" as he cracked the Purple Code. Friedman was wont to describe his team as "magicians" and consequently all intelligence deciphered from the Japanese Purple Code was in future referred to as "Magic."

Having broken the code, Friedman and his team set about constructing an operational replica which copied the actions of the Japanese original. They called it the "Purple Analog," a prototype produced in the basement of the home of an electrical engineer in SIS called Leo Rosen. The Navy, setting aside their rivalry, assisted in the construction.

Soon the Americans were gleaning important intelligence not just on Japan's military intentions but also those of Germany thanks to the regular communiqués sent from Berlin by Baron Hiroshi Oshima, a Japanese diplomat in the German capital who was acquainted with Hitler. He maintained a constant flow of information to Tokyo in the early years of the war on German weapons and technological advancements. All of these were read by the Americans, who offered a "free exchange of intelligence" with Britain even though in 1940 the USA was still neutral.

Admiral Isoroku Yamamoto, the commander-in-chief of the Japanese Combined Fleet during World War II, who was shot down and killed in April thanks to secret American intelligence.

But the British declined the invitation. Having only recently cracked the German Enigma code, the British wanted to ensure Ultra remained top secret and the reality was they didn't trust everyone in Washington to keep it that way, not out of any sense of misguided affection for Nazi Germany but because some Americans, unacquainted with the exigencies of wartime espionage, were blasé in their approach to intelligence.

Britain's concerns were warranted. One of President Roosevelt's aides, Major General Edwin Watson, on one occasion disposed of some top-secret intelligence by putting it in his office trash can, a shocking breach of security that fortunately didn't have serious repercussions. Not so the complacency of Colonel Bonner Fellers. Fellers, the US military attaché in Cairo, was in the habit of sending long and detailed radiograms from the Egyptian capital to Washington on the state of the British military's position in the war against Erwin Rommel in North Africa. Unfortunately the Americans were unaware that the Italian Secret Service—*Servizio Informazione Militari* (SIM), had broken into the American embassy in Rome in September 1941 and obtained a copy of the Black Code, the code by which US military attachés and ambassadors communicated the world over. It was a flagrant breach of diplomatic protocol on the part of the Italians but thanks to their skulduggery they and their German allies were able to decipher all Fellers' messages within a few hours of transmission. They proved so valuable to Rommel that in January 1942 his Afrika Korps launched a fresh—and successful—offensive against the British in Libya on the back of one of Fellers' decoded messages. Fellers eventually left Cairo in July 1942—partly due to the British, who suspected he was the source of the leaks—and his successor sent encoded reports to Washington in the M-138 strip cipher that was not known to the Axis forces. As a result Rommel lost a crucial source of intelligence just as the Desert War entered its decisive phase.

The Germans began to suspect that the Americans had cracked the Purple Code but the Japanese, and Oshima in particular, refused to believe this was possible. They continued to send message using the cipher and the Americans continued to decipher them, although they couldn't prevent the devastating attack on Pearl Harbor on December 1941 that brought the USA into the war.

How could the Japanese air force launch such a murderous assault on the US Pacific Fleet in Hawaii given that their top-secret military codes had been cracked by their foe? While some historians have claimed the US government were in fact alerted to an impending attack but ignored it, so that it would bring them into the war, most people dismiss this as a wayward conspiracy theory. Put simply: the US High Command expected an attack but assumed it would be come in the Philippines, where the American air force had several bases that posed a threat to the Japanese navy.

The onslaught at Pearl Harbor—Roosevelt's "Day of Infamy"—left 2,403 Americans dead, a further 1,178 wounded and eight battleships either lost or badly damaged. But the Americans were to have their

Colonel Bonner Fellers, the US military attaché in Cairo sent long-winded radiograms from the Egyptian capital to Washington on the state of the British military's position in the war that were gleefully intercepted by the Axis intelligence services.

revenge 18 months later—and their codebreakers played a large part in the deadly retribution.

Having deciphered the Purple Code, Friedman and his team of "magicians" also cracked the Japanese Fleet code, what the USA termed "JN-25," the means by which the Japanese navy sent tactical messages. One such decrypt in April 1943 tipped off the Americans that Admiral Isoroku Yamamoto, the commander-in-chief of the Combined Fleet, planned to fly to Bougainville in the South Pacific on a morale-boosting visit to his men after the defeat at Guadalcanal. The intelligence intercepted by the decoders gave Yamamoto's itinerary and even the number and type of aircraft his tour would entail. President Roosevelt ordered Frank Knox, secretary of the Navy, to "Get Yamamoto," which he did. On April 18 a squadron of Lightnings ambushed the Admiral's transport plane and its escort over the Solomon Islands and Yamamoto was shot down and killed. "Purple" had exacted its heaviest price yet on Japan.

FBI VERSUS ABWEHR IN AMERICA

Adolf Hitler had never liked the United States of America. Since coming to power in Germany in 1933 he had viewed the country with distaste, regarding it as degenerate and a diaspora of inferior races with the Jews all powerful. Following Japan's attack on Pearl Harbor, Hitler, and Benito Mussolini, the Italian fascist leader, declared war on the USA on December 11, the Fuhrer declaring that their aim—along with Japan—was the establishment of "a new and just order." He accused President Roosevelt of working to undermine Germany since as far back as 1937 and even said he believed America was secretly planning to invade the Fatherland in 1943.

The reality, however, was that it was Germany who for years had been conspiring against the USA. One of their first acts was to establish a network of "sleepers" in the USA, as they had in Great Britain (see page 40), spies who would assimilate into the local population until they were activated by their handlers in Germany.

One such sleeper was Carl Hermann Schroetter, to all intents and purposes the captain of a Miami charter boat and a respected member of his local community in Florida. In fact the Swiss-born Schroetter had been recruited into the Abwehr in 1939 during a vacation in Germany. The following year he embarked on his secret life as a spy, his everyday job as a sea captain was perfect for cruising the Florida coast and observing the movement of American military vessels. All that he saw he reported back to his handler in New York City, many of his messages written in invisible ink.

Having impressed the Abwehr with the quality and quantity of his research, Schroetter received the equivalent of an espionage promotion: he was instructed to spy on the naval air base outside Miami. Getting inside the base was impossible, so Schroetter used his initiative and got a job as the night chef at the Greyhound Club, a popular drinking den close to the base frequented by military personnel. In between cooking the sailors a steak, he would have a beer with them and talk about this and that, and what life was like as a sailor. Everything he gleaned from the beery sailors he reported back to Germany.

Schroetter was eventually caught by the FBI and confessed much information but throughout his interrogation he refused to reveal the names of other German agents operating in the USA, one of whom he had worked with in Florida. His name was Kurt Frederick Ludwig, head of the "Joe K" spy ring—so-called because it was the signature he used in the intelligence he sent to Germany.

Ludwig was based in New York, spying on the city's shipping movements, but by early 1941 the activities of the Joe K ring had come to the attention of the FBI. Ludwig was tailed to Florida, where he was seen in the company of Schroetter (sealing the latter's fate as up until then he had avoided suspicion as he worked alone). In August 1941 Ludwig, Schroetter and the rest of the ring were arrested and put on trial, all being found guilty of espionage in March 1942 and sentenced to terms ranging between 10 and 20 years. Schroetter received 10 years but hanged himself a short while into his sentence.

The collapse of the Joe K ring was a major setback for the Abwehr, but even as the members of the ring were being tried and convicted, the German Intelligence Service was concocting a far more dangerous and daring plot—one that entailed sabotage rather than surveillance.

In April 1942 a group of men assembled at the Abwehr sabotage school in the countryside close to Brandenburg, in eastern Germany. Their leader was Lieutenant Walter Kappe, a 37-year-old heavily built man who would be in command of Operation Pastorius. Having lived in the USA for more than 10 years, Kappe was well accustomed to American ways but, like Hitler, he was a committed Nazi who despised many aspects of American culture.

WILLIAM G. SEEBOLD

Another German recruited into the Abwehr was William G. Seebold, a veteran of World War I, who had emigrated to the USA in 1920, married an American and found employment as a draftsman with the Consolidated Aircraft Company. In the summer of 1939, while on vacation in Germany, he was coerced into the Abwehr after threats were made against his relatives still living in the country. Back in the USA, however, Seebold, immediately informed the FBI of his recruitment, handing over the $1,000 he had been given to buy radio parts as well as a list of names of a German spy network in America. The leader of the network was 62-year-old Frederick Duquesne, a respectable businessman with offices on Wall Street. So important did Seebold become to the FBI that their chief, J. Edgar Hoover, paid a personal interest in his activities, creating a "little brain trust" of his most capable agents to work on the case. Eventually 33 members of the Duquesne Spy Ring were convicted (the largest espionage case in the history of the USA), with those found guilty sentenced to serve a total of more than 300 years in prison.

WANTED
GERMAN SABOTEUR

Photo taken February 19, 1936

WALTER KAPPE, alias Walter Kappel   F.P.C. 16 M 28 W OOI
                                                 M 8 W III

Walter Kappe is known to be connected with **sabotage** activities being promoted by the Nazi Government. He was born January 12, 1905 at Alfeld, Leina, Germany, and entered the United States on March 9, 1925. He filed application for United States citizenship at Kankakee, Illinois, in June, 1935. He is known to be a member of the German Literary Club, Cincinnati, Ohio, and the Teutonia Club, Chicago, Illinois. Kappe was an agent in the United States for the Ausland Organization and editor "Deutscher Weckruf und Beobachter", official organ of the German-American Bund. Kappe left the United States in 1937 and may return to the United States as an agent for Germany. This individual is described as fol-

A reproduction of photo of the "Wanted" circular issued by the FBI during the countrywide manhunt for the German agents who landed on the east American coast. Their leader was Lieutenant Walter Kappe, the 37-year-old whose fingerprints are displayed on the poster.

The original caption on this FBI Wanted circular stated that Edward John Kerling, alias Edward John Kelly (near right), and George John Dasch, "are two of the eight Axis saboteurs captured by the FBI. Kerling led the group which landed at Pontevedra, Florida. Dasch led the group of four which landed by submarine at Amagansett, Long Island."

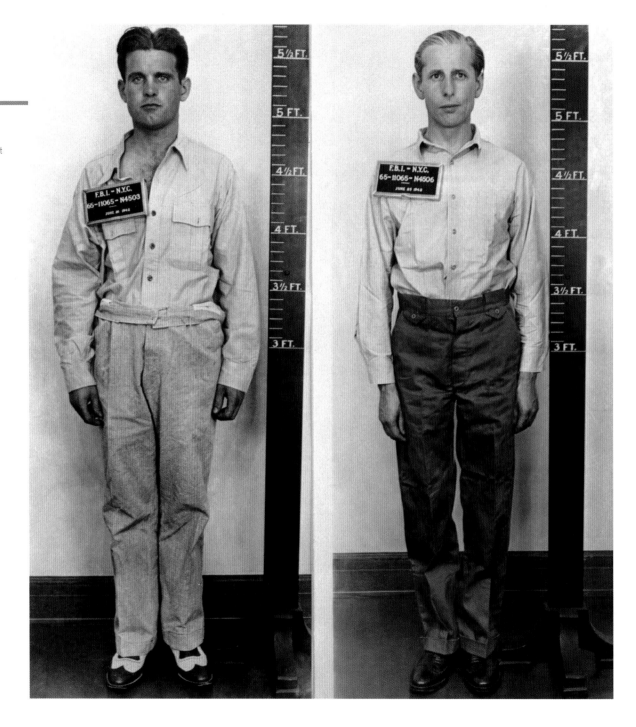

In selecting his men for the operation, Kappe had scrutinized the files housed in the Ausland Institute, the organization who had helped German expatriates return from the USA between 1939 and 1941. Picking eight men he thought fulfilled all the criteria to become saboteurs, Kappe divided them into two teams and gave command of one to 39-year-old George Dasch, a veteran of World War I who had emigrated to the USA in the 1920s and worked for many years as a waiter. One of the men selected to work in Dasch's team was Ernest Burger, a dedicated fascist who had taken part in Hitler's infamous Munich Putsch, the Fuhrer's initial ill-fated attempt to seize control of Germany.

Picked to lead the second team was 32-year-old Edward Kerling, who had lived in the States for 11 years before returning to Germany in 1940 and taking up an appointment with Josef Goebbels' Ministry of Propaganda. In Kerling's team was the youngest member of Operation Pastorius—22-year-old Herbert Haupt, who had emigrated to America aged five and spoke English without a German accent.

The saboteurs spent May 1942 training for their mission and on the 23rd of the month they learned of their targets: Dasch's team was tasked with blowing up the hydroelectric plants at Niagara Falls and three Aluminum Company of America factories in Tennessee, Illinois, and New York. Additionally they were to destroy the Philadelphia Salt Company's cryolite plant in Philadelphia, which was vital to aluminum manufacture.

For Kerling's team the targets were predominantly important transport links: the Pennsylvania Railroad station at Newark, New York Central Railroad's Hell Gate Bridge, the lock and canal complexes at St Louis and Cincinnati and sections of the Chesapeake and Ohio Railroad in Pennsylvania.

The two teams were also instructed to wage a terror campaign, planting bombs in busy railroad stations and

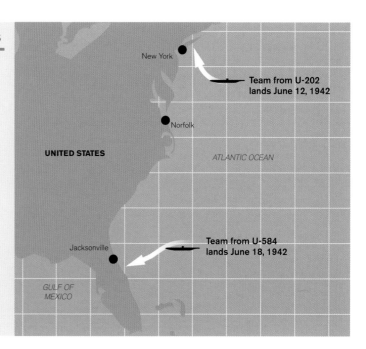

OPERATION PASTORIUS

The two landing points on the Eastern Seaboard of the two submarines that brought ashore the eight German agents as part of Operation Pastorius. All the spies were soon captured by the FBI and after a military tribunal six were executed in the electric chair on August 8, 1942.

New York

Team from U-202
lands June 12, 1942

Norfolk

UNITED STATES

ATLANTIC OCEAN

Jacksonville

Team from U-584
lands June 18, 1942

GULF OF
MEXICO

department stores so that the savagery of war would be brought home to the American public.

At the end of May the two teams—traveling independently of each other—left for the USA inside two German U-boats with the intention of rendezvousing in Cincinnati on July 4. They carried with them a sizable sum of American dollars and the requisite amount of explosives and fuses to sustain their sabotage mission. Kerling and Dasch also had handkerchiefs on which were written in invisible ink the names of their Abwehr contacts in America.

Dasch's team was the first to set foot on American soil, coming ashore on the evening of June 12 dressed as German marines. Within minutes Operation Pastorius began to unravel. Confronted by a "sand pounder," a coast guardsman who patrolled beaches looking for German submarines, the team tried to pass

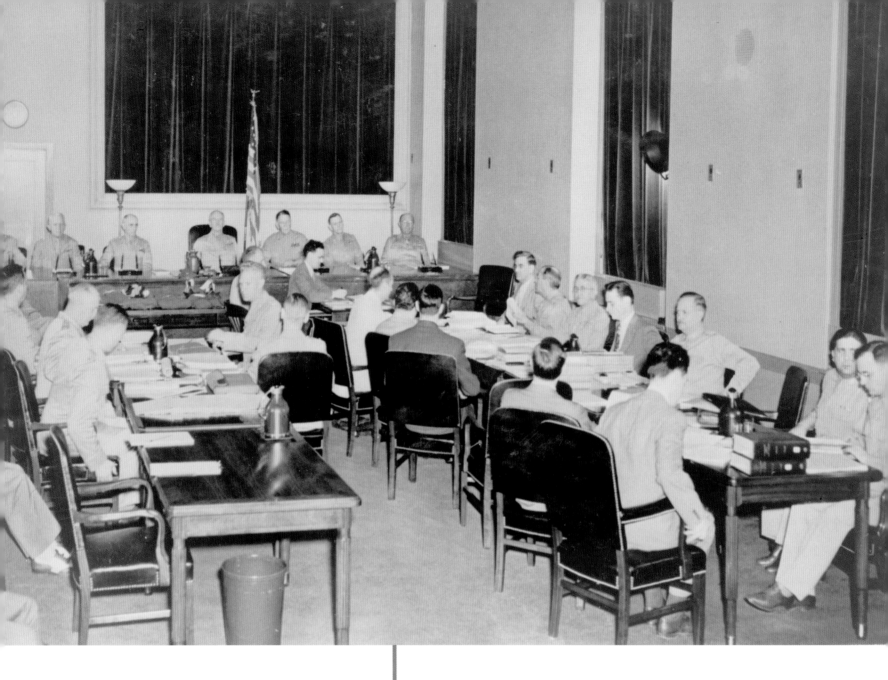

The US military commission sits in judgment on the third day of its proceedings in the trial of eight Nazi saboteurs. Left to right are: Brigadier General John T. Lewis; Major General Lorenzo D. Casser; Major General Walter S. Grant; Major General Frank R. McCoy, president of the commission; Major General Blanton Winship; Brigadier General Guy V. Henry; Brigadier General John T. Kennedy.

► The hydroelectric plant at Niagara Falls was one of the targets of the would-be German saboteurs.

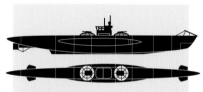

VII C U-BOAT

Crew 44

Type Attack U-boat

Length 220.1ft (67.1m)

Beam 20.3ft (6.2m)

Surface speed 7.6 knots

Crush depth 656ft (200m)

Torpedo capacity 14

A type VII U-boat of the sort which brought the saboteurs across the Atlantic to America. It was the most common U-boat type deployed by the German navy during the Battle of the Atlantic and had a maximum speed of 8.7mph when submerged.

themselves off as stranded fishermen and when that failed Dasch stuffed a wad of dollars ($260 in total) into the American's hands and told him to forget everything he'd seen. The guardsmen, who was armed only with a flare gun, complied and moved off, and Dasch thought they had got away with it. But as the saboteurs headed towards the Long Island Railroad station at Amagansett to catch the early morning train to New York City, the guardsmen—Seaman 2nd Class John Cullen—had alerted his superiors to his suspicious encounter, adding that he had heard one of the men speaking German. By midday the FBI had found some of the explosives buried by Dasch and his team on the beach and a huge manhunt was underway. But by then Dasch had already made the decision to turn himself in to the FBI.

Kerling's team, meanwhile, landed at Ponte Verdra Beach, 25 miles (40km) southeast of Jacksonville, on June 18 and encountered no inquisitive coastguard. Everything went smoothly for the four saboteurs and Kerling took one man to Cincinnati while Haupt and the fourth saboteur caught a bus for Chicago.

The same day Dasch arrived in Washington, handed himself in to the FBI and revealed all, allowing Hoover to tell President Roosevelt on June 22 that the FBI "had already apprehended all members of the group which landed on Long Island." He made no mention of Dasch's cooperation even though he had led the FBI to the other three members of his team, and handed over his handkerchief with the names of contacts written in invisible ink. One of those names was a Helmut Leiner, living in Cincinnati, and by tailing him the FBI eventually apprehended Kerling and his team.

Aware that to put the men on trial in a public court could comprise national security, Roosevelt decided that the spies would be tried by seven generals in a military tribunal—the first instance since the assassination of President Abraham Lincoln in 1865.

The eight were found guilty of espionage and all but Dasch and Burger—who had also cooperated fully and helped in the capture of his comrades—were executed in the electric chair on August 8, 1942. Burger was sentenced to hard labor for life and Dasch received 30 years, although both were deported to West Germany in 1948.

The coast guardsmen who blew the whole operation, John Cullen, died in 2011 aged 90. "The German fellow was nervous," he said in an interview about the capture of the spies, "but I think I was more nervous."

THE ROOTS OF FRENCH RESISTANCE

For the first months of the German occupation, France collectively had been almost too stunned by the scale of their subjugation to offer any resistance. For four years they had resisted German forces in World War I, only to be overrun a quarter of a century later in a matter of weeks. The armistice, signed in July 1940, divided France into the occupied and unoccupied zones; the former—the northern half—under the governance of Germany and the southern half controlled by a French government based in the spa town of Vichy under Marshal Philippe Pétain, the hero of Verdun in 1916.

There was the odd act of defiance, often extemporary, by individuals unable to stand the sight of Germans in their country. In Paris, however, a Resistance movement began to take root after the execution on December 23, 1940 of Jacques Bonsergent, a 28-year-old engineer whose only crime had been to witness an angry exchange of words between a group of Frenchmen and some German soldiers.

The Germans proclaimed the death sentence when he refused to name those involved in the confrontation on scores of posters spread across the French capital in

OCCUPATION OF FRANCE

Following the occupation of France the Germans divided the country into two zones, roughly north and south. The top half of the country was administered by a German regimen based in the capital, Paris, and became known as the Occupied Zone (Zone Nord). The southern half of France was the Zone Sud and was ruled by a puppet government with the French World War I hero, Marshal Philippe Pétain, at its head. This government was based in the spa town of Vichy and the southern half of France became better known as Vichy France.

- Atlantic Wall
- Demarcation line
- Occupied Zone from November 1942
- Closed Zone
- Territories annexed to the Reich
- Military administration of Belgium and Northern France
- Free Zone from November 1942
- Italian Occupation November 1942–September 1943
- Demilitarized Zone
- Italian Occupation Zone

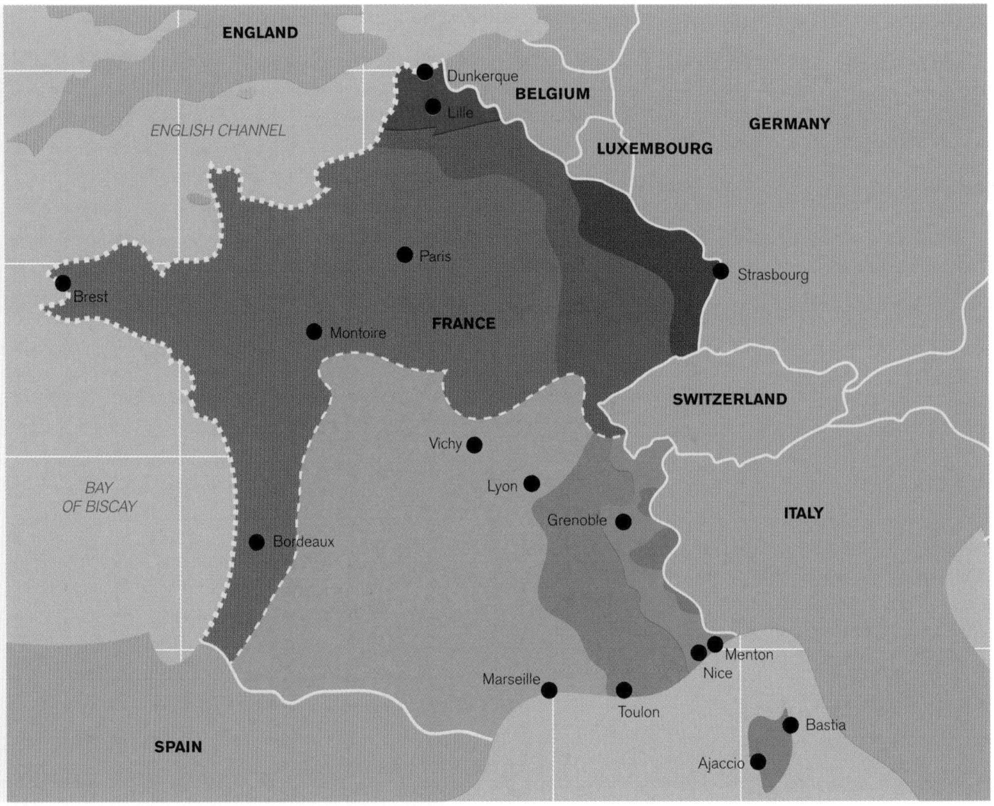

ENGLAND

ENGLISH CHANNEL

Dunkerque
BELGIUM
Lille
GERMANY
LUXEMBOURG

Paris

Strasbourg

Brest

Montoire
FRANCE

SWITZERLAND

Vichy

BAY
OF BISCAY

Lyon

Grenoble
ITALY

Bordeaux

Menton
Nice

Marseille

Toulon
Bastia

SPAIN

Ajaccio

the belief they would cower the population still further. It had the adverse effect. Flowers, candles, French flags, even British ones, were left alongside the posters as an act of solidarity for Bonsergent. The gesture reached the ears of General Charles de Gaulle, leader of the Free French in London, and a message was broadcast on the BBC wireless, asking French citizens to mark the New Year of 1941 by staying indoors between 3 and 4 p.m. on January 1. It was a small, innocuous act but for the first time the French felt as if they were defying their oppressor.

A few Frenchmen had been standing up to the Germans since the first days of the invasion, none more so than Jean Moulin, a 41-year-old prefect in the Eure-et-Loir department of France, with its administrative headquarters in the town of Chartres, 60 miles (97km) southwest of Paris. Refusing to blame a Nazi massacre of civilians on Senegalese troops serving in the French army, Moulin was arrested and tortured. Eventually he was released and Moulin

travelled via Spain to London where he told Charles de Gaulle "it would be insane and criminal, in the event of Allied action on the continent, not to make use of troops prepared for the greatest sacrifices, scattered and unorganized today, but tomorrow capable of making up a united army."

Recognizing his organization and administrative skills, General de Gaulle appointed Moulin his delegate-general in France, with responsibility for organizing the growing number of resistants in the country.

While in London Moulin was schooled in unarmed combat and small-arms training, and also learned to parachute, and then on the night of January 2–3, 1942, he dropped in to France to begin his work. Visiting Resistance networks in Marseille, Lyon, and Paris, Moulin helped to create an organized structure of secret armies within France, coordinated from de Gaulle's headquarters in London and supplied with arms from the British capital. It was no easy task and Moulin's superb diplomacy was put to the test as he

▲ **ABOVE LEFT** General Charles de Gaulle, leader of the Free French forces, gives an address to his countrymen from London via the British Broadcasting Corporation.

ABOVE RIGHT Jean Moulin, who formed the National Council of the French Resistance, reporting to de Gaulle, but who was captured and tortured to death by the Gestapo in 1943.

persuaded communists and right-wing groups to put aside their political differences and unite for the common good of France.

Between January and April 1943 one Resistance group alone—the Francs-Tireurs et Partisans (FTP)—derailed 158 trains and raided 110 engine yards. Escape lines were established to aid RAF crews shot down in France, and, in a few cases, British soldiers left behind from the evacuation at Dunkirk in 1940, to return to Britain across the frontier into neutral Spain or Switzerland. Volunteers known as "passeurs," some of whom were children, guided the Britons to safety. Money from London also helped finance dozens of anti-German essays, pamphlets, and newspapers, printed in every major French city, and secretly distributed to the population so they could see that, underground was a flourishing Resistance movement.

From February 1943 the number of young Frenchman willing to join Moulin's organized Resistance network increased when the Vichy government passed the *Service du travail obligatoire* (Compulsory Work Service) Act that required all able-bodied men between the ages of 18 to 50 and single women from 21 to 35 to be available to work for the German war effort. Almost overnight hundreds of French citizens left home to join one of the dozens of Resistance groups based in the countryside. Now, for the first time, the Resistance movement ceased to be just an urban phenomenon, centered on Paris, Marseille, Lyon, and other big cities, and instead spread to the French countryside.

Having returned to London to brief de Gaulle on his progress, Moulin parachuted into France again in early 1943 as head of the National Council of the Resistance (CNR). On May 27 he chaired its first meeting in Paris but the following month Moulin was betrayed to the Germans. Despite terrible torture he told the Gestapo nothing about the CNR's activities before dying of his injuries on July 8, 1943.

▲ This destroyed German tank was actually hit by US Air Force fighters, however it is an example of the type of military vehicle present on the soil of Northern France during 1944.

Moulin's sacrifice was not in vain. In February 1944 the *Forces Françaises de l'Intérieur* (FFI) expanded to encompass the Free French soldiers who had been fighting with the Allies since 1941 and the disparate Resistance groups within France.

In the weeks and months building up to D-Day the Resistance groups radioed important intelligence to London on the disposition and strength of German troops. Then, once the landings were underway in Normandy, their job was to delay German reinforcements reaching the beachhead by ambushing columns of vehicles and derailing troops trains. One German infantry division spent five days traveling 125 miles (201km) by rail from southern Brittany to Normandy because of Resistance attacks, while the notorious SS Panzer division known as "Das Reich" needed 16 days to travel north from Montauban instead of the seven it had estimated.

Prior to the invasion of France, the Resistance had received training from members of the Special Operations Executive (SOE) in the use of explosives and communications, allowing them to become—in some cases—self-contained units called Maquis, a word meaning the thick scrub terrain in southern France and the island of Corsica.

One of the most effective of such groups was Maquis Bernard, which operated in the Morvan, an area of rolling, wooded countryside approximately 75 miles (121km) west of Dijon in central France. For three months between June and September 1944 Maquis Bernard hosted A Squadron, 1SAS (the operation was codenamed "Houndsworth"), feeding them and passing on intelligence, and often fighting together against the Germans that passed north towards Normandy. "We had to train the Maquis, after a drop of arms, to fire the weapons," recalled David Danger, an SAS signaller. "A number of chaps shot themselves through the feet because they had no idea about safety, but overall the original Maquis blokes were pretty professional and trustworthy."

The French resistance to the occupation took other forms, more passive than the aggression of the Maquis, but nonetheless just as important. In September 1944 a large party of 2SAS troops parachuted into the Vosges region of France, in the east of the country close to the border with Germany. Their objective was to harry the Germans retreating through the rugged terrain into the Fatherland but unfortunately, just as the operation began, the advance of the American Third Army ground to a halt and the Germans dug in in the Vosges. The SAS soldiers found themselves in the midst of thousands of enemy troops and increasingly relied on the French civilians for assistance. One woman, Madame Bergeron, "a severe, conventional, serious, middle-aged spinster" who lived on a farm with her elderly mother, was the principal message bearer for the local Maquis group and also provided the SAS with food and shelter. Christopher Sykes, the SAS intelligence officer, recalled that Madame Bergeron was arrested by the Germans, who "heaped every humiliation on her to break her spirit … and they failed absolutely. They made her house into a brothel, they beat her, they tortured her, with no avail. This quiet, prim, very ordinary-looking, well-dressed woman had the strength of a tiger."

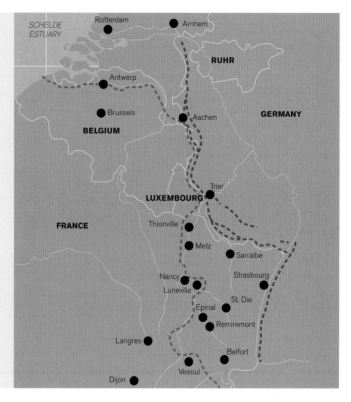

THE ALLIED FRONT, SEPTEMBER 15, 1944

In September 1944 the Allied advance east began to slow. So rapid had their drive been since breaking out of Normandy that the Americans overstretched their supply chain and the battlefield became temporarily static. The Germans needed the respite and used it to strengthen their new defensive positions along the banks of the River Moselle. On September 5 the US Third Army relaunched their advance east, liberating the city of Nancy 10 days later; but the Germans had been bolstered by the arrival of the 5th Panzer Division from Brussels and the Allied advance turned out to be painstakingly slow.

- - - **Allied front line**
- - - **West Wall**

Twenty years later, in 1964, Jean Moulin's remains were reinterred in the Pantheon in the presence of Charles de Gaulle and Andre Malraux, the Minister of Culture, who had worked with Moulin in the Resistance. Describing Moulin as the "leader of a people of the night," Malraux finished his oration by saying: "Today, young people of France, may you think of this man as you would have reached out your hands to his poor, unrecognisable face on that last day, to those lips that never let fall a word of betrayal: on that day, his was the face of France."

THE DOOLITTLE RAID

By March 1942 the Japanese were masters of all they surveyed. Since launching their deadly attack on the US Pacific Fleet at Pearl Harbor the previous December, Emperor Hirohito's forces had inflicted one crushing blow after another on the Allies, conquering Hong Kong, Malaya, Singapore, Indochina, and Burma. There was an air of invincibility about the seemingly tireless Japanese troops, with even the American magazine, *Reader's Digest*, carrying an account of the Japanese battalion that had set a world record for endurance marching in 1942 with a 100-mile (161km) dash down the Malayan Peninsula. It had taken them a mere 72 hours.

On March 8 Japanese troops landed in New Guinea, their ultimate goal being to invade Australia, while three days later they came ashore on Mindanao, the southern-most island in the Philippines and on March 14 they were in the Solomon Islands, their engineers working to build an airstrip on Guadalcanal to help increase the scope of their aggressive expansion in the Pacific.

The American public, still reeling from Pearl Harbor, began to wonder when—or indeed if—they would be able to strike back at Japan. An article in *Time* magazine captured this spirit of frustration, declaring that "the nation had taken a heavy blow."

No one was more aware of this than President Franklin Roosevelt. Desperate for a morale-boosting fillip, he assembled his military chiefs and demanded retaliation, something to shake the Japanese from their comfy complacency.

One of the chiefs present was Admiral Ernest J. King of the US Navy and it was his operations officer, Captain Francis Low, who proposed a means of hitting back at the Japanese. Like all the best ideas it was a simple one: an air attack against the Japanese mainland. This had of course been mooted before, but military chiefs thought only in terms of an attack using navy planes taking off from an aircraft carrier. Low's suggestion was to launch a fleet of army bombers from the deck of an aircraft carrier; with their longer range and great bomb-carrying capabilities they would be able to launch an attack and land in a friendly country before running out of fuel.

Low's plan got the go-ahead from the higher authorities and the man selected to lead the daring mission was Lieutenant Colonel James H. Doolittle, a 45-year-old aviation expert who had served his country in World War I. He was old, old enough to be the father of most of those who would be taking part in the raid, but it was made clear to Doolittle that his job was to plan the raid, not participate in its execution.

Doolittle soon produced a mission statement, writing that the "purpose of this special project is to bomb and

JAMES DOOLITTLE

Born in December 1896, James "Jimmy" Doolittle grew up in Alaska and then Los Angeles, where he attended an air show in 1910 that started his love affair with aircraft. Soon he began to build and fly his own gliders and in 1917 he enlisted in the Signal Corps Reserve as a flying cadet (the United States had yet to form its own air force). Commissioned a second lieutenant in March 1918, Doolittle never saw action in the last year of World War I but he remained in the service after the end of the conflict. As well graduating from the from the Massachusetts Institute of Technology with a doctoral degree in aeronautical engineering, Doolittle also built a reputation as a pioneer of aviation, introducing many innovations into flying such as the outside loop. In 1932 Doolittle established the world's high speed record for land planes at 296mph and although he had retired from active service by the time of World War II, he reenlisted in 1940 with the rank of major. Doolittle died in 1993 aged 96.

fire the industrial center of Japan." He envisaged 16 aircraft, carried by the navy to within 400 miles (644km) of the target, taking off shortly before dawn. The aircraft would be B-25s, twin-engine medium bombers with a crew of five that had the range to carry out the raid and also were able to carry four 500lb (227kg) bombs flying at 300mph. As for the targets, Doolittle picked out industrial objectives in the cities of Tokyo, Yokohama, Osaka-Kobe, and Nagoya.

Then there was the question of the return. As all bomber crew knew, the most fraught part of an air raid was after the bombs had been dropped and the aircraft turned for home. Returning to the aircraft carrier wasn't possible so it was decided the B-25s would continue west into China, guided by a radio signal at Chuchow, 200 miles (322km) south of Shanghai. From there, having refuelled, the American planes would fly a further 800 miles (1,288km) to the city of Chungking, China's wartime capital.

The most important element in the raid was the men who crewed the aircraft. Doolittle approached the Seventeenth Bombardment Group, stationed in Oregon, asking for volunteers. Nearly 150 men stepped forward— pilots, navigators, gunners, flight-engineers—all eager to participate even though none knew what exactly they would be asked to do. Doolittle addressed the volunteers when they arrived at Eglin Field in Florida to commence their training. He thanked them for their enthusiasm and apologized that because it was a top-secret mission he could say little more about the precise nature of the operation. It would be dangerous, he warned the volunteers, and he offered each man the chance to back out. No man took up the offer and throughout March they trained intensively, mastering short-field take-offs. "We practiced, over and over, ramming the engines at full power, taking off at 65 miles per hour in a five-hundred-foot run," recalled Copilot Jack Sims. "It could be done, as long as an engine didn't skip a beat."

While the crews practiced, the ground crew and specialist technicians modified the B-25s for the mission, increasing their range by installing 225-gallon auxiliary fuel tanks in the aircrafts' bomb bays and adding a 60-gallon tank in the bottom turrets in place of the gun.

From practicing on an airfield, Doolittle and his men progressed to taking off from the deck of an aircraft carrier, the *Hornet*, at its base in Norfolk, Virginia. Having led his men through weeks of strenuous training there was no way Doolittle was going to miss the operation, arguing to his superiors that it was imperative he took part in the raid because "I know

▲ Lieutenant Colonel James H. Doolittle and some of his men pose for the camera in China after their raid on Japan. Those present are, from left to right: Staff Sergeant Fred A. Braemer, Bombardier; Staff Sergeant Paul J. Leonard, Flight Engineer/Gunner; General Ho, director of the Branch Government of Western Chekiang Province; Lieutenant Richard E. Cole, Copilot; Lieutenant Colonel. Doolittle, Mission Commander and Lieutenant Henry A. Potter, Navigator.

The USS *Hornet*, a navy carrier, was one of the vessels involved in the Doolittle Raid.

more about this mission than anyone else. And I know how to lead it."

Doolittle was given permission to act as the raid's pathfinder, flying in first to drop some incendiary bombs and illuminate the target for the aircraft that followed.

On April 2 the *Hornet* and its escort sailed from California with the raiders and their aircraft on board. Only when the ship was safely at sea did its commander, Captain Mitscher, declare over the loud speaker that "the target of this task force is Tokyo." En route to the target, the *Hornet* rendezvoused with another Task Force, including the aircraft carrier *Enterprise*, and together the 18 vessels sailed across the Pacific.

Below deck Doolittle and his men continued to study their targets, memorized once more the flight paths and finalized the escape routes towards China.

On April 17 the Task Force was a little over 1,000 miles (1,609km) from Tokyo, every sailor and airman fearful that they could be attacked by the Japanese now they were closing in on their target. Shortly after dawn the next day they were spotted by an enemy patrol boat, which was sunk although not before it had time to send a warning back to Japan. Even though they were still nearly 700 miles (1,127km) from the Japanese capital there was no alternative but to launch the mission immediately—before the Japanese 5th Fleet had time to react to the threat. Admiral William F.

▶ Eight B-25Bs on the decks of the USS *Hornet* en route to Japan prior to the launching of the Doolittle Raid. The aircraft on the right (tail No. 40-2250) was mission plane No. 10 piloted by 2nd Lieutenant Richard O. Joyce. The light cruiser USS *Nashville* is visible in the distance.

Halsey, captain of the *Enterprise* and in overall command of the mission, signalled the *Hornet* at 0800 hours, declaring: "Launch planes x to colonel Doolittle and gallant command x good luck and god bless you."

The 16 aircraft, led by Doolittle as Plane No. 1, took off from the deck of the *Hornet* even though as one of the pilots, David Jones, recalled: "We knew we had a fuel problem. With the task force spotted, we would have to fly maybe four hundred miles farther than planned. Chances of reaching those airstrips in China were worse than bad."

One of the pilots waiting to take off was Ted Lawson in Plane No. 7, who subsequently wrote an account of the raid entitled "Thirty Seconds Over Tokyo." He recalled: "Doolittle picked up speed and held to his line, and, just as the *Hornet* lifted up on top of a wave and cut through it at full speed, Doolittle's plane took off. He had yards to spare. He hung his ship almost straight up on its props, until we could see the whole top of his B-25. Then he levelled off and I watched him come around in a tight circle and shoot low over our heads."

With all the aircraft successfully up in the air, the Task Force turned in the opposite direction to return to Pearl Harbor and await news of the raid. Meanwhile the 16 B-25s flew towards Tokyo no more than 50ft (15m) above the Pacific Ocean at a speed of 150mph in order to preserve their fuel as long as possible. There was no formation to their flight; they were flying independently, with ten (including Doolittle's plane) to hit targets in Tokyo while three raided Kanagawa, Yokohama, and the Yokosuka, and three made for Kobe, Nagoya, and Osaka.

Doolittle reached the Japanese capital a few minutes after noon on Saturday, April 18. From his bomb bay dropped four incendiaries. Materially it was a small and insignificant payload, nothing compared to what the RAF and the Luftwaffe had been dropping on British and German cities for the past two years, but those four bombs marked the opening of a new chapter

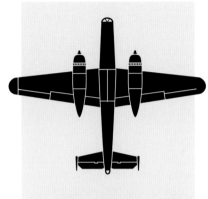

NORTH AMERICAN MITCHELL B-25

Type Medium bomber

Crew 6

Length 52ft 11in (16.3m)

Wingspan 67ft 7in (20.60m)

Speed 272mph (438km/h), 230mph (370km/h) cruising

Range 1,350 miles (2,174km)

Named after US aviation pioneer Major General Billy Mitchell, the B-25 started off life as a conventional medium bomber. Doolittle chose it for his celebrated raid because it was light enough to take off from an aircraft carrier, though it was too heavy to land on one. This meant that his B-25s had to fly on to land in nationalist China after their attack on Japan. Later, the aircraft revealed its substantial potential as a ground attack aircraft in the Pacific theater of war. It also served with the RAF and other Allied air forces.

in the war against Japan. No longer were they immune from attack.

As Doolittle "turned south and out to sea," the rest of the raiding force began dropping their bombs: on aircraft factories; on fuel works; on gas tanks; on munition warehouses, and in dockyards. The overall damage was minimal—an estimated 300 people killed or wounded and fewer than 100 buildings destroyed—but the psychological cost was immense. In addition, the Japanese defenders didn't manage to shoot down one of the enemy aircraft that had so brazenly attacked them in broad daylight.

The aircraft headed west over the East China Sea and though most kept flying until they ran out fuel, then baling out over China, one crew was not so lucky. The men of Plane No. 16 came down in territory occupied by the Japanese and were taken prisoner.

That was the only blemish on an otherwise daring and triumphant raid that was hailed by the American newspapers. Doolittle was garlanded with the Medal of Honor and all 80 raiders received the Distinguished Flying Cross, including the three fliers who were executed by the Japanese after months of brutal torture. One of them was 21-year-old Harold Spatz from Kansas, who wrote to his father on the eve of his execution: "I want you to know that I died fighting like a soldier. My clothes are all I have of any value. I give them to you. And Dad, I want you to know I love you. May God bless you."

A B-25B Mitchell bomber takes off from the aircraft carrier USS *Hornet* on its way to take part in first US air raid on Japan.

US CODEBREAKERS AT MIDWAY

The Doolittle Raid had enraged the Japanese. Those who bore the brunt of their fury were the blameless inhabitants of east China, subjected to scores of air raids on towns and villages as the Japanese sought retribution. But vengeance was also wanted on those who had perpetrated the daring assault on the Japanese mainland.

Admiral Isoroku Yamamoto, the commander-in-chief of the Japanese Combined Fleet, was instructed to select a suitable target for the revenge mission: he chose the atoll of Midway in the North Pacific, with the Aleutian islands chosen as the diversionary target.

Midway Naval Air Station was a large base with hangars, an artificial harbor, fuel storage tanks, and a population of several hundred civilian construction workers defended by a battalion of the Fleet Marine Force. They were stationed on Sand Island—one of Midway's two atolls—while on Eastern Island was a 5,250ft (1,600m) airstrip.

The force at Midway had first come under fire on December 7, 1941, a few hours after Japanese aircraft had bombed Pearl Harbor, but since then the war had passed by the defenders although they had been reinforced by the arrival of 17 Vought Vindicator dive bombers and 14 Brewster Buffalo fighters.

It was Admiral Yamamoto's intention to use Midway as the bait for a trap that would destroy once and for

▶ The Battle of Midway rages on the morning of June 4, 1942. In the center foreground is the *Soryu* (attacked by *Yorktown* aircraft), with *Kaga* and *Akagi* (both attacked by *Enterprise* aircraft), the two burning ships in the distance. The ship on flames on the far right of the photo is a light cruiser.

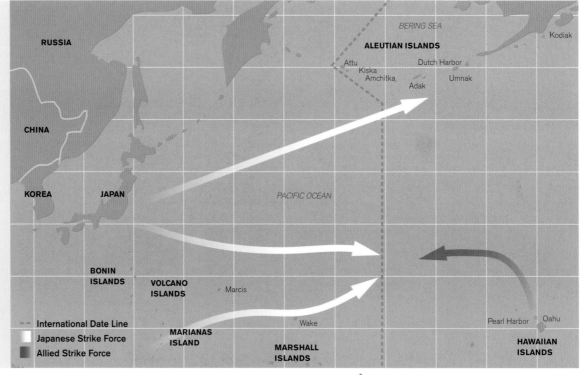

NAS MIDWAY

The Midway atoll in the North Pacific is situated 1,135 miles (1,827km) west-northwest of Pearl Harbor in Hawaii. Between them the islands of Sand and Eastern cover 6 miles (9.6km) in diameter and are encircled by a coral reef inside which is a shallow lagoon. The first recorded sighting of the atoll was in the summer of 1859 by Captain Middlebrooks (also known as Brooks) of the American sealing ship *Gambia*. Middlebrooks claimed Midway for the United States—named it after himself—and in 1867 another seafarer, Captain William Reynolds, formally took possession of the atoll, thereby making it the first Pacific island annexed by the US government. A short while later the name was officially changed to Midway because the atoll is approximately equidistant between North America and Asia. Between 1903 and the start of World War II, it had a dual purpose as a cable station on the Honolulu–Guam–Manila underwater telegraph line and an air base for Pan American Airways.

- - - International Date Line
▢ Japanese Strike Force
▢ Allied Strike Force

Midway Naval Air Station (BELOW LEFT AND RIGHT) was a large US naval base in the Pacific with a population of several hundred civilian construction workers defended by a battalion of the Fleet Marine Force. They were stationed on Sand Island—one of Midway's two atolls—while on Eastern Island was a 5,250ft (1,600m) airstrip.

all the US Pacific Fleet. Assembling an armada of eight aircraft carriers, 11 battleships, 23 cruisers, 65 destroyers and hundreds of fighters, bombers, and torpedo planes, Yamamoto's plan was to attack Midway and in doing so lure the US Fleet into the open where they would be sent to the bottom of the Pacific.

But such a large-scale operation required a great deal of logistical planning, involving the dispatching of radio messages to the relevant units and personnel. Having broken the Japanese Purple Code (see page 72), the Americans soon learned of the attack the Japanese had codenamed Operation MI.

So forewarned were the Americans of the impending attack that Admiral Chester W. Nimitz, commander-in-chief, Pacific Command, flew to the atoll on May 2, 1942, to inspect the defenses, though he didn't inform the 3,632 United States Navy and Marine Corps personnel of the attack. Instead he ordered the materials to improve security against a major amphibious assault. It wasn't until May 20 that Nimitz told Midway's commanders to expect a Japanese attack in eight days, describing in detail how the assault would unfold. That date was put back a few days later to some time between June 3 and 5 by when the atoll had been reinforced by tanks, Douglas Dauntless dive bombers, F4F Wildcat fighters and torpedo bombers.

Midway was bristling with coastal defenses and more than 120 aircraft, but all was not perfect. Their radar system was antiquated and inaccurate and there was scant coordination between the disparate squadrons of Marine, navy and air force crews.

Nimitz concluded that the best form of defense therefore was attack, launching an assault on the Japanese aircraft carriers as soon as they were spotted. "This meant exquisitely precise timing, a monumental dose of luck, or both," admitted Admiral Nimitz. "[Midway's] air force must be employed to inflict prompt and early damage to Jap carrier flight decks if recurring attacks are to be stopped …"

Having reinforced Midway, Nimitz had sent only a skeleton force of aircraft to the Aleutians, knowing this was a diversionary target for the Japanese. As for his Pacific Fleet, he divided into it two powerful carrier groups. The first comprised two of the carriers involved in the Doolittle Raid—*Hornet* and *Enterprise*—as well as six cruisers and nine destroyers. The second group consisted of the *Yorktown* aircraft carrier with an escort of two cruisers and five destroyers. On June 2 the two battle groups were approximately 250 miles (402km) northeast of Midway; the location of Yamamoto's fleet wasn't known until a little after 0900 hours the next day when an American aircraft on patrol 700 miles (1,127km) west of Midway spotted what the pilot at first thought were specks of dirt on his windshield. Looking again he realized what he was looking at. "Sighted main body," radioed the pilot to Midway.

The initial attacks by Midway's aircraft inflicted little damage on the Japanese fleet. A flight of nine B-17 bombers—the first to attack—registered no hits and a further raid by torpedo bombers resulted in minimal damage.

The next day, June 4, it was the turn of the Japanese to attack. At 0430 hours Vice Admiral Chuichi Nagumo, commander of the First Striking Force, launched his aircraft from the decks of his four carriers: *Akagi*, *Kaga*, *Hiryu* and *Soryu*. Soon more than 100 torpedo bombers, dive bombers and fighters were flying towards Midway; even the atoll's fragile radar system couldn't fail to detect such a force and at 0553 hours the air raid sirens sounded on Midway. Meanwhile the islands' fighter aircraft were scrambled and gallantly intercepted the attackers, shooting down some but suffering grievous loses of 15 Buffaloes and two Wildcats downed, with 13 pilots killed.

On the ground at Midway one marine, Private First Class Phillip Clark likened the approaching enemy formations to "three wisps of clouds far out on the

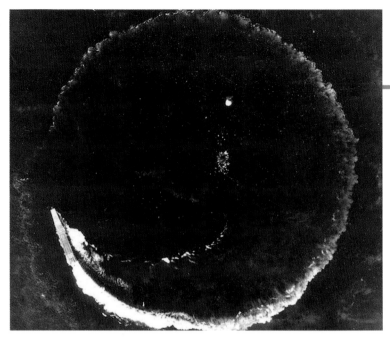
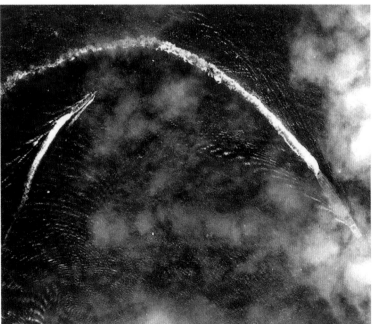

More photographs from the Battle of Midway, an engagement that ended disastrously for the Japanese Imperial Fleet. Having lost three carriers—*Akagi* **(BELOW LEFT)**, *Kaga*, and *Soryu* **(ABOVE RIGHT)**—a fourth was sunk when the *Hiryu* **(BELOW RIGHT AND ABOVE LEFT)** was caught by some Flying Fortresses from Hawaii. Admiral Yamamoto ordered his fleet to withdraw and the defeat gave the American navy control of the Pacific.

▶ Admiral Tamon Yamaguchi served in the Imperial Japanese Navy and his aircraft carrier force sheltered many of attacking planes at Pearl Harbor port. Yamaguchi went down with the sinking carrier *Hiryu* during the Battle of Midway.

horizon." The attack when it came was ferocious but the amount of forewarning had enabled the allies to construct defenses so strong that only 11 men on the ground were killed in the air assault that ended at 0648 hours.

Twenty minutes after the attack on Midway finished it was the turn of the Japanese fleet to come under bombardment. But the initial bombing sorties by the torpedo planes met with no success for the Americans, only heavy casualties; a similar story when the 11 dive bombers swooped out of the sky. Eight were lost. Finally the 15 Flying Fortresses tried to sink the fleet but none of their bombs found an enemy vessel as

around them swarmed Japanese Zero aircraft. The Americans returned to Midway crestfallen, with 19 of their 52 aircraft destroyed without any success on their part. Round one of the Battle of Midway belonged to the Japanese. Vice Admiral Nagumo was grimly satisfied even though he would need to order a second strike on Midway in light of the unexpectedly tough resistance in the first assault.

But there was an even bigger surprise in store for Nagumo. Neither he nor Admiral Yamamoto had any idea that the US Pacific Fleet was homing in on them. It wasn't until 0830 hours that Nagumo received a message stating: "Enemy force is accompanied by what appears to be a carrier." It was disturbing news, a disclosure that caused a fatal hesitation in Nagumo. His aircraft were being rearmed ready for a land attack; should he now order them to be rearmed preparatory to an attack against an enemy fleet? He decided on the latter course, instructing ground crews to arm his aircraft with torpedoes. But it was too late.

Soon torpedo bombers from the *Hornet* and *Enterprise* appeared from the east. Though none got through the barrage of antiaircraft fire and Nagumo's fighter screen, there were more to come—55 dive-bombers that caught the Japanese fleet unawares. The first carrier to be hit was Nagumo's flagship, *Akagi*. That was followed by the *Kaga* and *Soryu*. All three sank. As did the fourth carrier, *Hiryu*, when it was caught by some Flying Fortresses from Hawaii. A devastated Yamamoto ordered his fleet to withdraw as Japan reeled from another blow inflicted by the Americans. First they had bombed the Japanese mainland and now they had wrested control of the Pacific from their navy. The initiative now lay with America.

DESERT DECEIT IN NORTH AFRICA

As we saw in Chapter two, the Germans swept through western Europe in a matter of weeks thanks to their use of tanks and airborne troops. The British Expeditionary Force was forced into a humiliating retreat from the Channel port of Dunkirk at the end of May, leaving the country of the brink of defeat. But new Prime Minister Winston Churchill wasn't a man given to defeatism. On June 5 he wrote a memo to his chiefs of staff demanding that they propose "measures for a vigorous, enterprising, and ceaseless offensive against the whole German occupied coastline." From this memo arose the "commandos," Britain's first Special Forces Unit, established that same month under the command of Lieutentant-Colonel Dudley Clarke.

The commandos carried out their inaugural raid (unsuccessfully) on the Boulogne coast in June 24 and a couple of weeks later a second mission against German-occupied Guernsey was similarly inauspicious. Nonetheless the commandos grew in size throughout the early fall as they trained in earnest in Arran, off the Scottish coast. Clarke, meanwhile, was posted to the Middle East where he was instructed to form "a special section of intelligence for deception of the enemy" in Cairo. He had been requested personally by General Sir Archibald Wavell, commander-in-chief of British forces in the Middle East, and a man who despite his traditional military upbringing was a proponent of guerrilla warfare.

The previous June, in fact the day before the commandos' raid on Boulogne, Wavell had accepted a proposal from Major Ralph Bagnold for the formation of a Long Range Desert Group (initially the unit was called Long Range Patrol but this was subsequently changed). Bagnold made an unlikely leader of a special forces unit; a shy 44-year-old scientist, he was a former signals officer who had explored vast tracts of the Libyan desert by Ford motor car in the 1920s. Arriving in Egypt at the end of 1939, Bagnold had quickly appreciated that Britain's position in Egypt—and

therefore its control of the vital Suez Canal—faced a grave threat from the half a million Italian troops stationed in Libya. In the proposal he sent Wavell, Bagnold suggested using his expertise and experience to raise a 'mobile ground scouting force, even a very small scouting force, to be able to penetrate the desert to the west of Egypt, to see what was going on'.

Bagnold added that the Long Range Patrol would be more than just a reconnaissance force; if the

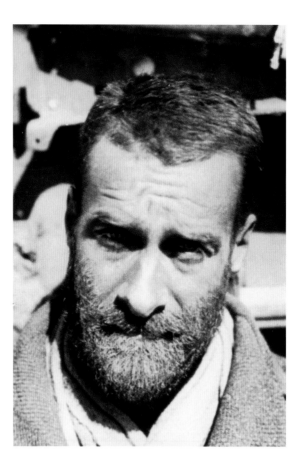

Members of Yeomanry Patrol of the Long Range Desert Group reading mail from home at Siwa Oasis in the Western Desert, circa 1942. Such was the secrecy surrounding the activity of the LRDG that they had to sign a confidentiality form on joining the unit.

◄ The Long Range Desert Group (LRDG) was the idea of Major Ralph Bagnold (pictured), a veteran of World War I and a renowned desert explorer in the 1920s. He pioneered many of the routes across the Libyan desert that were subsequently used by the LRDG to launch surprise raids on Italian forces.

opportunity arose, there would be "some piracy on the high desert." Wavell was so won over by Bagnold's idea that he asked him to have it ready to begin operations in six weeks. Time was of the essence but Bagnold was a brilliant administrator as well as explorer and by the start of August everything was in place for the Long Range Desert Group (LRDG) to embark on its first operation. Bagnold had divided his 80-strong force (composed predominantly of British officers and New Zealand men) into three patrols, in which there would be two gunners, two navigators, one fitter, one mechanic, eleven drivers, ten machine gunners, one wireless operator, and one medic.

For the first three months of their existence the LRDG was used mainly to reconnoiter on Italian positions deep inside the Libyan desert. Then in October Wavell ordered them to change strategy. From now on, as Bagnold noted, they were to "stir up trouble in any part of Libya we liked, with the object of drawing off as much enemy transport and troops as possible from the coastal front to defend their remote and useless inland garrisons."

The LRDG relished their opportunity to be more pugnacious. While some patrols mined roads, others blew up bomb dumps or attacked isolated desert outposts manned by bored Italians. Their response, believing that the British were planning an attack through the desert, was to divert troops from the coastal regions into the interior to escort supply columns and reinforce outposts. This was just as Wavell hoped, for he was in the throes of planning a big offensive that he hoped would drive the Italians out of Libya and bring the British victory in North Africa.

A patrol of the Long Range Desert Group set out over the sandy wastes of the Libyan desert in November 1942, a few weeks after the British had launched their large-scale offensive at El Alamein, the beginning of the end of the war in North Africa.

RIGHT The LRDG gunner on this vehicle is wearing an Arab headdress, a common occurrence for the soldiers who had to operate among the desert sandstorms in North Africa.

BELOW RIGHT Both the Axis powers and the Allies used dummy tanks, mounted on trucks, to fool the enemy during the North African war. These fakes (pictured) belong to the British.

The LRDG wasn't the only method of Wavell's into duping the Italians. Since the summer of 1940 he had been using dummy tanks to fool his foe into believing he had more than the 50,000 troops at his disposal. The fictitious 10th Battalion Royal Tank Regiment was formed from soldiers of the real 1st Battalion Durham Light Infantry, whose tanks were "made out of wood and canvas which they carried folded in the unit transport."

Wavell had requested Dudley Clarke to assist him in this subterfuge although when he arrived in Cairo on December 19, the British offensive had already begun and the Italians were retreating in chaos, caught completely by surprise by Wavell's thrust west across the desert.

British superiority in North Africa was fleeting. They had won the battle but not the war, and the arrival in February 1941 of the German Afrika Korps, commanded by the superb General Erwin Rommel, changed the dynamics in the desert. Rommel wasn't averse to using similar tricks to Wavell, particularly as his force was initially very small. He had Italian workmen build 200 dummy tanks from the chassis of old cars and he marched his same body of men three times through Tripoli to make it appear to any watching enemy spies that a considerable force had arrived from Germany.

At the end of March 1941 Rommel felt confident enough to launch his first offensive, and within three weeks the British had been driven back across all the ground they had won from the Italians three months earlier. Part of the problem for the Allies was that, following their victory over the Italians, the cream of its

▲ David Stirling, the man who founded the Special Air Service in the summer of 1941. Though he was captured in January 1943 and spent the rest of the war a prisoner, his creation expanded into a brigade and still exists today as Britain's elite—and most secretive—fighting force.

force had been transferred to Greece in expectation of the German invasion. In an attempt to dissemble this shortage in manpower, Dudley Clarke created "A Force." Though it was never made officially clear what the "A" denoted, Clarke encouraged the idea it was "A" for Airborne and that a large unit of airborne troops had just arrived in Egypt. To give the idea further credence, Clarke arranged for a number of dummy gliders to be appear at an airfield near Cairo, fully aware that one of the many German agents in the Egyptian capital would report the news to his handlers.

What Clarke craved, however, was some genuine airborne troops to finish the deception. He was in luck. The commando units that had been raised in June 1940, trained at Arran, and then shipped out to the Middle East, had been disbanded 12 months later after a series of disappointing raids against inappropriate targets. While a number returned to their parent unit, others remained in the Middle East waiting for

something to turn up; two who did were Lieutenants David Stirling and Jock Lewes. Between them they came up with an idea for a small airborne unit to parachute into enemy territory to wage a guerrilla war; they procured a handful of parachutes destined for India and made some trial jumps, during which Stirling injured his back. As he recovered in hospital, convinced more than ever of the validity of his idea, he drafted a memo to General Claude Auchinleck (who had replaced Wavell as commander-in-chief) in which he stated:

"I argued the advantages of establishing a unit based on the principle of the fullest exploitation of surprise and of making the minimum demands on manpower and equipment. I argued that the application of this principle would mean in effect the employment of a sub-unit of five men to cover a target previously requiring four troops of a Commando, i.e. about 200 men. I sought to prove that, if an aerodrome or transport park was the objective of an operation, then the destruction of 50

SPECIAL INTERROGATION GROUP

Another of the clandestine units that emerged in the desert war was the Special Interrogation Group (SIG), a unit consisting largely of German Jews who had fled Palestine that was commanded by a British officer called Captain Herbert Buck. Comprising fewer than 40 men initially, the SIG were trained by two German POWs in the techniques of the Wehrmacht as well as marching songs and other minutiae. Their first assault mission ended in disaster, however, when one of two POWs betrayed the SIG to the German sentries as they attempted to attack an airfield near Derna in Libya. In July 1942 the SIG did succeed in raiding Axis airfields at Fuka and Mersa Matruh, destroying a large number of enemy aircraft. In September 1942, however, the SIG was all but wiped out during an overly ambitious raid on the Libyan port of Tobruk during which they had masqueraded as German soldiers bringing in a detachment of captured British personnel (in reality commandos). Following the failure of the raid on Tobruk, the SIG was disbanded and its few surviving members transferred to the SAS and SBS.

aircraft or units of transport was more easily accomplished by a sub-unit of five men than by a force of 200 men. I further concluded that 200 properly selected, trained and equipped men, organised into sub-units of five, should be able to attack at least thirty different objectives at the same time on the same night."

Stirling's proposal idea was accepted and Dudley Clarke had them designated "L Detachment, Special Air Service Brigade" even though the unit totalled just six officers and 60 other ranks. But when one of the many Axis spies in Cairo learned of the airborne "brigade" he would report the news to Rommel's headquarters.

Throughout the next 18 months of the desert war, the LRDG and SAS were at the forefront of the "secret" war against Rommel. Stirling was christened the "Phantom Major" by the Germans, such was his unit's ability to steal onto an airfield in the dead of night and plant bombs on dozens of aircraft; in the first six months of 1942 the SAS destroyed 143 aircraft. They did it not by parachuting into enemy territory (their inaugural operation in November had been a spectacular failure) but with the connivance of the LRDG, who used their unparalleled knowledge of the desert to transport Stirling and his men to within marching distance of the target. The SAS dubbed the LRDG the "Libyan Taxi Service," but it was a jest born out of respect.

When they weren't assisting the SAS, the LRDG reverted to their original role as a reconnaissance force and their surveillance of enemy troop movements— usually undertaken within a couple of hundred yards of German roads—proved vital after Bernard Montgomery launched his offensive at El Alamein in October 1942. When the war in North Africa was finally won six months later, Montgomery wrote to the LRDG, telling them: "I would like you to know how much I appreciate the excellent work done by your patrols … without your careful and reliable reports the launching of the 'left hook' by the NZ Division would have been a leap in the dark; with the information they produced, the operation could be planned with some certainty and as you know, went off without a hitch. Please give my thanks to all concerned."

LEFT An SAS patrol embarks for the desert interior using one of the secret routes pioneered by the LRDG. Note the sand channels stacked on the bonnet to help extract the wheels from deep sand, and also the water condenser on the vehicle's radiator grill.

BELOW LEFT A group of SAS soldiers pose for the camera after another successful raid in 1942. Paddy Mayne, the former Ireland rugby international and the unit's second in command, is far right and next to him is David Stirling.

OPPOSITE Graham Rose and Jimmy Storie, two of the original recruits to the SAS in the summer of 1941, clean their weapons a year later prior to raiding a remote German airfield.

WILD BILL AND THE OFFICE OF STRATEGIC SERVICES

In June 1942 the war in North Africa hung in the balance. General Rommel's successful June offensive had pushed the British back into Egypt and caused them to dig hurried defensive positions at El Alamein. But the German commander had shot his bolt, and never again was Rommel to enjoy such dominance. As the Allies shipped in thousands of reinforcements and tons of fresh supplies, British and American chiefs of staff began drafting the operation that they hoped would crush the Axis forces once and for all in North Africa.

▼ Lieutenant Colonel George S. Patton, junior in his days as an officer in the 1ˢᵗ Tank Battalion during the summer of 1918. Behind him is a French Renault tank.

After much arguing and amendment it was finally agreed that the operation, codenamed Torch (as in the Torch of Liberty), would entail an all-American force of some 24,500 troops under Major General George Patton landing on the Atlantic coast and capturing the Moroccan city of Casablanca, while 18,500 American troops led by Major General Lloyd Fredenall would seize the Algerian city of Oran on the Mediterranean coast. Finally an Anglo-American force of 20,000 soldiers would capture Algiers, of whom 2,000 would be British commandos interspersed with American troops.

This was considered a necessity because of the belief among the chiefs of staff that French forces would be more likely to surrender to an invasion force if they considered it American rather than one that was clearly Anglo-American. The reason was simple: many Frenchmen had not forgiven Winston Churchill for ordering the Royal Navy to attack the French fleet at anchor in the French Algerian naval base of Mers-el-Kebir in July 1940. Churchill had ordered the action to prevent the German navy subsuming the French fleet into its own. Nearly 1,300 French sailors had died in the attack and their naval commanders vowed never to forgive Churchill. With this in mind it was agreed by the Allies that the Americans would subtly sound out the French in the lead-up to Operation Torch, using a mixture of gentle diplomacy and hard-nosed espionage to ascertain the likely reception from French forces when the invasion began.

Tasked with carrying out this mission was the newly formed Office of Strategic Services, America's first organized intelligence-gathering agency that had been formed in July 1941 on the instruction of President Roosevelt.

Appointing a decorated World War I veteran its commander—William "Wild Bill" Donovan—the civilian office was initially called the Coordinator of Information (COI). Its purpose was to collect and assess intelligence that might affect the interests of the United States.

▲ **ABOVE LEFT** William Donovan, aka "Wild Bill," the chief of the Office of Strategic Services (OSS). An abrasive character, Donovan was responsible for turning intelligence gathering into art form and the OSS was later used as the template for the Central Intelligence Agency.

ABOVE RIGHT General Dwight D. Eisenhower gives the order of the day, "Full victory—nothing else," to paratroopers somewhere in England, just before they board their airplanes to participate in the first assault in the invasion of the continent of Europe in June 1944.

Following America's entry into the war, the COI was renamed the Office of Strategic Services (OSS) in June 1942, with its scope of activities extended—at the encouragement of Winston Churchill—to fomenting guerrilla resistance and subversion against the enemy.

Donovan had relied greatly in the first year in his role on cooperation and assistance from Britain's Special Operations Executive (SOE), but with the forming of the OSS he was determined to make the agency self-sufficient. An agreement was reached with the SOE that the OSS would assume responsibility for two major theaters—North Africa and the Far East (in fact, however, the OSS set up more than 40 overseas offices during World War II, from Morocco to China to South Africa).

At the time of this agreement in June 1942 the SOE had just achieved a major coup with two of its agents assassinating Reinhard Heydrich, a leading figure in the Nazi party who was the ruthless Reich Master of Czechoslovakia. OSS was under pressure therefore to demonstrate its own capabilities and Operation Torch presented it with an opportunity to prove its worth.

OSS began its work by collating intelligence from the 12 American vice-consuls stationed in the region, including in Algeria, Morocco and Tunis. The information was gathered and analyzed by Colonel William Eddy, who then reported to General Dwight Eisenhower, the Supreme Commander, Allied Expeditionary Force, of the North African Theater of Operations. OSS also compiled a detailed dossier on the topography of the beaches of North Africa where the landings would take place and recruited anti-Vichy Frenchmen, with the purpose of training them to launch guerrilla attacks as the landing had gotten underway.

Meanwhile Robert Murphy, the chief American diplomat in North Africa, used his influence and contacts to sound out the senior French officers whom he considered most likely to welcome an American invasion. At his insistence General Mark Clark, the deputy commander-in-chief for Torch, came to Algeria in October to meet General Mast, commander of the troops in the Algiers Sector. Under the utmost secrecy Clark was brought to Algeria in a British submarine where he gave the Frenchman a carefully worded overview of the operation, neglecting in the interests of security to reveal the time and place of the landings. At one point the villa in which they were meeting was raided by local police and Clark and his party had to take refuge in the wine cellar where fortunately they were not discovered.

Operation Torch was launched on November 8 and was a success for the invaders. Fewer than 500 Allied soldiers were killed and only at Oran did they encounter any serious resistance. The OSS's strategy of organizing resistance among anti-Vichy Frenchmen bore fruit in Algiers when hundreds of them rose up in the first hours of the invasion and took control of key installations in the city, ready for the Americans.

The Germans reacted to the landings by reinforcing Tunisia with more troops and it took several months of bitter fighting before the Allies cleared North Africa of Axis soldiers. In May 1943, however, pressed from the east by the British Eighth Army and from the west by the US 2nd Corps, nearly a quarter of a million German and Italian prisoners were taken.

Although OSS had made misjudgments during their intelligence gathering for Operation Torch—notably, overestimating the number of Frenchmen who would fight against the Vichy regime—overall they had passed their first test. In December 1942 General George Marshall, the US chief of staff, wrote to William Donovan to tell him that OSS's role in the operation had received special notice.

An aerial view of the port of Casablanca, Morocco, at the time of the Allied landings in North Africa in November 1942. Note the sunken ship in the centre of the harbor and the French battleship *Jean Bart* on the left.

▼ American troops come ashore behind a large American flag on the beaches near Algiers as part of Operation Torch in November 1942. Casualties were light, with the Vichy French choosing not to offer serious resistance to the Allied invasion of North Africa.

In OSS's other sphere of operations, the Far East, there had also been success thanks to the activities of Detachment 101—named to give the unit more gravitas than had it merely been named "1." Formed in 1942, Detachment 101 comprised 12 officers and nine NCOs and was led by Major Carl Eifler, a former customs official on the Mexico border. The detachment spent the early summer of 1942 in Canada, undergoing specialist training with British commandos and members of the SOE. They also devoured small libraries of books on Burma and its customs and peoples so that when they arrived in the China–Burma–India (CBI) theater in August 1942 they were ready to begin immediate operations. One of the OSS officers, Ray Peers, recalled that they were briefed by the American general in command of CBI, Joe Stilwell, as to their remit: "He said he was anxious to have us get behind Japanese lines. Information was scarce and he believed anything we could reveal about the enemy would influence forthcoming operations. What he wanted was a group eager to prove to pieces the myth that a white man could not survive in the jungle."

In December 1942 Detachment 101 launched its first guerrilla operation in Burma to blow up railroads and bridges that served the strategically important town of Myitkyina, where the Japanese 18th Division headquarters was based. Two officers from A-Group parachuted into the jungle 100 miles (161km) south of Myitkyina and, after establishing a base, called in 10 more operatives, who jumped at a height of 600ft (183m). The 12 saboteurs then marched 100 miles (161km) through thick, snake-infested jungle in a little over two days. Then, splitting into two teams, they blew the railroad in 30 places using time-delay fuses and also destroyed a railroad bridge near the town of Namhkwin.

By the end of 1943 Detachment 101 had expanded its operations in Burma to six intelligence bases in the north of the country and had infiltrated wireless operators along the main transportation routes that cut through the rugged countryside. These agents radioed their information to the main CBI headquarters in India. Additionally Detachment 101 had embarked on a massive recruitment program of local natives, particularly those belonging to the Kachin tribe, of whom nearly 10,000 worked for Detachment 101.

Once such lone operator was Captain Vincent Curl, a red-bearded Texan who had known Eifler from their days serving together in the infantry before the war. In March 1944 a 3,000-strong American force—nicknamed Merrill's Marauders (see page 142)—was sent into Burma to support a major Anglo-Chinese offensive.

▼ Detachment 101 was a small section of the OSS that operated in Burma from 1942 until the end of the war. As well as intelligence gathering, the operatives seen here were responsible for coordinating and fomenting armed resistance to the Japanese occupation among the native population.

SPECIAL OPERATIONS EXECUTIVE

When the Special Operations Executive was established in July 1940 it came under the auspices of Hugh Dalton's Ministry of Economic Warfare with a remit to "coordinate all action, by way of subversion and sabotage, against the enemy overseas." Nicknamed in some quarters "the Baker Street Irregulars" after a cabal of spies encountered by the fictional detective Sherlock Holmes, SOE went under the official cover name of the Inter-Services Research Bureau. Gradually it grew into an organization employing or controlling 13,000 people around the world, of whom more than a quarter were women. As the war set aflame more regions of the world, so SOE expanded from a Europe-centric network to an organization that had agencies in, among others, Algiers, Singapore, Abyssinia, and Egypt. The nature of its work was similarly varied with it operatives responsible for the destruction of the heavy water plant in Norway (see page 114) and the assassination in Czechoslovakia of Heinrich Himmler's deputy, Reinhard Heydrich.

But it was in Western Europe where the SOE was most active, with an estimated 3,733 parachute landings and 81 pick-up operations conducted in France alone by "F" Section. In total nearly 500 SOE agents were sent to France on espionage or sabotage operations or to organize and train the French Resistance ahead of the invasion. Records show that more than 5,000,000kg of equipment was supplied by the SOE to Resistance groups, including 307,023kg of explosives. The cost, however, was heavy, with 104 agents killed or executed, among them 13 women, one of whom was Violette Szabo, whose life story later became the subject of a book and a film.

▲ The caption on the poster in the background says it all: "Practice makes Perfect." The OSS recruits seen here were rigorously trained before being allowed into the field.

Deep in the jungle one Marauder battalion encountered Curl, who loaned them his 300 Kachin guerrilla force. 'It specialized in ambushes, information gathering and rescuing downed Allied flyers,' wrote Lieutenant Charlton Ogburn, one of the Marauder officers. 'The Kachins not only knew the country and the trails, but they also knew better than anyone but the Japanese where the Japanese were, and often they knew that better than the higher Japanese commands.'

By late 1944 OSS was employing approximately 15,000 men and women, and its expenditure for that year was $57 million. Its operations had also inflated to include Morale Operations—also known as "Black Propaganda"; CounterIntelligence, a branch of its operations referred to as "X–2"; and Research and Analysis (R&A), staffed by around 900 scholars and led by Harvard historian William Langer, whose role was to collate data from open sources and all departments of the government. As the official website of the Central Intelligence Agency—the successor to the OSS—says of R&A: "The Office of Strategic Services virtually invented the discipline of non-departmental strategic intelligence analysis—one of America's few unique contributions to the craft of intelligence."

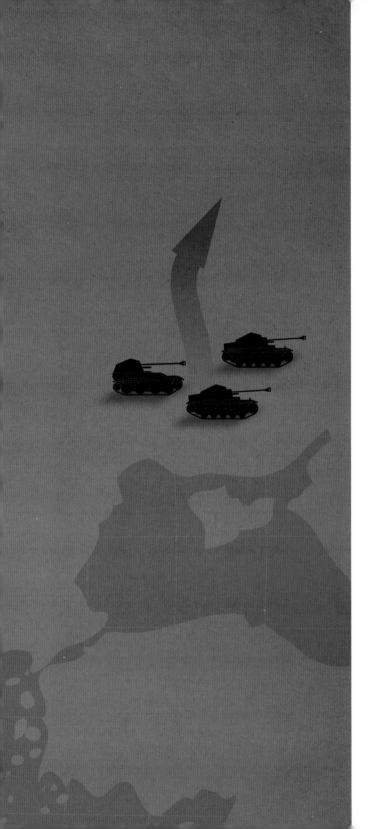

TURNING THE TIDE

By 1943 the Axis forces were on the defensive as the Allies' superior air power began to prove decisive—and not just the aircraft. The top-secret "bouncing bomb" destroyed the German dams in the Ruhr and provided the Allies with a wonderful propaganda coup. Meanwhile the Russians were taking the fight to the Germans in Kursk while the Nazis were also shaken by a Jewish uprising in the Warsaw Ghetto that took them weeks to crush. The war was also going badly for Japan, with Allied gains in Burma and the Pacific, and even a daring commando raid in Singapore Harbor.

OPERATION GUNNERSIDE

Deutrium oxide doesn't sound very dramatic but the substance sparked one of the most secret—and audacious—operations of World War II. More commonly known as heavy water, deuterium oxide has a hydrogen isotope that contains a neutron, making its molecules heavier than those in normal water. As a result in nuclear reactors it slows down neutrons, boosting the possibility of nuclear-fission reaction. It is also cheaper and easier to extract plutonium for use in nuclear weapons.

Fearful that Hitler was using heavy water to develop the world's first nuclear bomb, the British began planning ways to disrupt production at the Norsk Hydro plant. The challenge they faced was the building's location. Situated in a valley (60 miles [97km] west of Oslo), the plant had nature as its sentries. In one of the most inhospitable regions in Norway, the plant was 1,000ft (305m) above the valley floor, on a rocky ledge surrounded by steep heavily forested hills. The approaches to the plant would entail a grueling ski across mountains in temperatures that at times could be brutal.

▼ Before the outbreak of war, the Norsk Hydro plant at Vemork in southern Norway was producing heavy water (as much as 12 tons a year) as a by-product of manufacturing fertilizer. Following the German occupation of Norway in April 1940, the Nazis took over the running of the plant to the great consternation of the Allies.

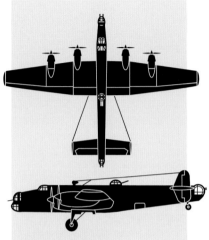

HANDLEY PAGE HALIFAX HP57 III

Type Heavy bomber

Crew 7

Length 71ft 7in (21.81m)

Wingspan 104ft 2in (31.74m)

Speed 282mph (454km/h)

Range 1,860 miles (3,000km)

Though overshadowed by its counterpart, the Avro Lancaster, despite having entered service more than a year before it, the Halifax nevertheless was one of the most versatile aircraft produced for the RAF during World War II. As well as serving as a strategic bomber, it flew as a pathfinder, air ambulance, glider-tug, transport and maritime reconnaissance aircraft. The first Halifaxes, however, were too slow. They also suffered from rudder problems that could throw the aircraft into an uncontrollable spin. It was not until the Type III was produced that these problems were fully rectified.

HORSA GLIDER

Type Horsa 1

Crew 2

Length 67ft (20.4m)

Wingspan 88ft (26.8m)

Speed 150mph on tow, 100mph gliding

Constructed from 30 separate parts primarily made out of wood, the Horsa glider had been ordered by the British government in 1940 as the means to transport its special forces troops into battle. The first Horsa (pictured) was designed to carry 25 soldiers while the later model had a hinged nose and was capable of transporting vehicles and guns as well as soldiers.

The first task for Combined Operations headquarters in London was to obtain detailed intelligence on the plant's defenses and the feasibility of a commando attack. So in March 1942 a Norwegian member of the Special Operations Executive (SOE), Einar Skinnarland, parachuted into the area and, with the help of local Resistance fighters, made notes of the plant's defenses and the strength of the garrison. Having decided that a commando attack might succeed, the British decided to begin planning a raid using gliders and specially trained Royal Engineers.

While these men started their training, a four-man team of Norwegians parachuted into their country to carry out a further reconnaissance, codenamed Operation Grouse. Jens-Anton Poulsson, Knut Haugland, Claus Helberg and Arne Kjelstrup were all expert skiers who had been trained by the SOE in sabotage, wireless communication and guerrilla warfare. They dropped on the night of October 18, 1942 and spent the next 15 days trekking towards the target.

The four men of Operation Grouse selected a suitable site for a glider to land—on a frozen lake near Mosvatn—and radioed the information back to London. On November 19 two RAF Halifax bombers left England, towing Horsa gliders; inside each were 15 Royal Engineers from the 1st Airborne Division. The mission was a disaster, with bad weather and poor visibility contributing to its failure. Both gliders crashed well short of the target and those not killed on board were captured, tortured, and then executed by the Gestapo. Worse, the Germans were now alerted to the British determination to attack the Norsk Hydro plant.

Meanwhile the four members of Operation Grouse had evaded capture but were now stranded on the remote Hardanger Plateau with winter closing in and temperatures as low as minus 4°F (minus 20°C). Although the quartet had grown up in the Norwegian mountains none had been forced to survive in the wild for so long, and by Christmas 1942 they were digging through the snow and scraping reindeer moss off the rocks to eat. Their only shelter was a small, unheated mountain hut, in which ice coated the ceiling and reached halfway down the walls. The radio operator, Knut Haugland, constructed a transmitter using a car battery and fishing rods taken from other mountain huts, and with this he received confirmation from London that they still intended to sabotage the plant in a new operation codenamed "Gunnerside" (named after the village in Yorkshire, England where the SOE director, Sir Charles Hambro, liked to shoot grouse). On the night of February 16 six more Norwegian members of the SOE parachuted into the region, along with arms and explosive equipment, under the command of Joachim Ronneberg. "We jumped out at midnight and the landscape was covered with snow," he recalled in 2013. Ronneberg soon realized they had been dropped miles off course and it took five days of hard traveling before they made contact with their four compatriots.

On the night of February 27–28 the 10 saboteurs set off on their mission. Though the Germans had responded

▼ Deuterium oxide, more commonly known as heavy water, was considered by the Germans cheaper and easier to extract than plutonium in the construction of nuclear weapons.

▲ Captain Jens Anton Poulsson **(LEFT)**, was the leader of the sabotage team who parachuted into Norway in October 1942 as part of Operation Grouse. Arne Kjelstrup **(ABOVE)** and Knut Haugland **(ABOVE RIGHT)** were also part of the team.

to the failed glider operation by installing additional mines and floodlights around the plant, the extra security measures had induced in the guards a fatal complacency. After all, who on earth could possibly infiltrate a building perched on a 1,000ft (305m) high ledge encircled by a thick forest, mines and searchlights, the only approach being a 246ft (75m) bridge spanning the ravine. Sentries paced up and down the bridge so the Norwegians dropped into the ravine, waded across the freezing river and climbed through the forested mountainside until they encountered the single railroad track that led straight inside the plant. Furnished with plans of the plant from the earlier reconnaissance, Ronneberg and one other man accessed the basement room through the cable tunnel and found the cells producing the heavy water. Two other saboteurs, having become separated in the tunnel, climbed in through a window. There wasn't a German to be seen, only the Norwegian caretaker, who was happy to help. Ronneberg instructed his team to cut the two-minute detonating fuses to 30 seconds, and they then made their rapid escape. "The snow was hard so we left no footprints," recalled Ronneberg. "We stopped for a rest at about 7 a.m. No one speaking, the sun was rising. It was marvelous, actually. We had the Norwegian mountains as our best friends."

Though a German division was dispatched to hunt down saboteurs, the Norwegians made good their escape, with five skiing 200 miles (322km) to Sweden, two reaching Oslo and the rest remaining in the region to continue Resistance operations.

The damage caused to the Norsk Hydro plant was considerable, with more than 500kg of heavy water destroyed as well as much vital equipment in the electrolysis chambers. Production ceased for more than two months and the knowledge gained during the operation enabled the raiders to brief Allied aircrews on the layout of the plant, resulting in several damaging air raids on it. Eventually in 1944 the Germans abandoned heavy water production in Norsk Hydro.

Reflecting on the secret mission in 2013 at an event to mark the 70th anniversary of Operation Gunnerside, Ronneberg (the last surviving member of the 10-man team), remarked of his fellow saboteurs: "We were a gang of friends doing a job together."

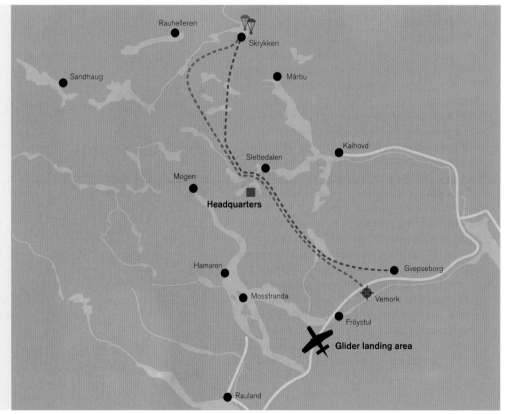

VEMORK, NORWAY

The Norwegian plant in Vemork, situated in a valley 60 miles (97km) west of Oslo, was built by Norsk Hydro and opened in 1911, the main purpose of its operation to mass-produce heavy water. Though British intelligence realized that the Nazis were protecting the plant because of its heavy water production they couldn't bomb Vemork for fear of incurring heavy civilian casualties if the liquid ammonia storage tanks exploded.

- - - **Helberg's Route**
- - - **Sabotage Party's Route**

Bergen **NORWAY** Oslo
Vemork
SWEDEN
BALTIC SEA
NORTH SEA
DENMARK

Rauhelleren
Skrykken
Sandhaug
Mårbu
Kalhovd
Slettedalen
Mogen
Headquarters
Hamaren
Gvepseborg
Mosstranda
Vemork
Fröystul
Glider landing area
Rauland

WARRIORS OF THE WARSAW GHETTO

The Germans believed it would be an easy task to clear the Warsaw Ghetto of Jews in April 1943. They, after all, were the "Master Race," and ever since the Ghetto's creation in the summer of 1940 the Nazis had controlled the Polish Jews with ruthless dominance. Enclosed by a brick wall 10ft (3m) high and 11 miles (18km) in circumference, the Ghetto was sealed off from the rest of Warsaw, with its 360,000 Jews left to die of disease and hunger in an area approximately 3.5 square miles.

Tens of thousands of Jews died in the first two and a half years of the Ghetto's existence so that by early 1943 only around 60,000 remained (estimates vary from 55,000 to approximately 65,000). Still too many, declared SS Commander Heinrich Himmler, whose job it was to purify Europe by killing all Jews. On January 9 that year Himmler demanded that the SS employ "intensified measures" to cleanse the Ghetto, removing all the remaining Jews to either slave labor camps or death camps.

On January 18 the Germans entered the Ghetto expecting to remove the first batch of Jews without meeting any resistance. They were wrong. Men and women attacked the Germans with anything they could find, often just knives and iron bars, but there was also a small quantity of arms. One grenade was thrown by 17-year-old Emily Landau into a group of SS soldiers, killing and wounding several. Elsewhere small-arms fire cut down astonished Nazis who hadn't believed the Jews capable of resisting. On January 20 the Germans withdrew from the Ghetto; they had removed 5,000 Jews but suffered 70 soldiers killed or wounded.

The resistance had been led by the Jewish Military Union or Zydowski Zwiazek Wojskowy (ZZW), a small secret army formed at the end of 1939 by four Jewish officers from the Polish Army determined to fight back against the Nazi invader. The ZZW started in 1940 with just 39 volunteers but gradually over the next two years its numbers increased to nearly 350 and cells emerged in Polish cities other than Warsaw.

But it was in the Polish capital that the ZZW had its nerve center under the command of David Apfelbaum. In the summer of 1942 huge numbers of Jews had been taken from the Ghetto and sent to the Death Camps as the ZZW looked on helplessly. Virtually without weapons, the Secret Army also believed that to resist would only result in a massacre; additionally, it was still believed that those Jews removed were being sent to labor camps, not liquidated as part of the Nazis' Final Solution.

By 1943, however, word had reached the ZZW of the fate of those removed from the Ghetto. Word had also reached those Poles outside the Ghetto of the courage shown by the Jews during the Nazis' incursion in January. Now the Polish Home Army (Armia Krajowa or AK) began to smuggle in weapons to their fellow

This photograph was included in a report from Brigadier General Jürgen Stroop, SS commander to Heinrich Himmler, head of the SS, showing the destruction of the Warsaw Ghetto in April 1943.

▼ Some of Warsaw's Jewish population who have been forcibly assembled sit close to the wall of the Ghetto, awaiting deportation. Most would never return to Poland.

resistors—not just the ZZW but also the Zydowska Organizacja Bojowa (ZOB), an underground organization founded the previous summer from mainly young men and boys. By April 1943 the Ghetto resistance groups had a modest array of heavy machine guns, light machine guns, rifles, pistols, and hundreds of grenades.

They knew another attempt to cleanse the Ghetto was imminent and sure enough, on April 19, the Nazis came again, nearly 3,000 of them, ordered to annihilate the Jews within 20 hours so that Himmler could present Hitler with his birthday present the following day—a declaration of "a Warsaw clean of Jews."

Ranged against them were around 600 armed men and women belonging to ZOB and 400 men of ZZW. The odds were stacked against the Ghetto's defenders but they had on their side surprise and an intimate knowledge of the terrain.

On the evening of Sunday, April 18, the first night of the Jewish Passover, the Germans began to encircle the Ghetto, allowing the Resistance leaders precious time to prepare their defense. When the assault was launched in the early hours of April 19 the Nazis were met with a furious fusillade of small-arms fire and grenades. The Germans fled, reappearing with three armored cars, two of which were destroyed by Molotov cocktails. "The faces that only yesterday reflected terror and despair now shone with an unusual joy which is difficult to describe," wrote one Jewish combatant. "This was a joy free from all personal motives, a joy imbued with the pride that the ghetto was fighting."

Meanwhile Brigadier General Jürgen Stroop, the SS officer in charge of clearing the Ghetto, had to break the news to Himmler that the initial operation had not gone according to plan. "At our first penetration into the ghetto the Jews and Polish bandits succeeded, with arms in hand, in repulsing our attacking forces, including the tank and armored vehicles," he wrote in his report. "The losses during the first attack were: 12 men."

Stroop launched a fresh assault around noon, calling up artillery support as his soldiers worked their way cautiously inside the Ghetto. But the Jewish Resistance fighters continued to inflict casualties on the Nazis, hurling grenades from rooftops onto the streets below and sniping at the enemy as they darted from doorway to doorway. His anger growing hourly, Stroop enlisted the help of the Luftwaffe and their bombs pushed back the defenders, although they managed to set alight a German warehouse in which hundreds of Jews had

▼ Facing Stroop's Nazi soldiers inside the Ghetto were 600 armed men and women belonging to ZOB and 400 men of ZZW. Though lightly armed, they put up ferocious resistance for nearly a month.

This photo was also included in Stroop's report on the destruction of the Ghetto. It shows two female members of the Jewish Resistance movement. Incredibly, Malka Zdrojewicz (right) survived the Majdanek extermination camp and later raised a family in Jerusalem.

been forced to work. The Germans advanced, exacting as they inched forward a terrible revenge on all those they found. Inside the Ghetto hospital Ukrainian SS troops bayoneted pregnant women in the stomach and battered new-born babies to death.

The Luftwaffe continued to bomb the Ghetto in the days that followed, setting alight large swathes of the artificial city with incendiary bombs. On the ground German engineers started to demolish buildings with explosives, forcing civilians to flee into the open where they were either shot dead or captured. The Resistance fighters fought on, some donning the clothes of dead Germans and opening fire on unsuspecting troops as they advanced.

By now, however, food, water, and ammunition were running low in the Ghetto. On April 26, a week after the Germans had attacked, Mordechai Anielewicz, the 24-year-old leader of the ZOB, dispatched his last message to the outside world. "This is the eighth day of our life-and-death struggle. The Germans suffered tremendous losses. In the first two days they were forced to withdraw. Then they brought in reinforcements in the form of tanks, armor, artillery, even airplanes, and began a systematic siege … sensing the end, we demand this from you: Remember how we were betrayed. There will come a time of reckoning for our spilled, innocent blood. Send help to those who, in the last hour, may elude the enemy—in order that the fight may continue."

As the net tightened on the defenders, 40 fighters managed to escape the Ghetto through the sewers but the majority chose to fight against the Nazi barbarity. On May 8 the Germans assaulted a bunker at 18 Mila Street, inside which was the headquarters of ZOB containing Anielewicz and more than 100 of his fighters along with 80 civilians. As SS troops started to pour gas into the bunker those trapped inside were faced with a terrible choice, knowing that they would be shot if they fled on to the surface: asphyxiation or suicide. Most

chose to kill themselves, including Anielewicz, who was subsequently awarded the Order Wojenny Virtuti Militari, Poland's highest military honor for courage.

Eventually, on May 16, Himmler was able to tell Hitler the Ghetto had been cleansed, with an estimated 7,000 Jews killed during the uprising after Stroop had personally blown up the Great Synagogue of Warsaw. Seven thousand more were sent for immediate liquidation at Treblinka Death Camp and the rest— around 42,000—were transported to Lublin/Majdanek concentration camp and to Poniatowa forced labor camp, where nearly all were murdered by being shot in trenches in November that year during the Nazis' "Operation Harvest Festival."

It had taken nearly a month and cost the lives of as many as 350 Germans. The Resistance had shaken the Third Reich, another blow to their morale in a year when the tide of war turned decisively against them. As Joseph Goebbels, the Nazi Minister of Propaganda, wrote in his diary: "It shows what the Jews are capable of when they have arms in their hands."

In 1968, on the 25th anniversary of the Ghetto uprising, one of the ZOB survivors, Yitzhak Zuckerman, was asked to put their rebellion into a military context. He replied: "This was a war of less than a thousand people against a mighty army and no one doubted how it was likely to turn out. This isn't a subject for study in military school … If there's a school to study the human spirit, there it should be a major subject. The important things were inherent in the force shown by Jewish youth after years of degradation, to rise up against their destroyers, and determine what death they would choose: Treblinka or Uprising."

The Warsaw Uprising of July 1944 led to the virtual destruction of the Polish capital and resulted in the death of 200,000 civilians. This photograph captures some of the bitter street fighting that erupted in the streets of Warsaw.

THE MAN WHO NEVER WAS

Lieutenant Colonel's Dudley Clarke's deception extended beyond just North Africa. As we saw in the previous chapter, his inventive and secret mind had created "A" force to harass General Rommel—in the German commander's imagination if not in actuality— and with the war in the desert all but won Clarke was presented with his next challenge: how to fool the Germans into believing the Allies' next target was Greece and not Sicily and Italy.

British Prime Minister Winston Churchill and American President Franklin Roosevelt had decided at their Casablanca conference in January 1943 that the Allies would take their first footsteps in liberating Europe in Sicily in an operation codenamed "Husky." For that to succeed, however, the Germans and Italians must be tricked into thinking the assault would be launched through Greece and the Balkans. This was Clarke's task, to plan a fictitious invasion of Crete and Greece, codenamed "Operation Barclay." Naturally, Clarke set about his mission with relish, assembling along the North African coast a dummy armored division belonging to his still make-believe "A" Force: dummy tanks, dummy gliders, dummy camps, and dummy wireless communications. Fake aircraft were also assembled on airfields, in among real aircraft that were scrambled to intercept any inquisitive German reconnaissance aircraft that came too close to be able to spot the difference.

Meanwhile Clarke ordered that real soldiers, Greek ones, should start practicing amphibious landing training while notices were pinned out indiscreetly in barracks, asking for Greek-speaking British officers. Clarke even organized the purchase of a large sum of Greek drachmas on the Cairo stock exchange; in short, even the slowest of German spies couldn't fail to notice a Greek flavor to the Allies' preparation.

Of course, Allied headquarters appreciated that Clarke's deception alone wasn't enough. The Germans would take note but their suspicions would be aroused that it was all part of a sophisticated ruse. Something even more cunning was needed. In London Sir John Masterman and his Double Cross Committee were asked for ideas, and what they came up with produced one of the most brilliant and successful deceptions of the entire war.

The pair responsible for what came to be known as Operation Mincemeat were an RAF officer, Charles Cholmondeley, on secondment to MI5, and Ewen Montagu of Naval Intelligence; but their inspiration came from an incident the previous year when a plane carrying a Free French officer, who had on his person documents with the names of Allied secret agents, crashed off the Spanish coast. The body washed up in neutral Spain and though it was eventually returned to

Dummy aircraft, like this one, were built of wood and later covered with cloth to dupe enemy reconnaissance aircraft. When the photographs were studied by German intelligence they appeared to show several squadrons' worth of aircraft.

◄ Lieutenant Colonel Dudley Clarke was a master at military deception. Having proved his cunning in the war in North Africa, his next remit was to fool the Germans into believing the Allies' next target was Greece and not Sicily and Italy.

the British in Gibraltar, this was not before the Germans had had the opportunity to photograph the documents.

Cholmondeley and Montagu proposed something similar—a corpse washed ashore in Spain and the Germans reaching it before the British had time to retrieve the important documents.

There was one overriding challenge in such a scheme: the dead man. The corpse must fulfill several criteria, a middle-aged man who had died recently from an affliction that wouldn't look suspicious to a Spanish pathologist. They sought advice from a coroner called Sir Bentley Purchase and he produced the corpse of a 34-year-old Welshman he described as "a bit of a ne'r-do-well." He had died in January 1943 from pneumonia and exposure, and a top London pathologist assured Cholmondeley and Montagu that a Spanish counterpart would not be able to determine that the man under his scalpel had not died from pleural effluvia as a result of drowning at sea after a plane crash.

To maintain the crucial secrecy required to pull off their deception, MI5 dressed their corpse in the uniform of a Royal Marine commando major and put it in a steel container packed with dry ice on which was written "Optical Instruments." There was a black leather briefcase chained to the major's belt and the next task for Cholmondeley and Montagu was to fill it with documents subtle enough to fool the Germans into believing Greece was the invasion target without making it obvious it was all a hoax. There were the obvious papers—Royal Navy identity card (although they had a slice of luck when Montagu bumped into a junior officer who resembled the dead man and had him pose for a photograph) and a pass to Combined Operations Headquarters, confirming his identity as Major William Martin—but there were also two letters tucked inside the briefcase. One was a covering letter to Admiral Sir Andrew Cunningham, commander-in-chief Mediterranean, from Lord Louis Mountbatten, chief of Combined Operations, vouching for Martin's expertise in landing craft and barges. The main letter was from the vice-chief of the Imperial General Staff, General Archie Nye, to General Harold Alexander, the man who had masterminded the defeat of Rommel in North Africa, discussing the forthcoming operations, in which he skillfully alluded to the main assault aimed at Greece with the feint directed at Sicily.

To bring Major Martin fully to life, Cholmondeley and Montagu added the accoutrements of every man's life: personal letters, a photograph of a sweetheart, a box of cigarettes, a ticket stub from a recent theater performance in London's West End, and even a letter from Lloyds Bank, warning he had exceeded his overdraft limit.

On April 19 "Major Martin" left Britain on his top-secret mission, slipping out of Scotland aboard the submarine *Seraph* bound for Spanish waters. On the last day of the month, the submarine surfaced off Huelva in the Gulf of Cadiz and, after the naval officers had said a short prayer, the corpse of Major Martin with a life preserver was placed in the water along with a rubber dinghy. MI5 had chosen the south-east of Spain because of the presence in Huelva of Adolf Clauss, an Abwehr spy who had cultivated excellent contacts with Spanish officials, and who would almost certainly be tipped off about the corpse. The timing was important, too, approximately two and a half months before the intended invasion of Sicily, thereby allowing the Germans time to move their forces east towards Greece.

The events that followed went entirely according to plan. The British vice consul in Huelva was informed that a body of a British officer had been washed ashore, and Francis Haselden duly identified it and made it clear to the Spanish authorities that London demanded the return of the briefcase as a matter of extreme urgency.

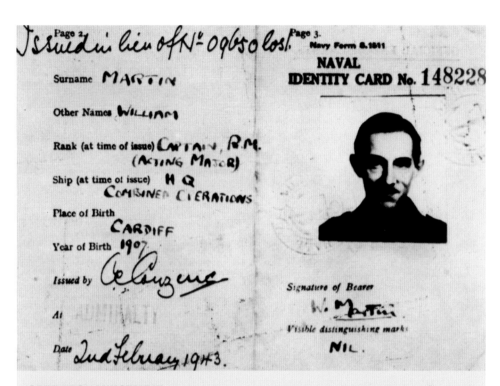

OPERATION MINCEMEAT

It wasn't until 2010 that the true identity of Major William Martin was definitively established. The corpse used in Operation Mincemeat was that of Glyndwr Michael, a jobless and homeless man who took his own life in January 1943 by swallowing rat poison. Michael's body was discovered in an abandoned warehouse in King's Cross, London, with his death certificate giving the cause of death as "phosphorus poisoning. Took rat poison—bid [to] kill himself while of unsound mind."

It was finally received by the British naval attaché in Madrid on May 13, four days after Berlin received a signal from Adolf Clauss that he had seen what was inside the briefcase. There were high level meetings and consequently Hitler ordered that month the transfer of the 1st Panzer Division from France to Kalamata in Greece, a fleet of torpedo boats were sent from Sicily to Greece and three German minefields were laid off

Greece. General Jodl, head of the German supreme command operations staff, could barely contain his glee at the coup, declaring: "You can forget about Sicily. We know it's in Greece!" The appearance in June 4 in the *Times* Casualty List of Major William Martin, Royal Marines, was final proof to the Germans that they had outmaneuvered the British.

Not everyone was convinced. Benito Mussolini, leader of Italy, continued to believe the Allies would attack Sicily but he was overruled by Hitler. On July 10 Mussolini's fears proved correct and Operation Husky was launched against Sicily. Within 38 days the Allies had conquered the island and on July 25 Mussolini was arrested. His reign as Il Duce was over, all thanks to Major Martin and Operation Mincemeat.

THE BOUNCING BOMB

At first glance Barnes Neville Wallis didn't look like the sort of man capable of inventing arguably the world's most ingeniously destructive bomb. Gray-haired and mild mannered, the Englishman spent the 1920s as chief designer for the armament firm Vickers Armstrong, helping build the R100, a giant airship, later creating a lightweight aircraft design that resulted in the manufacture of the Vickers Wellesley and the Wellington Bomber.

Working on aircraft aroused Wallis's curiosity about bombs. His orderly, scientific mind considered the conventional means of dropping a stick of bombs inefficient and callous. What was needed was a bomb that would detonate below the surface, reducing civilian casualties but causing immeasurably more damage to buildings and infrastructures. In effect, it would be like creating an earthquake. Wallis hawked his idea around the corridors of Air Ministry but it was too advanced, too complex, for military minds at this stage of the war. The "Earthquake" bomb would eventually be designed, and used to impressive effect in the last few months of the war, but it was another bomb that Wallis was asked to work on that made his name synonymous with genius.

Much of Germany's steel output came from the water in the dams of the Ruhr Valley. There were three dams, the Mohne, Eder, and Sorpe, and on them Germany's war effort relied for coal, armaments, and hydroelectric power. The British wanted the dams destroyed to severely disrupt their enemy's output—but how? A conventional bombing mission would stand little chance of success, their bombs neither accurate nor powerful enough to breach the huge concrete dams.

The British formed an "Air Attack on Dams Committee" to study the problem and Wallis was invited to give his thoughts.

Drawing on his research into the "Earthquake" bomb, Wallis asked himself how best to produce a bomb with a sufficient shock to breach the dam. A bomb dropped

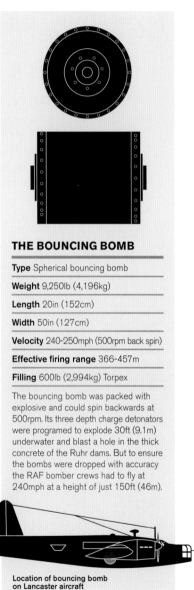

THE BOUNCING BOMB

Type Spherical bouncing bomb

Weight 9,250lb (4,196kg)

Length 20in (152cm)

Width 50in (127cm)

Velocity 240-250mph (500rpm back spin)

Effective firing range 366-457m

Filling 600lb (2,994kg) Torpex

The bouncing bomb was packed with explosive and could spin backwards at 500rpm. Its three depth charge detonators were programed to explode 30ft (9.1m) underwater and blast a hole in the thick concrete of the Ruhr dams. But to ensure the bombs were dropped with accuracy the RAF bomber crews had to fly at 240mph at a height of just 150ft (46m).

Location of bouncing bomb on Lancaster aircraft

from above wouldn't achieve the purpose but what about a bomb that exploded against the wall? Then Wallis realized that if a bomb was detonated close to the water line against the wall, the water would conduct the bomb's blast effect into the wall instead of allowing its energy to dissipate.

A picture began to form in Wallis's mind of what was needed, a bomb of about five tons exploding against the wall but one that wouldn't be snagged by the torpedo nets. How to achieve that? Then he recalled that the famous British admiral of the early 19th century, Horatio Nelson, had invented a way of attacking French warships by skimming cannonballs across the sea's surface. Inspired by Nelson's example, Wallis started to experiment by catapulting marbles off water in a bath tub. He was encouraged by what he found, progressing to firing larger projectiles in a similar fashion, all the while making notes on distance, height, speed, and backspin.

Finally, on December 4, 1942, Wallis was able to observe the first trial run of his new invention that was codenamed "Upkeep." It was a disaster. The Wellington bomber released the mine and it shattered on impact with the water. Other tests were carried out but with the same result. Skeptics within the "Air Attack on Dams Committee" began to titter behind Wallis's back, dismissing him as a "crackpot." Few could see how a bomb, 4ft (1.2m) in diameter and 5ft (1.5m) in length, and which in shape resembled an oil barrel, could achieve what its inventor claimed.

Wallis went back to the drawing board and strengthened the bomb's casing, and in January 1943 he looked on in triumph as his bomb fell from the Wellington, hit the water and then skimmed 20 times towards the dummy target.

Yet there was still resistance within official quarters. Air Chief Marshal Arthur Harris wrote to the chief of staff, Charles Portal, in February, complaining that Wallis's bouncing bomb was "just about the maddest

LEFT A practice run of the Upkeep bouncing bomb being dropped during a training fight by members of RAF 617 Squadron at Reculver bombing range, Kent. The bomb's designer, Barnes Wallis, and others watch the practice bomb strike the shoreline.

BELOW LEFT A Lancaster aircraft carries one of Barnes Wallis's "bouncing bombs." Just 4ft (1.2m) in diameter and 5ft (1.5m) in length, the bomb resembled in shape an oil drum and despite initial skepticism from RAF High Command it proved to be incredibly effective.

proposition as a weapon that we have come across." Wallis met with Harris, head of Bomber Command, at the end of the month, and was curtly informed: "My boys' lives are too precious to be wasted by your crazy notions."

The Vickers company, still Wallis's official employers, began to fear he was getting the firm a bad name with his "crazy notions" and ordered him to close down his bouncing bomb workshop. But a few days later Charles Portal informed Wallis that his bomb would be used on an attack on the dams; the raid was scheduled for May (when the water in the valley would be at its highest) so he had just three months to perfect his invention.

While Wallis beavered away in his workshop, the RAF began selecting the air crew for what they described to the mission's leader, Wing Commander Guy Gibson, as "perhaps one of the most devastating [operations] of all time." Gibson, a highly decorated 24-year-old, who had flown 173 operational sorties, chose 22 of the best crews from Britain, Canada, Australia and New Zealand, known from now on as "617 Squadron."

The mission was shrouded in such secrecy that no one—not even Gibson—knew what was the target. All Wallis was permitted to reveal was the mine, explaining that the bomb, packed with 6,600lb (2,994kg) of explosive, could spin backwards at 500rpm and that its three depth charge detonators were set to explode 30ft (9.1m) underwater. Then he showed Gibson footage of it in action. "Well, that's my secret bomb," said Wallis, when the short clip was over. "That's how you're going to put it in the right place. Now, can you fly at 240 miles per hour, at 150 feet, over water?"

Gibson took his squadron to Derwent Water in the Midlands to practice, flying first at day and then at night. In the dark it was found impossible to keep to the right height so someone had the clever idea of fitting two spotlights to the underside of each aircraft, which would converge at 150ft (46m) and allow pilots to measure their height from the water as they flew at a speed of 232mph. But 150ft (46m) proved still too high. Mines continued to disintegrate and Wallis had to reluctantly inform the air crews that they must approach the target even lower. How low? they asked. At 60ft (18m), replied Wallis.

The date set for the mission was the night of May 16–17. At last the target was revealed and in the final briefing instructions issued: Gibson would lead a flight of nine Lancaster bombers to attack

▶ Guy Gibson was the leader of the famous "Dam Raid." A supremely courageous bomber pilot, Gibson was awarded the Victoria Cross as a result of the raid's success. He was shot down and killed in 1944.

the Mohne Dam, and once breached they would continue on to the Eder. Meanwhile a further flight of five bombers would target the Sorpe Dam and five would act as reserve aircraft.

En route to the target three of the aircraft were lost but Gibson's aircraft reached the target unscathed, the wing commander dropping his bomb first amid a barrage of antiaircraft fire. As they had practiced over the Derwent, the bomb was dropped 1,275ft (390m) from the dam, the distance calculated by Wallis for the bomb to hit with the maximum impact.

Gibson's mine hit the 130ft (40m) high and 112ft (34m) thick dam but appeared to have little effect. The second aircraft, piloted by Micky Martin, swooped in and was hit by ground fire, its bomb bouncing wide of the target, and the third aircraft's mine exploded short of the dam. The fourth, dropped by Melvin "Dinghy" Young exploded on the parapet, cracking the concrete, and then David Malty dropped his bomb. It hit the dam in the center and suddenly the concrete collapsed and water began pouring through. "Hell, it's gone!" roared Martin. They flight roared up the Ruhr Valley to Eder, and breached that dam too. There was no such luck at Sorpe; only two aircraft managed to

BARNES WALLIS

After the war, Wallis was at the forefront of aeronautical research and development at the British Aircraft Corporation for many decades. The release in 1955 of the film *The Dambusters*—in which he was played by Michael Redgrave—turned Wallis into something of a household name in the UK. Elected a fellow of the Royal Society in 1954, Wallis was knighted in 1968 and died in October 1979 aged 92.

▶ **RIGHT** An RAF reconnaissance photograph taken in the immediate aftermath of the raid shows the damage caused to the Eder Dam.

BELOW RIGHT AND FAR RIGHT One significant upshot of the damage caused by the Dambusters was Hitler's instruction to transfer more than 25,000 forced laborers from their construction of the Atlantic Wall along the French coast and instead restore production in the Ruhr disrupted by the raid. As a result when Allied soldiers came ashore on the Normandy beaches on June 6, 1944, they found half-finished coastal defenses.

reach the target (the others being shot down or forced to return to base with mechanical problems) and their bombs had no effect.

Wallis, there to greet 617 Squadron upon their return, was deeply affected when he realized nine of the 19 bombers would never come back. "If I'd only known, I'd never have started this," he said. The surviving air crews consoled the inventor, explaining gently that death was a companion they lived with every day. Gibson was awarded the Victoria Cross and was sent as a reward to Australia on a lecture tour. The Germans meanwhile embarked on a huge clean-up operation. The torrent of water that gushed through the two breached dams at 50ft (15m) per second swept away everything in its path, including power stations, bridges and railroad viaducts. Whole industrial areas were submerged and the German steel industry came to a halt. Labeling it a "dark picture of destruction," the official report into the raid likened the damage inflicted on production to the loss of 100,000 men for several months. To help repair the damage, Hitler ordered more than 25,000 workers to curtail their construction of the Atlantic Wall on the French coast and instead restore production in the Ruhr. Consequently when Allied soldiers came ashore on D-Day on June 6, 1944, they found half-finished coastal defenses that were far easier to surmount than if they had been completed.

The "Dambusters" hadn't just shattered two dams, they'd also helped halt a wall, all because of Barnes Wallis and his "crazy" invention of a bomb that bounced.

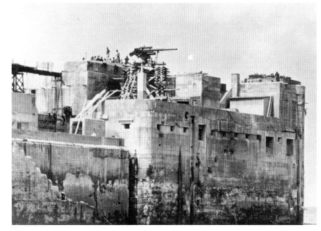

THE COMET LINE

Twelve months before the Dambusters raid the RAF had carried out another attack in northwest Germany but one that was more powerful and far less precise. On the night of May 30, 1942, 1,000 RAF bombers laid waste to the city of Cologne in what became known as the "1,000 Bomber Raid." It was a deadly attack that left nearly 5,0000 civilians dead or wounded and severely damaged the city's infrastructure.

For the Third Reich it was a prelude to a bombing campaign that three years later would devastate large swathes of the country's cities and towns. For the airmen of RAF Bomber Command and the American aircrews who began arriving in Europe in 1942, the raids also took a heavy toll. From Bomber Command alone 55,000 men lost their lives and a further 10,000 baled out over occupied Europe and spent the rest of the war in prisoner of war camps; several hundred more were more fortunate. Having parachuted from their stricken aircraft, landing—usually at night—behind enemy lines, their chances of evading capture were slim, and their chances of returning to Britain to continue the war effort even less likely.

But help was at hand for those aircrew shot down. Also across Occupied Europe escape lines were established by courageous men and women, determined to do their bit to resist the Nazi war machine. They were formed in the months following the collapse of France and the Low Countries, first by people who provided shelter for Allied soldiers, usually British, who had escaped from their guard during transportation east into Germany. The help was basic, food, clothes, and a roof over their heads. But by the end of 1940 Baron Jacques Donny, a 57-year-old Belgian businessman, had started organizing a chain of safe

Andrée de Jongh, one of three friends who in the spring of 1941 began working for an escape line in Belgium. Over time this would become the Comet Line and would result in the deaths of dozens of brave Belgians.

houses in Brussels where the escapees were sheltered. But the problem remained of how to move this increasing number of soldiers—most of whom were so conspicuous they couldn't easily blend into the local population—out of Belgium and into neutral Spain, whence they could be transported back to Britain.

Then in the spring of 1941 three friends, Henri de Bliqui, Arnold Deppe (Bliqui's cousin), and Andrée de Jongh began working for Donny's organization. Calling themselves the "Three Ds" on account of their surnames, the trio decided they might be able to provide a solution to the problem of smuggling the escapees out of the country. Before the war Deppe had worked in the Basque region of southwest France, in around the fashionable resorts of Bayonne, Biarritz, and St-Jean-de-Luz, which were very close to the Spanish border. He visited the area again, and reconnoitered a route over the Pyrenees into Spain. In the meantime, however, the Belgian escape committee had been infiltrated by the Nazis and de Bliqui was arrested in April 1941 and subsequently executed. Undeterred, de Jongh and Deppe began expanding their escape line, with de Jongh's father, Frédéric, using his contacts in Brussels to establish a new chain of safe houses.

In the summer of 1941 the escape line ("Comet" didn't become its official moniker until 1943) was trialled by Deppe, de Jongh and the British SOE agent, the party crossing into northern France, then taking the overnight train from Paris to Bayonne before heading to the safe house in Anglet, 15 miles (24km) north of the Spanish frontier, owned by a sympathetic Belgian family. They then traveled on foot across the Bidassoa River and over the Pyrenees into San Sebastian.

The next month the escape line took its first quarry, four Belgian army officers, but they and Deppe were arrested at Lille railroad station. De Jongh escaped capture, having traveled by a different route but it was clear there was a traitor somewhere in the system. Nonetheless, de Jongh, a slightly built 24-year-old

daughter of a schoolmaster, successfully saw her three escapees—a Scottish soldier called James Cromar and two Belgians, over the Pyrenees and to the British consulate in Bilbao.

The British, initially skeptical that a woman as young as de Jongh could have achieved such a feat, soon agreed to pour resources into the escape line, asking in return that aircrew were given priority over soldiers as their specialized training was considered more important to the war effort than an infantry soldier.

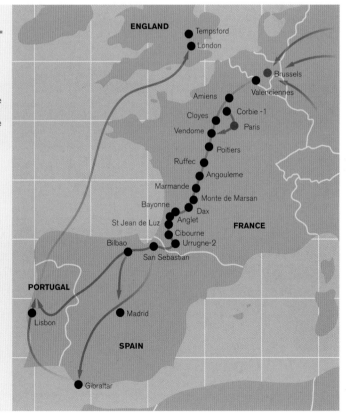

THE COMET LINE

The Comet Line differentiated between "escapees" and "evaders." The former had escaped from Germany or Italian custody, usually a POW camp or their transport en route to the camp, and were usually army personnel. Evaders, on the other hand, had never been captured and were more likely to be aircrew who had baled out of their damaged aircraft and were evading capture in the hope of returning to their squadron.

ENGLAND
Tempsford
London
Brussels
Valenciennes
Amiens
Corbie-1
Cloyes
Vendome
Paris
Poitiers
Ruffec
Angouleme
Marmande
Monte de Marsan
Bayonne
Dax
St Jean de Luz
Anglet
Cibourne
Urrugne-2
Bilbao
San Sebastian
FRANCE
PORTUGAL
Madrid
Lisbon
SPAIN
Gibraltar

● Collecting Area
● Safe House

Soon de Jongh started to receive more and more aircrew into her safe houses as the British stepped up their bombing of German targets. With most of the targets located in Germany's industrial heartland, in the northwest of the country, this meant the bombers flew over Holland and Belgium so any fliers forced to bale out would do so over those two small countries. The increased escape activity caused an upsurge in Gestapo activity as they sought to infiltrate the escape lines with Abwehr secret agents and local collaborators. The risk run by those running the safe houses was just as great as the people helping the escapees into Spain; one Belgian family who offered to shelter Allied personnel were the Maréchals. The mother, Elsie Bell, was English and her husband Georges, a Belgian, whom she had met in London during World War I. Their daughter, also called Elsie, was 16 in 1940 and together the family hid 14 men in their "safe" house. Eventually they were betrayed. Georges was shot and the two women sent to a concentration camp. "They reduced us to nothing," recalled the young Elsie. "We didn't even feel like we had the value of cattle."

Sensing the increasing danger, de Jongh moved her operational base to Paris and personally escorted dozens of aircrew to safety through the Pyrenees. But the Germans seemed to be always just a step behind; arrests were made in February 1942, and again in August and November (including Suzanne de Jongh, sister of Andrée) that year, and de Jongh's luck finally ran out in January 1943 when she was detained at a Pyrenees farmhouse as she prepared to lead her 34th escape group towards Spain.

Tortured relentlessly by the Gestapo, de Jongh revealed nothing and was despatched to Ravensbrück concentration camp. The breach in the line, however, remained, with the worst damage inflicted by the French Gestapo agent Jacques Desoubrie, using the alias name Jean Masson. In June 1943 Frederic de Jongh was arrested in Paris and executed in the spring of 1944. He was one of 23 members of the Comet Line shot by the Nazis, while a further 133 (more than 60 per cent of those captured) died in captivity, most in concentration camps.

But despite the arrests and executions there was never any shortage of men and women willing to take their place; by the summer of 1943, as the Allied bombing of Germany intensified, new escape routes into Spain were pioneered, with one in particular, the Larressore (a town midway between Biarritz and the Spanish border) route, delivering into British hands 83 Allied aircrew and several French agents between September 1943 and January 1944.

Andrée de Jongh survived Ravensbrück and returned to Belgium in 1945. By then the Comet Line had been closed down for a year, the escape route no longer needed following the Allied invasion of France in June 1944.

It was a heavy price to pay but the achievements of the Comet Line were staggering; an estimated 800 airmen and soldiers had been spirited out of Occupied Europe and back to Britain to rejoin the war against Nazi Germany. None had ever known the real name of Andrée de Jongh; to them she was just "Dédée," the pet name given in Belgium to girls called Andrée. Yet everyone who encountered the young Belgian woman was struck by her courage. "She was the force, the power, and the inspiration that brought us from Belgium to Spain."

Andrée de Jongh was caught by the Gestapo and sent to Ravensbrück concentration camp (LEFT) in northern Germany. Miraculously she survived and died in 2007 aged 90.

ENIGMA/KURSK AND OPERATION BAGRATION

By the start of 1943 the war was no longer going Germany's way. On the verge of defeat in North Africa, German forces had also suffered a crushing and costly defeat at Stalingrad during the winter of 1942–43. In January 1943 the situation in Russia was grave. The advancing Soviet forces had punched a 180 mile (290km) hole between the German Army Group B and the Army Group Don, and as the Red Army continued their offensive the German troops south of the Don River were threatened with entrapment. In response Hitler reorganized his forces in Russia, disbanding Army Group B and reconstituting Army Group Don as Army Group South under the command of field marshal Erich von Manstein. Hitler and von Manstein rarely agreed about strategy in Russia but the Field Marshal was eventually granted his request to operate without interference from Berlin.

Von Manstein believed that the Soviet forces were dangerously overstretched, susceptible to a large scale counterattack that would win back for the German army the cities of Kharkov and Kursk. Kharkov was duly retaken on March 15, 1943 and though Kursk still remained in Russian hands when the German offensive ran out of momentum, Von Manstein had gone a long way in wresting the initiative from the Russians.

What he now planned was a decisive summer offensive—codenamed Operation Citadel—that would capture Kursk and extend into Soviet territory a 70-mile (113km) salient that would result in the destruction of thousands of enemy soldiers and force the Red Army onto the defensive, giving German troops time to reinforce their tired and depleted ranks with men and equipment.

But there were two crucial factors working against the German preparations for the forthcoming offensive. The first was their underestimation of Russian organization; not only were generals such as Konstantin Rokossovsky, Nikolai Vatutin, Ivan Konev, and Georgy Zhukov far more competent than those

MARDER II TANK

Crew 3

Weight 23,809lb (10.8 tonnes)

Length 20ft 10in (6.36m)

Armour 0.19–1.38in (5–35mm)

Main armament 1 x 7.5cm Pak 40 37 rounds

Speed 25mph (40kmh)

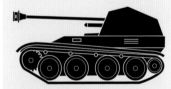

MARDER III TANK

Crew 4

Weight 23,523lb (10,670kg)

Length 15ft 3in (4.65m)

Armor 0.4–2in (10–50mm)

Main armament 1 x 7.5cm Pak 40 37 rounds

Speed 26mph (42kmh)

The Marders were tank used by the German army with a Panzer II chassis. They were introduced to counter the formidable Russian T-34 tank and were armed with captured Soviet guns in order to penetrate the thick T-34 armor. The Marders were used extensively in 1943 and 1944 but their weakness was the lack of armor on the top that left crews dangerously exposed.

Though Operation Citadel was a resounding success for the Soviet army, thanks in part to intelligence provided by the British Ultra decryption network, thousands of Russian soldiers were captured by the Germans. This group are being marched into captivity on June 21, 1943.

high-ranking officers who had been in command two years earlier when Germany launched its invasion of Russia, but the country's war production was also reaching its potential by the summer of 1943. Factories located in the east of the Soviet Union, beyond the range of the Luftwaffe bombers, were producing a vast quantity of arms and ammunition, including the powerful new T-34 tanks that were resistant to German antitank shells.

Secondly, the Soviet Union had superior intelligence to the Germans thanks, in part, to special-purpose radio battalions that had been deployed in the front to monitor German radio traffic and jam it whenever possible. Of more significance, however, was the information Russia received from Great Britain. Though trust between the two Allies was never great, in 1942 and early 1943 the British were so desperate to keep the Germans fighting on two fronts that they passed on to the Soviets messages that had been decoded through Ultra at Bletchley Park.

The extent of the British intelligence, and its effect on the outcome of Operation Citadel, remains a matter of conjecture. Some historians claims that because of Ultra, the Soviets knew the exact time and location of von Manstein's offensive. Others took a different view; for example, American Colonel David M. Glantz, of the Soviet Army Studies Office, wrote a paper in 1988 in which he said: "The British did provide the Soviets with Ultra-derived materials, without revealing the source of the data, via the British Military Mission in Moscow. This information did little to improve Soviet performance prior to 1943. After April 1943, the information diminished in volume and importance, and after July 1943 it virtually ceased."

But the intelligence provided by the British to the Russians in the first few months of 1943 undoubtedly allowed the Red Army to position itself for the imminent German offensive. On April 8, for instance, General Zhukov, in command of all combat forces to the south of Kursk, telegrammed Josef Stalin, telling him: "The enemy will attempt to cut off the Kursk salient, to encircle and destroy the Soviet forces of Central Front and Voronezh Front deployed here. At the moment, both fronts only have 15 tank divisions, meanwhile the German forces in the

Belgorod-Kharkov direction have already gathered 17 tank divisions—most of them include the new types of tanks, such as Tiger I, improved Panther, Jagdpanzer IV, and some kinds of tank destroyers such as Marder II, Marder III."

With such intelligence at his disposal it was little surprise that Operation Citadel—launched at dawn on July 5, 1943—ended in defeat for Germany. The climax of the campaign was the Battle of Kursk, the largest tank battle in history, in which an estimated 6,000 tanks, 4,000 aircraft, and two million soldiers fought each other. The outcome was a German withdrawal that continued over the summer and into the fall. Kharkov fell to the Russians in August and Kiev in October as the Germans dug defensive positions in Belorussia.

But the German troops were far from defeated despite their defeat at Kursk, leading the Russians to start preparations in early 1944 for a huge offensive of their own with the objective of pushing German troops out of the western Soviet Union once and for all. There were approximately 850,000 German soldiers still in the Soviet Union and facing them on the four fronts in Belorussia were around one million Soviet troops.

The operation was codenamed Bagration, after the Georgian prince, Pyotr Bagration, the brilliant commander of Russian forces during the 19th century war with Napoleon's France.

By now the Russians no longer had access to Britain's Ultra intelligence reports, the trust between the two countries having become increasingly fraught, but what the Soviets did have was a complex deception program in place known as maskirovka. In the early

MASKIROVKA

The Russian translation of camouflage is "maskirovka," although whereas in the English language this definition, as applied militarily, is generally restricted to the method of deceiving the enemy by painting or screening objects so they are lost to sight in the background, in Russian the "maskirovka" has a broader meaning and covers not just distorting uniforms and armaments but also strategic disinformation designed to confuse the enemy. The official Soviet definition for maskirovka was: "The means of securing combat operations and the daily activities of forces; a complexity of measures, directed to mislead the enemy regarding the presence and disposition of forces, various military objectives, their condition, combat readiness, and operations, and also the plans of the command … Maskirovka contributes to the achievement of surprise for the actions of forces, the preservation of combat readiness, and the increased survivability of objectives." One of the most enthusiastic champions of maskirovka was General Zhukov (pictured), who used the tactic to great effect during the Battles of Khalkhyn Gol against the Japanese in the summer of 1939, when the Soviet Union defeated the Japanese Sixth Army in a series of engagements on the Soviet–Japanese border.

Red Army soldiers go into action **(ABOVE)** alongside T-34 tanks during the battle of Kursk in July 1943. It was the T-34's combination of speed, ruggedness, agility, and its 76.2mm high-velocity gun that made it so feared among German Panzer crews, such as the ones pictured **(BELOW LEFT AND RIGHT)** in their Tiger I tanks.

months the vast deception began to be implemented against the German Army Group Center dug in on the wood and marshy ground that stretched across Belorussia and into eastern Poland (officially Russian territory following their 1939 invasion).

The Germans for their part knew a great offensive would be launched and they were confident they knew where it would be launched—further south, in northern Ukraine. It was the Russians' intention to maintain this belief, a ruse of gargantuan proportions that entailed concealing from the enemy the moving of approximately 1.7 million soldiers, and the Soviet High Command (Stavka) knew this figure was not enough. Their aim was to reinforce the front opposite the Germans with five combined arms armies and two tank armies, as well as two mechanized corps and four cavalry corps, all of which meant more than 3,000 tanks, 12,000 guns and mortars, and hundreds of thousands of tons of fuel, rations, and ammunition had to be moved in secret to Belorussia, while giving the appearance of massing their forces hundreds of miles south in northern Ukraine.

Once all the reinforcements were in place the first phase of the Soviet battle plan would commence with the 1st Baltic and 3rd Belorussian Fronts assaulting from Vitebsk in the north, while the 2nd Belorussian Front, supported by the 1st Belorussian, advancing towards Minsk. This would result in the encirclement of the Army Group Center and precipitate the second phase of Operation Bagration, a frontal assault across the entire Minsk front.

As the deception was put into operation, the vast majority of the Soviet army were as ignorant of where the offensive would be launched as the Germans. General Sergei Shtemenko, 1st Deputy of the Stavka Operations Department, described how: "Precautions were taken to keep our intentions secret. Only a very narrow circle of people were directly engaged in working out the plans of the summer campaign as a whole and the Belorussian operation, in particular … All correspondence on this subject as well as telephone conversations or telegraph messages were strictly forbidden and a very strict check was kept on this. Proposals from the front concerning operations were also dealt with by only two or three people, were usually written by hand and reported, as a rule, by the

◄ Two Destroyed Panzer IVs belonging to the 20th Panzer Division near Bobruisk. The two dead crew were among approximately 900,000 Germans killed or captured during Operation Bagration in the summer of 1944.

commanders in person." Soldiers and vehicles moved only at night by rail and soldiers arriving from other parts of the Soviet Union were not brought up to the frontline but were held back in the east, 40 miles (64km) or more behind where the offensive would begin. Even there they contributed to the maskirovka with Konstantin Rokossovsky, commander of the 1st Belorussian Front, remembering that: "In many places we built fake crossings and roads. Guns were concentrated on secondary lines, from which they launched artillery attacks and were then removed to the rear: dummies being left there on the firing positions."

Meanwhile more than 600 miles (966km) further south in northern Ukraine, the Soviets were being far less discreet in their "preparations" for their imminent offensive. The Soviet air force began patrolling more frequently, reconnaissance planes were sent over enemy lines, while German spotter planes were allowed to fly across Russian lines and photograph the dummy tanks (approximately 100 in every rifle division) and dummy vehicles (approximately 75 in every rifle division). Railroad traffic in the Ukraine increased, so too wireless communication, while at night small teams

of Russian soldiers armed with torches wandered over the front at specific intervals, flashing their lights as German aircraft flew overhead, deceiving the pilots into thinking they were directing the movement of large numbers of troops towards the front line.

When Operation Bagration finally began on June 22—three years to the day since Germany had launched its invasion of Russia—the Red Army smashed through the German defenses in Belorussia. Six days later the Russian armor had reached as far as the Berezina River, a distance of 200 miles (322km), while in the first week of fighting the Germans had 50,000 killed and half that number captured. The Germans fell back and by the end of Operation Bagration had suffered losses (killed and captured) of more than 900,000 soldiers. *Maskirovka* had utterly fooled them, as the German general Friedrich von Mellenthin later admitted: "The horrible counterattacks, in which huge masses of manpower and equipment took part, were an unpleasant surprise for us," he said. "We did not … detect even one minefield or antitank area until … the first tank was blown up by a mine or the first Russian antitank guns opened fire."

AMERICA'S NISEI INTELLIGENCE

The *Los Angeles Times* editorial of February 1942 warned that now that the United States was at war with Japan they faced a danger from within. "A viper is nonetheless a viper wherever the egg is hatched," thundered the newspaper. "So a Japanese American born of Japanese parents, nurtured upon Japanese traditions, living in a transplanted Japanese atmosphere and thoroughly inoculated with Japanese … ideals, notwithstanding his nominal brand of accidental citizenship almost inevitably and with the rarest exceptions grows up to be a Japanese, and not an American."

The *Los Angeles Times* was responding to the decision by President Franklin D. Roosevelt to sign Executive Order 9066, authorizing the internment of tens of thousands of people of Japanese ancestry, two-thirds of whom were American citizens known as "Nisei," second generation Japanese who called the USA home. The majority, more than 100,000, were locked up in one of 21 internment camps throughout the USA— euphemistically described in the cold, hard language of government bureaucracy as Relocation Centers. The government also suppressed a secret FBI intelligence report asserting that in their opinion the overwhelming majority of Japanese-Americans posed no threat to national security.

Even serving Japanese-Americans were affected by the wave of bigotry sweeping the country in early 1942, with those Nisei in the ranks of the Hawaii National Guard reclassified as "enemy aliens ineligible for the military." In protest more than 1,400 of them formed the "Hawaii Provisional Battalion," which in time was reconstituted as the 100th Infantry Battalion before coming the 442nd Regimental Combat Team in 1943. That same year the US government reversed its decision on Japanese–Americans serving in the armed forces subject to each soldier filling out a questionnaire on where their allegiance lay.

In 1944 the 442nd RCT shipped out to Europe, fighting in bitter engagements in Italy and France during 223 days of combat action in which 21 soldiers were awarded America's highest decoration for valor, the Medal of Honor.

Although the government had relaxed its policy of allowing Nisei to serve in the armed forces officially in 1943, the previous year it had started to recognize the important role Japanese–Americans could play in the war in Military Intelligence Service (MIS). In 1942 a Nisei language school was opened at Camp Savage, Minnesota (later designated the Military Intelligence Service Language School) in which Japanese–Americans were educated in Japanese military techniques and vocabulary, taught how to be interpreters and how to translate military documents. The first class of 42 students graduated in May 1942 and by the end of the war hundreds were graduating at a time.

One of the early students at the Camp Savage Language School was 29-year-old Roy Matsumoto, born and brought up in Los Angeles and a product of Long Beach Polytechnic High School. Despite being an American citizen, Matsumoto was interned in early 1942 in the Jerome Relocation Center in Arkansas. 'I lost just about everything, almost all my personal property and financial assets, including my bank deposits,' he recalled. "The government's excuse: It was enemy alien property. They were never returned to me. I was so mad."

Yet despite this shameful treatment he volunteered for the MIS Language School at Camp Savage in August 1942. He breezed through most of the classes and was waiting to be posted to an intelligence unit when in the summer of 1943 his eye was caught by a notice posted on the camp bulletin board seeking Nisei with a "high rate of physical ruggedness and stamina" and a good command of the Japanese language. The volunteers were asked about their "marital status, health, language proficiency." When it came to Matsumoto, he was given no choice. "I did well at the language school, so without an interview I was ordered

Nisei soldiers from the 100th Infantry battalion receive training in the use of grenades in 1943. The following year the battalion saw action in Italy, including participating in the bitter fighting to defeat the German defenders at Monte Casino.

▼ The Congressional Gold Medal, America's highest civilian award, was bestowed on the Nisei by the US government in 2011. The design depicts Nisei soldiers, second-generation Americans of Japanese ancestry, from both the European and Pacific theaters of war.

OPPOSITE Nisei infantrymen of the 442nd Regimental Combat Team hike up a muddy French road in the Chambois Sector, France, in late 1944. During World War II, 21 members of the 442nd regiment were awarded the Medal of Honor, America's highest medal for battlefield gallantry.

RIGHT Members of the 442nd Regimental Combat Team build a pontoon bridge as part of their training at Camp Shelby in the USA. The bridge completed, a company of infantry rush with fixed bayonets to the opposite shore and enter the "enemy's" heavily wooded territory.

BELOW RIGHT The training over, the 442nd Regt were shipped to Europe for their first taste of action. Here some of them seek cover as German artillery shells rain down during the final stages of the battle for Italy in April 1945.

▲ Roy Matsumoto, right, was one of 14 Nisei interpreters who volunteered to serve with Merrill's Marauders when they shipped out to Burma. Unlike the Nisei fighting in Europe, Matsumoto knew that if he fell into Japanese hands he could expect no mercy.

to join," he recalled. A few days later, Matsumoto and the other 13 Nisei selected were on a train with shades down headed for San Francisco under a cloak of great secrecy.

Once in San Francisco the 14 Nisei were escorted under armed guard on board the SS *Lurline*, a once luxury passenger liner converted by the exigencies of war into a troopship. On September 21, 1943 the vessel slipped out of California and a couple of days later the Nisei were introduced to their shipmates: more than 2,000 men belonging to the a volunteer unit called the 1688th Detachment (a further 1,000 volunteers would join in New Caledonia).

Neither the 14 Nisei, who were assigned to the three battalions comprising the 1688th Detachment, nor the rest of the outfit knew where they were headed. Since volunteering a few weeks earlier, secrecy had been paramount and two officers caught idly discussing their unit with sailors were dismissed and soon on their way home. It wasn't until the *Lurline* had left western Australia, having taken on supplies, that the ship's safe was opened "and sealed material from Washington was delivered to the various battalions indicating what kind of equipment we were to have and what kind of organization we would finally become."

The orders also revealed their destination—India. From India, after a period of extensive training and acclimatization, during which the outfit was named the 5307th Composite Regiment (Provisional), they deployed to northern Burma in February 1 under the overall command of General Joseph Stilwell, in charge of Americans in the China–Burma–India theater.

The 5307th were to form part of an operation, codenamed "Capital," which entailed a three-pronged attack against the Japanese, who had been in possession of Burma for two years. While the Chinese attacked from the northeast and the British Fourth Corps struck from the west across the Chindwin, two further Chinese divisions would drive down the

middle of northern Burma and seize the strategically important town of Myitkyina supported by force of 3,000 Americans. Their presence was more than just symbolic: they were to act as a rapid-reaction guerrilla force, attacking the Japanese in their rear as and when required.

Not long after the unit marched south into enemy-held territory they had their first engagement with the Japanese when a patrol from the 3rd Battalion, led by Lieutenant Logan Weston, was attacked by a superior force from the elite Japanese 18th Division.

Several Americans were killed or wounded as the Japanese began creeping towards their positions. The situation was desperate and then the patrol's Nisei interpreter, Henry Gosho, a 23-year-old from Seattle, came to their rescue. He had been sent by his father to Japan in the late 1930s to learn the language but while at college he had been forced to join the cadets. As a result he knew all Japanese military commands and he was now able to call on that knowledge to ease his unit out of their dire predicament. "I was amazed to find that this firing order was exactly the same order that I had learned [in Japan] while going to college," recalled Gosho. "So I said to Weston, 'I'm not sure this is right, but he's giving firing orders.' So Logan turned round and said, 'What are they?' I told him, and he rearranged our firepower so we were able to respond to theirs."

The precious inside information checked the Japanese encirclement, allowing Weston a small window of opportunity to withdraw his men to safety before they were overrun. He also radioed for reinforcements and soon the Japanese were taking heavy casualties of their own as they were ambushed in pursuit of Weston's patrol.

Meanwhile Roy Matsumoto was also putting his Japanese to good use with the 2nd Battalion, instructed to hold a road not far from Weston's engagement. Spotting something in the trees above his position, Matsumoto shinned up the trunk and discovered a

telephone line connecting the Japanese 18th Division's headquarters in Kamaing with one of their field commanders. Matsumoto tapped into the line with a field phone handset and spent several hours eavesdropping. "I was able to get very important enemy troop movements and 18th Division orders," recounted Matsumoto. "I then heard a sergeant talking to his captain, and I learned they were guarding an ammo dump. There were only three or four of them, and the sergeant said, 'What shall we do?' Their captain said a position, and I reported this." Merrill passed this message to Stilwell, requesting an airstrike against the dump, which was duly delivered with excellent results.

The last intelligence Matsumoto picked up was also the most valuable: Forward elements of the 18th Division were ordered to withdraw south from Maingkwan. To cover this retreat, a force of Japanese troops was instructed to attack the Americans dug in

on the road below where Matsumoto was listening to their conversation. The Japanese launched their attack a short while later and the 2nd Battalion was waiting, killing more than 100 of the enemy thanks to Matsumoto's intelligence.

A few weeks later and much further south, Matsumoto performed one of the most courageous acts of the whole campaign in Burma. In pursuing the Japanese south, the 2nd Battalion had been counterattacked and were ordered to dig in on the tiny hilltop village of Nhpum Ga, blocking the Japanese from pushing north and allowing the Chinese time to bring up thousands of troops. Dysentery was sweeping through the 2nd Battalion and Matsumoto was the only one of their four Nisei fit enough for active service. One night in early April noises came from the Japanese positions just yards from where the Americans were crouching in their foxholes. Where they preparing an

▲ The 3,000 men who comprised Merrill's Marauders sailed from San Francisco for Burma in September 1943 aboard the former cruise liner SS *Lurline*. Their mission was top secret and even the men didn't know their destination until they were approaching India.

attack? Under his own initiative Matsumoto crawled down the slope in the black of night to within yards of where the Japanese lay. He was close enough that he could almost reach out and touch them. "The Japanese were talking in their foxholes just as soldiers do," he said. Girls, food, family. Matsumoto remained motionless, listening for a clue as to what had them so animated. Then it came: an anxious soldier asking his buddy if he reckoned their dawn attack would finally break the Americans.

He returned with news of the impending attack, giving the 2nd Battalion a precious couple of hours to noiselessly vacate their frontline foxholes—booby-trapping them in the process—and moving further back up the hill. They also concentrated what heavy machine guns they had on the direction from which the Japanese would attack.

The assault unfolded just as the Japanese had unwittingly revealed to Matsumoto, dozens of them dying as they leapt into empty foxholes that exploded. Matsumoto looked over the top of his carbine and saw the second wave of enemy soldiers hesitate, unsure whether to go on or fall back. Matsumoto had studied Japanese infantry tactics as a cadet in Japan. He knew the order to now issue. "Prepare to charge," he yelled in perfect Japanese. He paused, then hollered, "Charge!" The Japanese charged and dozens died on the American guns. Within days the siege of Nhpum Ga had been lifted and the 2nd Battalion saved from annihilation.

Matsumoto and his 13 Nisei interpreters in the 5307th Unit weren't alone in their courage and endeavor. Scores of graduates from the MIS language school performed magnificent deeds in the Pacific campaign, such as Sergeant Hoichi "Bob" Kubo on the island of Okinawa. Hearing that 100 civilians faced being made to commit involuntary suicide by their Japanese captors, he crept towards their position and in two hours of negotiations persuaded the soldiers to release the civilians, appealing to their sense of honor as warriors.

In all an estimated 26,000 Japanese-American men and women served in the United States armed forces during World War II but few received recognition of their sterling deeds after the conflict. Not until the Civil Liberties Act of 1988 did the US government formally apologize to all those who had been interned.

The Americans of Merrill's Marauders and their Chinese allies march side by side down the Ledo Road in northern Burma in February 1944. It was the first time that the two nations fought side by side against a common enemy.

GENERAL FRANK MERRILL

Originally known as the 1688th Detachment, then the 5307th Composite Regiment (Provisional), the 3,000 men who volunteered to embark on what the recruitment posters termed as a "dangerous and hazardous mission" came to be best known as Merrill's Marauders after their commanding officer, General Frank Merrill. It was a newspaper correspondent, visiting the unit as they trained in India, who suggested the nickname. After all, 5307th Composite Regiment (Provisional) hardly tripped off the tongue and readers would find Merrill's Marauders altogether more thrilling. Yet ironically, Merrill never actually led his Marauders into combat and was invalided out of Burma with a bad heart not long into the six-month mission. Instead it was his second-in-command, Colonel Charles Hunter, who was the real leader of the Marauders, though he never received the recognition he deserved. "A better name for the outfit would probably have been Hunter's Harbingers or Hunter's Hawks, or something like that rather than Merrill's Marauders," reflected Sam Wilson, a Marauder's lieutenant who rose to be a lieutenant general after the war. 'But … history doesn't always work like that.'

AUSTRALIA'S Z SPECIAL UNIT

"Set Europe ablaze!" That was prime minister's cry to his chiefs of staff in the summer of 1940 when he demanded Britain hit back at Germany following their conquest of most of the continent. As we saw in earlier chapters, one result of Churchill's edict was the formation of the commandos but there was another organization formed in 1940 that would in the next five years contribute to the Allied triumph. And like the commandos, their range of operations would expand throughout the course of the war so that it wasn't just Europe being set ablaze but also the Far East.

The Special Operations Executive was established initially to infiltrate secret agents into Occupied Europe to help foment and organize resistance among the civilian population. But in May 1941 the SOE opened its Singapore branch as Japan's military ambitions became clearer in the Far East. In December 1941 Japan entered the war with its attack on Pearl Harbor and its subsequent conquest of former British colonies such as Burma, Hong Kong, and Singapore. In March 1942 Japan raided the airfield and harbor at Broome, Western Australia, and a few days later landed at Huon Bay, New Guinea, the prelude to a push towards Port Moresby, the capital of New Guinea, from where they planned to use its air bases as a means of isolating Australia from American forces in the Pacific, in effect besieging Australia so its contribution to the Allied effort would be negligible.

One response from Australia was to establish in April 1942 an Australia Special Operations Executive, which was given several cover names in the course of its life to protect the secret nature of its operations, including the Services Reconnaissance Department, the Inter-Allied Services Department (ISD) and perhaps the most famous of all—Z Special Unit. In its short existence the Z Special Unit launched more than 80 missions into Japanese-held territory of which Operation Jaywick was the most successful and the most audacious.

Its objective was the destroy enemy shipping in to Singapore Harbor, deep behind the Japanese lines and surrounded by enemy-held islands with aircraft and ships continuously patrolling the sea. Codenamed Operation Jaywick (Jaywick was a popular air freshener at the time, marketed before the war in Singapore with its claim that it would remove unwanted smells from the home), the mission's leader was Major Ivan Lyon, a British infantry officer whose wife and young son had been interned by the Japanese following their conquest of Singapore. As his second-in-command Lyon appointed another Briton, Lieutenant Commander Donald Davidson of the Royal Navy.

Lyon asked for volunteers for a top-secret mission from the Flinders Naval Depot in Victoria and selected 17 men from more than 40 applicants. For the next six weeks, still in the dark as to the nature of the mission for which they had volunteered, the men underwent a harsh training regime to weed out the weak and unsuitable. As well as learning how to live off the land

Most of the men who volunteered for the highly secretive Z Special Unit were Australian. Here some of them pose for the camera during training on Fraser Island. Left to right: Corporal Jim Abbott, Mick Lappin, Private Leslie Watkins, John Hodges, and Len Blair.

◄ Major Ivan Lyon, the British infantry officer in charge of Operation Jaywick. Departing from Australia in a small fishing boat, Lyon and his raiding party sunk Japanese shipping in Singapore Harbor in a raid of stunning audacity.

in south-east Asia, they practiced canoeing and the art of laying limpet mines. At the end of the training 12 men were selected for the mission.

While the men had been training Lyon had been addressing the difficulty of getting them to the target without being detected by the strong Japanese defenses. His solution was to sail to Singapore in a small fishing boat, the *Krait*—just over 20m long with a top speed of six and a half knots—which was sturdy and well used to navigating the Java Ocean.

The *Krait* departed from Cairns, northern Australia, in August 1943, picking up supplies on the west coast before heading north, the vessel flying a Japanese flag and the crew having darkened their bodies with pigment and donned sarongs to give the appearance of local fishermen. Even their rations and everyday essentials were Japanese so that if anything should fall overboard the suspicions of the enemy would not be aroused.

The *Krait* headed north without incident and on September 17 Davidson wrote in his log: "Spirits have been excellent; very high morale, which is a very satisfactory feature. It's a good bunch this."

The next day the raiders came ashore at the small uninhabited island of Pompong around 90 miles (145km) south of Singapore where they spent a couple of days, exercising their bodies after more than two weeks at sea. They made final preparations, slipping into their black two-piece suits of waterproof silk closed at the ankles and wrists. On their feet they wore black sandshoes and each raider carried a revolver with 100 rounds. Additionally, they each had a knife, compass, first-aid kit, and a cyanide pill that would kill in a matter of seconds. Their canoes, when full loaded, carried more than 600lb (272kg) of equipment including the limpet mines.

The *Krait* was to remain hidden on the island while six of the raiders in three teams of two paddled north to Singapore. They set out on September 20 and three days later reached the small unpopulated island of

Dongas, 8 miles from Singapore and with a small hill in its center that proved an ideal observation point. "By night Singapore appears as brightly lit as of yore," wrote Davidson in his log. "Even motor car lights do not appear to be dimmed."

The original plan had been to attack the harbor on the night of September 26–27 but when Lyon saw through his telescope 13 ships at anchor he decided to strike immediately. But the raiders hadn't appreciated the strength of the tides and it proved impossible to paddle the 8 miles (12.9km) to Singapore. They hid up in another island and reverted to the original plan of each two-man canoe attacking different sections of the harbor. Davidson had in his canoe Able Seaman Walter Falls, and in his log he described how: "We attacked in each case on the port side as it was away from Singapore lights. Fortunately our work was dead silent without any hitches or clanging. Falls with our magnetic holdfasts was absolutely expert … our time to approach, limpet & get away averaged 20 minutes per ship, a lot this being taken up by the approach. Ships were lying 4 cables (800 yards) apart about."

Davidson and Falls slipped out of Singapore Harbor as stealthily as they had entered and at dawn on September 27 were concealed at Batam Island. There they listened to the sound of several explosions, congratulating each other but also aware that now every Japanese in the region would be hunting them. But despite a tropical storm Davidson and Falls rendezvoused with the *Krait* on October 1, having paddled nearly 90 miles (145km) in four nights. To their delight the other four raiders also returned safely, having also found plenty of targets in the harbor. Between them they sank seven enemy ships, nearly 40,000 tons in total, and scored a huge psychological victory over the Japanese, who felt humiliated at a commando raid within what they termed their "Southern Resources Area." If they weren't safe from attack there, then where were they safe?

On October 19 the *Krait* reached the American base in Exmouth Gulf, some 48 days and 5,000 miles (8,047km) since setting out from its original starting point in Cairns, northern Australia. Thirty three of those days had been inside waters controlled by the Japanese.

Emboldened by the success of Operation Jaywick, Lyon and Davidson hatched a plot for another top-secret mission the following year, codenamed "Rimau" (the Malay word for "Tiger"). It was bigger in scale than the attack on Singapore, entailing 23 men in all, and instead of being self-contained the raiders would rely on two submarines to take them to and from the target. Though the target was again Singapore, this time the commandos would penetrate the harbor in 15 one-man motorized submersible canoes (nicknamed "Sleeping Beauties,") having first captured a local fishing boat. This was because it was deemed too risky for the submarine to enter the harbor. It was an added complication, an unknown factor, that further stacked the odds against Lyon and his men.

The raiding party set out from Perth on September 11, 1944, and on the 28th they commandeered an Indonesian junk, the *Mustika*. Once again they made themselves look like local fishermen in appearance, but this vessel, unlike the *Krait*, had no engine so the winds dictated their progress towards Singapore. It was slow and painstaking progress but on October 10 they were primed and ready to attack. But as they started to prepare to clamber into their submersible canoes they were spotted by a Malay patrol boat. Opening fire as it approached, the raiders repulsed the attack but knew that the element of surprise was now gone and that the Malays would warn the Japanese. Destroying the junk, Lyon aborted the mission and ordered his six men into the canoes and to head to the rendezvous with the submarine.

As the raiders paddled for their lives away from Singapore events were unfolding 1,000 miles (1,609km) south that would have a tragic bearing on the outcome of *Rimau*. The Allies' Ultra decryption service intercepted a Japanese message giving details of the

OPERATION COPPER

One of Z Special Unit's last missions was to reconnoiter the Japanese defenses on the island of Muschu, a tiny island off the coast of Papua New Guinea in April 1945. Codenamed Operation Copper, eight Australian commandos paddled ashore but the next day encountered some of the estimated 1,000 Japanese troops on the island. Five of the commandos managed to evade the enemy for several days before constructing some rafts and putting out to sea in the hope of signalling patrolling aircraft. But the rafts soon broke up and four of the soldiers decided to return to the beach and try again. One, Mick Dennis (pictured far left), whose sister was a 1932 Olympic swimming champion, remained in the sea, and after

hours in shark-infested waters was eventually rescued by Australian forces. Two of the men who returned to the beach, Spence Walklate, a well-known Australian rugby league player, and Ron Eagleton, tried again using logs but they simply vanished without trace. It wasn't until 2013 that an Australian investigator located their remains on a neighboring island called Kairiru, and after studying Japanese records, concluded that the pair had been caught, tortured, and executed. Their killers then burned their bodies and buried them in the hope their crimes would never be discovered. In 2014 Walklate and Eagleton were laid to rest in Lae War Cemetery alongside their five comrades.

patrol boat stumbling upon the commandos as they prepared to attack Singapore Harbor. The Australians now faced a terrible choice: if they reacted to the message by ordering the submarine into Singapore to collect the raiders it would reveal to the Japanese that they had broken their codes, prompting them to change the cipher system. The Allies couldn't run that risk so no message was sent to the submarine. The raiders were on their own.

Over the course of the next few days the raiders were hunted down by the Japanese, encountering them first on Soreh Island where a vicious firefight took place. Davidson and another soldier, Corporal Archie Campbell, were wounded, so Lyon ordered them to evacuate by canoe to the nearby island of Tapai. To cover their withdrawal Lyon and his remaining men provided covering fire, killing more than 60 enemy

soldiers in a four-hour gun battle. All except Doug Wane were killed. He was captured and later died when his Japanese captors used him as a human guinea pig in their experiments to find an antitetanus injection.

Davidson and Campbell reached Tapai but they knew their situation was hopeless. They knew too what would happen if caught alive. They ended their lives with cyanide. The raiders of Rimau were laid to rest after the war at Kranji War Cemetery, which was visited by Prince William, the Duke and Duchess of Cambridge during a tour of the Far East in 2012. According to Group Captain Clive Coombes, the British Defense Advisor in Singapore, the prince asked specifically to see the graves of Z Special Unit. "Prince William was well aware of the force's heroics and was keen to see their resting place," said Coombes.

▲ Some unidentified members of the Z Special Unit (**ABOVE LEFT**) about to board *Motor Launch 1321* in Aitape Harbor, on the north coast of Papua New Guinea, ahead of their mission to reconnoiter Japanese defenses on the island of Muschu. The same motor launch at anchor (**ABOVE RIGHT**) after the failure of the raid that resulted in the deaths of seven of the eight commandos.

THE NAVAJO CODETALKERS

More than any other of the major combatants in World War II Japan had the greatest experience of code breaking. In fact, Imperial Japan had three separate organizations dedicated to decrypting enemy code under the jurisdiction of the army, navy and the Foreign Ministry. Ironically, because of all these resources, from which inevitably sprang jealousies and petty rivalries (not unlike the antagonism that existed between the American army and navy codebreakers), the Japanese didn't enjoy as much success decrypting their enemies' communications as they should have.

Because of their expansionist ambitions stretching back to the 1920s—a decade when the Western Powers were still recovering from the ruinous costs of World War I—Japan had cause to dedicate resources to codebreaking years ahead of other nations. In 1921 a nascent army cryptologic service came into being with the objective of deciphering British and American codes. The following year Japan, while negotiating with the Soviet Union over Siberia, gained an advantage when it decrypted the communications being sent by the Russian delegation back to Moscow. This success only strengthened Japan's belief in the efficacy of decryption and more money and resources were poured into the department, so that by the mid-1930s the army's codebreaking department numbered more than 130 people.

The navy's codebreakers pre-dated even the army's, tracing its roots back to the Russo-Japanese war of 1905, and in 1929 they centralized their codebreaking department as tensions began to mount between Japan and the United States.

The Japanese Foreign Ministry's department of decryption was the smallest of the three but it complemented the decoding carried out by the army and navy, so that by 1941 Japan's intelligence services were confident they could crack most codes. They had already enjoyed success with the US diplomatic codes, Gray and Brown, as well as the navy's CSP-642 strip

cipher and (thanks to the Germans) the codes used by American merchant ships. The Americans were concerned that, as 1942 dawned, an already precarious situation in the Pacific could be exacerbated if the Japanese continued to crack their codes. As one officer noted: "Military communications were made available to the enemy like sand sifting through a sieve."

The solution for the leaky "sieve" came from an unlikely source. Philip Johnston, a World War I veteran, had grown up on a Navajo reservation, the son of a missionary who had made it his role in life to convert Native American Indians to Christianity. Johnston was one of the few non-Navajos fluent in the language, and therefore he knew how difficult a language it was to master. It was "an unwritten language of extreme complexity" because as the Naval

Navajo codetalkers Henry Bake and George Kirk are photographed in action in 1943. The men of the 382nd participated in some of the bloodiest fighting in the Pacific, including Guadalcanal, Bougainville, Guam, Peleliu, Okinawa, and Iwo Jima.

▼ The first batch of 29 Navajo US Marine Corps codetalker recruits are sworn in at Fort Wingate, New Mexico. Designated the 382nd Platoon, US Marine Corps, the men used their Native American language to great effect against Japan.

▲ A CRI 43007 transmitter-receiver of the type used by the Navajo codetalkers. Their two-part code consisted of a 26-letter phonetic alphabet and a 211-word English vocabulary, and was so arcane it proved indecipherable to the Japanese, who had hitherto prided themselves on their codebreaking abilities.

History and Heritage Command in Washington explained: "Its syntax and tonal qualities, not to mention dialects, make it unintelligible to anyone without extensive exposure and training. It has no alphabet or symbols, and is spoken only on the Navajo lands of the American Southwest."

Reading an article about the need to protect military codes from Japan, Johnston obtained an interview with Lieutenant Colonel James E. Jones, the Marines' Signal Corps Communications Officer at Camp Elliott near San Diego in February 1942. He listened as Johnston expounded his idea about recruiting Navajos as codebreakers. He could sense Jones's skepticism so explained how intricate the language was, that it contained "a number of words that, when spoken with varying inflections, may have as many as four totally different meanings." It was practically incomprehensible to any non-Navajo, a series of strange gurgling noises that resembled "a partially blocked sink drain."

Jones was unconvinced, telling Johnston that: "In all the history of warfare, that has never been done. No code, no cipher is completely secure from enemy interception. We change our codes frequently for this reason." Nonetheless, he agreed on a trial demonstration and so Johnston went to Los Angeles to begin recruiting bilingual Navajos, returning to Camp Elliott at the end of February with four volunteers. They were split into pairs and installed in two rooms at opposite ends of a corridor. The first pair were given a standard military order in English and told to transmit it to their two comrades in Navajo. When this had been received at the other end of the corridor, the two Navajos translated it back into English—almost word for word for the original order.

Sensing the potential, Major General Clayton Vogel, commanding general of Amphibious Corps, Pacific Fleet, staged a second test under simulated combat conditions, and was impressed when the Navajo were able to decode a three-line English message in 20 seconds. The average time for encrypting machines at this stage of the war required 30 minutes to execute the same task. Vogel applied to Washington for the immediate recruitment of 200 Navajos to serve as Marine Communications specialists but was told he could select just 30.

This small but nonetheless significant number were recruited in the spring of 1942 from agency schools on the Navajo Reservation in New Mexico and Arizona (in 1942 there were about 50,000 Navajo tribe members in total in the USA). All had to be fluent in both English and Navajo, physically fit and young enough. Proving a Navajo's age, however, was something of a challenge as there were no birth records on the Reservation. The chosen few reported for basic training at the San Diego Marine Corps Recruit Depot in April and were designated the 382nd Platoon, U.S. Marine Corps, known colloquially as "The Navajo School." Once they had passed Boot Camp—and only one of the 30 failed despite the sudden and shocking confrontation with military discipline—the 29 remaining recruits were sent to Camp Pendleton, Oceanside, California, in May 1942 where they created the Navajo code containing a dictionary and different words for military terms that had to be committed to memory during training.

The code devised by the Navajos was short and easy to learn—a necessity when it would be required during moments of great duress in combat—and the result was a two-part code composed of a 26-letter phonetic alphabet and a 211-word English vocabulary; its Navajo translations comprised the second part of the code. It was complex (see box). Most letters had more than one Navajo word representing them so, for example, the letter "A" was represented by any of three Navajo words: "ant," "apple," or "axe"; while J had three possibilities in "Jaw," "Jerk," and "Jackass." "Q," on the other hand, had just one representative—"Quiver."

Common military terms had words of their own: a fighter plane was a hummingbird (*da-he-tih-hi*), a battalion a red lion (*ta-chee-ne*), and America was *ne-he-mah* ("our mother"). "In developing our code, we were careful to use everyday Navajo words, so that we could memorize and retain the words easily," recalled Chester Nez, one of the original Navajo recruits. "I think that made our job easier, and I think it helped us to be successful in the heat of battle."

The code proved an immediate success and a message that took an hour to encrypt, transmit, and decrypt using the existing and conventional American Shackle system could be transmitted orally by the Navajo codetalkers in around 40 seconds. American army and navy codecrackers tried without success to crack the Navajo code.

Having passed out of Camp Pendleton the Navajos reported in August 1942 for combat duty with the First Marine Division on Guadalcanal. Chester Nez, born in 1920 to a mother from the Black Sheep Clan and a father of the Sleeping Rock People, had been made to speak English at the agency school and was punished whenever he lapsed into Navajo by having his mouth washed out with soap by the matron. He went into action in Guadalcanal on November 4, 1942, carrying a radio the size of a shoebox that weighed around 33lb (15kg). The first message he had to send was: "Enemy machine gun nest on your right. Destroy."

Nez went on to serve in some of the bloodiest battles of the Pacific campaign, as did the rest of the Navajo codetalkers (between 375 to 420 in total while a further 500 or so served as Marines). Their primary job was to transmit intelligence about tactics and troop movements and other battlefield communications over telephones and radios. But they also acted as runners and infantrymen as the US Marine Corps fought its way through Bougainville, Guam, Peleliu, Okinawa, and Iwo Jima.

On Iwo Jima, the brutal five-week battle in the spring of 1945 that ended in a crucial victory for America providing them with the airfields required for

NAVAJO CODE

Japan liked to think that it was able to crack to some degree most of its enemies' codes but the Navajo code proved beyond their capabilities. After the war a Japanese general, Seizo Arisue, informed by his interrogator that the code was based on a Native American language, replied: "Thank you, that is a puzzle I thought would never be solved." It's not surprising that the Japanese failed to decipher the Navajo Code, given its complexity. Their dictionary, declassified after the war, is evidence of what the Japanese were up against. Here are some examples:

MILITARY UNITS	NAVAJO WORD	LITERAL TRANSLATION
Corps	Din-Neh-Ih	Clan
Division	Ashih-Hi	Salt
Regiment	Tabaha	Edge Water
Battalion	Tacheene	Red Soil
Company	Nakia	Mexican
Platoon	Has-Clish-Nih	Mud
Section	Yo-Ih	Beads
Squad	Debeh-Li-Zini	Black Sheep

NAMES OF COUNTRIES	NAVAJO WORD	LITERAL TRANSLATION
America	Ne-He-Mah	Our Mother
Australia	Cha-Yes-Desi	Rolled Hat
Britain	Toh-Ta	Between Waters
China	Ceh-Yehs-Besi	Braided Hair
France	Da-Gha-Hi	Beard
Germany	Besh-Be-Cha-He	Iron Hat
Japan	Beh-Na-Ali-Tsosie	Slant Eye
Russia	Sila-Gol-Chi-Ih	Red Army

NAMES OF AIRPLANES	NAVAJO WORD	LITERAL TRANSLATION
Planes	Wo-Tah-De-Ne-Ih	Air Force
Dive Bomber	Gini	Chicken Hawk
Torpedo Plane	Tas-Chizzie	Swallow
Fighter Plane	Da-He-Tih-Hi	Humming Bird
Bomber Plane	Jay-Sho	Buzzard
Patrol Plane	Ga-Gih	Crow
Transport	Atsah	Eagle

NAMES OF SHIPS	NAVAJO WORD	LITERAL TRANSLATION
Ships	Toh-Dineh-Ih	Sea Force
Battleship	Lo-Tso	Whale
Aircraft	Tsidi-Moffa-Ye-Hi	Bird Carrier
Submarine	Besh-Lo	Iron Fish
Mine Sweeper	Cha	Beaver
Destroyer	Ca-Lo	Shark

A detachment of the US Marine Corps march away **(ABOVE LEFT)** from the fighting on Guadalcanal for some well-earned rest. No such let-up for the men of 3ʳᵈ Defense Battalion, seen here **(ABOVE RIGHT)** operating a SCR-268 radar, the first of its kind installed on Guadalcanal. The naval battle for Guadalcanal in November 1942 was a bitter struggle and in this photograph **(BELOW)** the USS *President Jackson* (AP-37) is seen maneuvering under Japanese air attack.

air attacks on the Japanese mainland, six Navajo codetalkers sent and received more than 800 messages in the first two days of the battle. None contained an error. "Were it not for the Navajos, the Marines would never have taken Iwo Jima," declared Major Howard Connor, 5th Marine Division signal officer.

The Japanese tried desperately to break the Navajo code but they couldn't. The only Navajo they captured during the Pacific campaign wasn't a codebreaker and, to their fury, couldn't make head nor tail of the Navajo code when forced to under torture.

After the war the Navajo codetalkers were forbidden from talking publicly about their work; the US military reasoned that the code might come in useful again and so it remained a secret. It wasn't until 1992, shortly after the end of the Cold War, that the Navajo received the recognition they deserved with a ceremony at the Pentagon in which 35 veterans were present.

The last of the original codetalkers to die was Chester Nez, who passed away in June 2014. A few years before his death he said in an interview: "Our Navajo code was one of the most important military secrets of World War II. The fact that the Marines did not tell us Navajo men how to develop that code indicated their trust in us and in our abilities. The feeling that I could make it in both the white world and the Navajo world began there, and it has stayed with me all of my life. For that I am grateful."

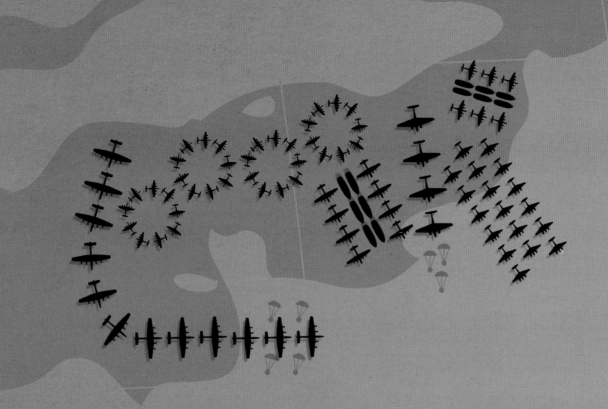

THE COMING OF THE END

The summer of 1944 was the date fixed for the largest invasion force in history to cross the Channel to France but in the months beforehand the Allies spun a web of intrigue to mislead the Germans as to the exact location. Once the Normandy bridgehead had been successfully established the Allies began their inexorable drive east towards Germany, into the heart of a rotting Third Reich that launched its V-weapons against Britain in a final desperate attempt to win the war. Meanwhile an altogether more deadly secret weapon was about to be unleashed on Japan that would finally bring the war to an end.

GHOST ARMIES

The main item to be discussed at the Quebec Conference of August 1943 was the invasion of France, codenamed Operation Overlord. The Americans, present along with the British and Canadians, had been pressing for an invasion of France since 1942 but their original wish to launch the operation in 1943 had been deferred at the behest of Winston Churchill to 1944. Far better, insisted the British prime minister, to attack first the soft underbelly of Europe—Italy.

By the time the three Allied leaders met in Quebec, Sicily had already been occupied by the Allies and the invasion of Italy was about to begin. Attention, therefore, could turn to the landings in France.

The Allied chiefs of staff had decided that the most suitable spot for a large scale invasion was a 50 mile (80.5km) stretch of coast in Normandy, a proposal that was further refined at the next Allied Conference, in Tehran, at the end of November 1943. In overall charge of Overlord was the American general, Dwight Eisenhower, while the actual invasion itself would be under the command of Bernard Montgomery, the British field marshal who had defeated Rommel in North Africa. He redrew the invasion plan, preceding the sea landings with an operation by three airborne divisions and not the original three brigades. As for the sea landings, five divisions would land on five beaches with two further divisions in reserve.

Now that the Allies were sure where the invasion would take place they needed to fool the Germans into thinking otherwise, a grand deception plan that was codenamed Operation Bodyguard. This was a nod to a comment made by Churchill to Soviet leader Josef Stalin at the Tehran Conference. Discussing the need for the utmost secrecy the British leader exclaimed: "In wartime, truth is so precious that she should always been attended by a bodyguard of lies." To which Stalin had responded: "This is what we call military cunning."

As we saw in chapter 20 the Russians actually called it maskirovka, a concept which was helping them drive the Germans out of the Soviet Union. Now the Allies aimed to push the Germans out of France using their own version of maskirovka, what the British secret service described as resembling "an elaborate jigsaw puzzle, each piece would contribute to a picture, the full significance of which was only confirmed when it was complete."

This "puzzle" was codenamed Operation Fortitude and consisted of "North" and "South." The former, relying on bogus radio information and misinformation from the network of double agents operating for MI5, was to keep some of the Germans' focus on Scandinavia, in particular Norway. Messages from double agents warned their German handlers of a likely attack on the Norwegian towns of Narvik and Stavanger from the fictitious British Fourth Army in Scotland.

Fortitude South also used double agents to draw the Germans into the belief that the Pas-de-Calais—200 miles (322km) east of the Normandy beaches—would be where the Allies landed. But in addition one of the cleverest and most cunning deceptions of the war was created to mislead the Nazis in the weeks and months building up to D-Day.

It was called the First United States Army Group (FUSAG), and it was under the command of Lieutenant General George S. Patton, "Old Blood and Guts" himself, one of the Allies' top commanders. Comprising 11 divisions, a total of 150,000 highly trained men, FUSAG was assembling in the southeast of England, in the counties of East-Anglia, Essex, and Kent, ready to storm ashore on the Calais shore, at only 20 miles (32km) from Dover, the nearest French port to England.

There was indeed an army massing in this corner of England, one that was visible to the Germans in reconnaissance photos, but it was an inflatable army or what the Americans called a "Ghost Division."

Patton arrived to take command of the First United States Army Group in January 1944, just a few months after he had been rebuked for slapping a soldier suffering

The First United States Army Group (FUSAG), under the command of the formidable Lieutenant General George S. Patton, worried the Germans in the early months of 1944. Had they known the truth, however, their fears would have been evaporated. FUSAG was in fact a "Ghost Army", composed of dummy tanks and fictitious units and not the 11 divisions that the Germans had led to believe. The tanks that enemy reconnaissance photographed amassing in England were either inflatable or wooden, such as the ones photographed. But the Germans also pulled off similar stunts, as the British discovered when they invaded France in June 1944 and found a collection of German dummy tank turrets and antitank guns.

from combat fatigue during the invasion of Sicily. Relieved of his command, Patton was sent on a series of publicity tours in around the Mediterranean, ostensibly to punish the firebrand but also to keep the Germans guessing. What was one of the Allies most experienced generals doing touring southern Europe? It made more sense when at the start of 1944 they learned he had been appointed commander of FUSAG. That could mean only thing, surmised the Germans, that they would be in the vanguard of any invasion of France.

Initially FUSAG was known in official communiqués as "Army Group Patton," containing real units that would in time take part in the genuine invasion under Montgomery's command. These units, British, Canadian, and American, boosted the actual soldiers preparing to invade France by some 70 per cent, and inevitably they came to the attention of the Germans from one of their reconnaissance planes. It was a skill on the part of the RAF to allow the enemy spotter aircraft to photograph the build-up of troops 30,000ft

A concrete caisson or "Phoenix", part of the Mulberry artificial harbor for D-Day, under construction, January 27, 1944 (see box) while the photograph depicts the Mulberry in operational use off Arromanches in Normandy, September 1944. The artificial harbor was in continual use for eight months and was estimated to have accommodated around two million men and half a million vehicles.

ARTIFICIAL HARBORS

The greatest natural challenge facing the Allies at Normandy was the notorious Channel tide which varied between high and low tide as much as 20ft (6m). Landing the vehicles and heavy equipment would be impossible because the cargo ships wouldn't have the depth of water under their hulls that they required. For that the Allies needed a deep-water harbor but there wasn't one anywhere near the Normandy beaches. So it was agreed at the Quebec Conference that the Allies would construct their own artificial harbors, codenamed "Mulberries." One British and the other American, both would be ready days after the first troops had come ashore at Normandy. Under the utmost secrecy work began on building two jetties using a floating roadway made from waterproof canvas and tensioned by cables supported on pontoons. Tests ironed out imperfections. On June 9, three days after the invasion, the two artificial harbors—the American "A" at Omaha Beach and the British "B" at Arromanches—were built and the roadways and jetties installed, having been pulled across the Channel by tugs. Though the American harbor was wrecked in a fierce storm 10 days later, the British Mulberry was in continual use for eight months and was estimated to have accommodated around two million men and half a million vehicles.

below without causing the Luftwaffe to suspect they were being deliberately allowed access.

Nonetheless if the Allies were really assembling as many men as the Germans had been led to believe, there would be need to be evidence on the ground of a million troops. To facilitate the deception huge camps began appearing over southeastern England. They were more than camps, they were virtual cities, with hospitals, cinemas, barracks, and supply dumps. But the camps needed vehicles if they were to fool the German reconnaissance planes so trucks, tanks and jeeps were constructed from wood and rubber. At night they were moved and following in their wake through the muddy fields were teams of men with equipment to replicate tyre and tank tracks.

The FUSAG deception was made even more authentic in the letters' pages of local papers, with residents writing to complain about the behavior of the "foreign troops." Some of the "foreigners" were then seen strolling through London wearing the insignia of a black Roman Numeral I on a blue background inside a white and red pentagon. The insignia denoted nothing more than the ingenuity of the US Army's heraldry department but word soon reached Germany of the new shoulder patches being worn around town. The jigsaw puzzle was becoming ever more elaborate, and it was close to completion.

As the invasion date neared so activity increased on the rivers and in the harbors of eastern England, with landing craft arriving every day—or at least that's what they looked like from the camera of a German reconnaissance plane. Up close they were just hundreds of flimsy wooden structures floating on oil drums. Similarly the jetties and storage tanks that were built on the south coast were a result of a noted architect, Basil Spence, and again they were dummies. Dover bore the brunt of the fictitious army and every evening throughout the spring of 1944 the port was illuminated with blackout lights to give the impression that

important work was being carried out preparatory to the embarkation of the invasion fleet

In reality the real invasion fleet sailed from a couple of hundred miles further west along the coast, from Portsmouth, Southampton, and Poole among others. They arrived on the five Normandy beaches on June 6, some 156,000 soldiers by the end of the "Longest Day," and despite heavy fighting secured the beachhead with the help of a further 23,000 airborne troops who had dropped a few miles inland to attack and eliminate key German installations. But whether they would be able to push inland depended on keeping some 21 German Divisions in Pas-de-Calais. For this to happen Fortitude South continued well after D-Day, with agent "Arabel" warning Germany that the Normandy landing was just a diversionary assault and the real attack would indeed come in the Calais area. Meanwhile in the ports of eastern England FUSAG continued to prepare for its "invasion." More dummy landing craft arrived, as did genuine navy minesweepers who laid smokescreens to conceal from the reconnaissance planes was what happening below. Radio traffic diminished—always a clue as to the prelude of an impending attack—and on June 9 Hitler ordered the German 15th Army to remain in Pas-de-Calais and prepare for the main invasion.

But there was no invasion in Calais, although Patton did make it to France, not with the First United States Army Group but as commander of the US Third Army. In August 1944 Patton led his army 60 miles (96.5km) in under two weeks, from Avranches to Argentan, his armour most definitely not consisting of inflatable tanks. But FUSAG had played a critical role in fooling the Germans, as Bernard Montgomery acknowledged in his memoirs *21 Army Group: Normandy to the Baltic*. He wrote: "These deception measures continued, as planned, after D-Day and events were to show that they … played a vital part in our successes in Normandy."

Thanks to Operation Fortitude, the Germans were utterly duped as to the true intention of the Allied invasion force. In August General Patton—now in charge of the very real US Third Army—advanced 60 miles (96.5km) in under two weeks, from Avranches to Argentan. The speed of the push east led to the surrender of thousands of Germans, like these ones surrendering in St Lambert on August 19, 1944.

D-DAY DOUBLE CROSS

The British believed they had Germany beaten when it came to the spying game. As we saw in chapter four, by the end of 1941 the success of British intelligence in the espionage duel with the German Abwehr was reflected by Sir John Masterman's boast that MI5 "actively ran and controlled the German espionage system in this country."

Masterman, the Oxford don, was the chief of the Twenty Committee or what was also known as the Double Cross system, whereby every German agent that landed in Britain was caught and either executed or—as was usually the case—"turned" so they became a double agent. Thirteen German spies were executed by the British but three times that number opted to switch allegiance. Some, like John Moe, as we saw in chapter four, (codename "Mutt") actually turned themselves in and willingly gave their services; others, such as the Danish-born Wulf Schmidt, who arrived in England by parachute in September 1940, did so because to refuse would have meant death on the end of a rope.

Given the codename "Tate," Schmidt became part of the elaborate Operation Bodyguard, the aim of which was to fool the Germans into believing the invasion of France would take place in the Calais region. Obtaining a job in a farm in the southeast of England, Schmidt relayed intelligence to the Germans on the build-up of troops in the area, American troops, belonging to the First United States Army Group (FUSAG). Their destination was Calais and Schmidt even provided his handler with the approximate date of their embarkation for the invasion. This confirmed Hitler's view, first expressed in 1943, that Calais was where "the enemy must and will attack."

There was no such thing as FUSAG. It was a "ghost army" (see page 164) but the Germans fell for it. But that wasn't the biggest intelligence gaffe committed by the Nazis in the lead-up to the invasion of France.

Ironically they were suckered by a man who, initially, had also caused the British to make a rare mistake in their espionage program. In January 1941 Jean Pujol Garcia was a 29-year-old with little to suggest he would turn out to be the greatest double agent of the war— possibly any war. A native of Barcelona, Pujol had little interest in politics and even less inclination to be a soldier; during the Spanish Civil War of the late 1930s he deserted and refused to take up arms even when imprisoned. At the outbreak of World War II this bespectacled and benign man had never held down a job for any length of time and was in many ways the archetypal idealist. But the savagery of the Nazi war machine stirred something deep within Pujol's soul. The more he heard, the more he read of what Germany was doing to the Jews and the oppressed citizens of countries such as Poland, Czechoslovakia, and the Low Countries, the more determined he became to contribute to Hitler's defeat. To do that he would use his greatest weapon: his imaginative verbosity.

In January 1941 Pujol paid a discreet call to the British embassy in Madrid offering his services as a secret agent but he was politely turned away by the staff. The rejection only made the Spaniard more determined—and devious. He decided to change tack and so approached the Germans offering them his services as a spy. Initially reluctant, the head of the Abwehr in the Iberian Peninsula, Gustav Leisner, decided eventually to employ Pujol as a spy though they still had reservations that this seemingly fickle, fragile man could be of much use. He was told to get himself to London and, if he managed that task, to contact Luis Calvo, an agent working for a right-wing newspaper in the British capital.

Pujol was furnished with $3,000 in cash and a blank questionnaire to be filled in about what he observed once in Britain. He was also given the codename "Arabel." Pujol left Spain on the first leg of his trip and made his way to Lisbon. Once in the Portuguese capital he remained there, visiting bookshops where he used some of his money to buy travel guides and histories of

The challenge facing the Allies was how to conceal from the Germans the massive build-up of troops and tanks (RIGHT) prior to June 1944. It was the task of the spies involved in Operation Bodyguard to fool the Germans into believing the invasion of France would take place in the Calais region.

the British Isles. From these he made up a series of fictitious reports that he radioed back to Leisner. He read agent "Arabel" reports (most of which were written in invisible ink in between the visible lines of ordinary letters) with mounting excitement—the intelligence was not only voluminous; it was also important.

The British were also excited by the reports emanating from agent "Arabel," all of which had been intercepted from the outset by their Ultra team of codebreakers. The Double Cross committee were alarmed by the accuracy of the occasional report—such as the departure of a convoy to Malta—but they were puzzled on other occasions by statements that were so obviously fictitious, such as Glaswegians desperate "for a litre of wine" and his inability to get a grip on the British currency of pounds, shillings, and pence. It was almost as if, the British mused, agent "Arabel" was making it all up from far away and occasionally getting lucky with his outlandish reports.

In early 1942, a year after his first approach to the British embassy in Madrid, Pujol decided to try again, this time sending his wife to the American embassy in Lisbon. The Americans were non-committal in their response but passed the information onto the British; suddenly the penny dropped! Pujol must be agent "Arabel."

Within a few weeks Pujol had been secretly ferried to England by MI5 where he was taken under the wing of Tomas "Tommy" Harris. What followed between the pair was described by the *Official History of British Intelligence in World War Two* as "one of those rare partnerships between two exceptionally gifted men whose inventive genius inspired and complemented each other."

Given the codename "Garbo" by MI5, Pujol with Harris at his side began sewing an elaborate tapestry of deceit with the ultimate aim of deceiving the Germans when the time came for the invasion of France. The pair concocted 27 fictitious subagents, men living in the UK who were passing information to agent 'Arabel', which he in turn radioed to Lisbon. As well as a South American Nazi sympathizer living in Glasgow, there was a loud-mouthed American sergeant and a Welsh nationalist in charge of a secret fascist organization called the 'Brothers of the Aryan World Order' based in Swansea. None of them existed in reality but over the course of the next two years Pujol and Harris wrote 315 letters averaging 2,000 words each to the Abwehr. Some of the intelligence supplied had to be true, to lure the Germans even further into the trap, but nothing sent to the Germans posed any substantial threat to the Allied war effort. According to

JEAN PUJOL GARCIA

Pujol was awarded the MBE in December 1944 in recognition of his espionage services to Great Britain. Having been bestowed with an Iron Cross first class, the Spaniard has the rare distinction therefore of being decorated by two countries for his spying activities. Fearful of Nazi reprisals (in fact the Germans never discovered that agent "Arabel" was a double agent), Pujol settled in Africa immediately after the war, but later emigrated to Venezuela where he remained for the rest of his life, enjoying his anonymity. It wasn't until the 1980s that his past caught up with him when the historian Rupert Allason—whose pen name is Nigel West—began researching agent "Garbo." With Tomas Harris long since dead, Allason had little to go on until he discovered in 1984 that Garbo's surname was "Pujol." Contacting everyone of that name in Barcelona, Allason finally got through to Pujol's nephew, and later that same year he flew to New Orleans to meet Juan Pujol. Unaware of the esteem in which he was held in Britain, Pujol had to be persuaded to come to London where he was thanked for his wartime work by the Duke of Edinburgh at Buckingham Palace. Pujol died in Caracas in 1988.

the official MI5 records: "This rich vein of fantasy was maintained and enlarged under Security Service control to provide as much 'confusing bulk' as possible for the enemy to assimilate. The assessment of the *Official History of British Intelligence in WW2* is that the Germans, in Spain at least, became so flooded with information from GARBO's agents in Britain that they made no further attempt to infiltrate the UK."

By January 1944 the Germans had come to rely on Pujol so much that they asked him to focus his efforts on unearthing information about any plans for the invasion of France. The Germans were sure a large-scale landing would take place that year but they were uncertain where; Hitler suspected the Calais region but several of his generals—more experienced military men—believed it would be in Normandy, 200 miles (322km) west of Calais.

Normandy was indeed the proposed site for Operation Overlord, the invasion of France, but for the next six months Pujol was used by the Allies as part of Operation Bodyguard, the complex deception plot to fool the enemy into concentrating its force in Calais. Between January 1944 and June 6 (D-Day) over 500 radio messages (four transmissions a day) were sent by Pujol to his German handlers, while other double agents such as "Tate" and "Tricycle" (a.k.a. Dusko Popov, a wealthy Yugoslavian womanizer who operated out of the Savoy hotel) also did their bit in duping the Germans into believing the invasion would come in the Pas-de-Calais region.

The final stitch in Pujol's tapestry was a message from him to his German handler to stand by for an important communiqué at 0300 hours on June 6, just as the invasion fleet crossed the Channel towards Normandy. He would warn the Germans that one of his subagents in Southampton had informed him that the invasion fleet was assembling. Incredibly, however, the German radio operator forgot to tune in and the message was never received. Only when the invasion

was underway did they realize agent "Arabel" had tried to warn them—thereby enhancing his reputation as their most effective and reliable spy in Britain. Pujol feigned disgust as this missed opportunity, telling his German handler: "I cannot accept excuses or negligence. Were it not for my ideals I would abandon the work." In reality this lapse in German efficiency worked mightily in the Allies' favor for now the Germans hung on Pujol's every word—even though the invasion was underway.

But did the landings in Normandy mark the real invasion? Or were they simply a diversion? On June 9, three days after Allied troops had come ashore, Pujol

▲ Despite the success of the Allies in fooling the Germans on D-Day, the landing forces suffered substantial casualties in the first days of the invasion. These British airborne troops were captured after parachuting behind the Normandy beachhead to secure bridges over the Orne River.

sent what MI5 described as "perhaps his most important message of all." It was characteristically long-winded and Pujol demanded it be conveyed urgently to the German High Command immediately. "Pointing out that the First US Army Group under Patton had not yet moved from Southeast England, (Pujol) reported authoritatively that the purpose of the diversionary Normandy landings was to help ensure the success of the forthcoming assault on the Pas de Calais."

The Germans fell for it, and instead of moving Field Marshal Rommel's 15th Army west from Calais Hitler ordered it to remain where it was in readiness for the main Allied landings. In total 21 German divisions were retained in Pas-de-Calais, not just for a few days but until the end of July when the Nazi High Command finally appreciated the Normandy landings had been the main invasion. Even then it never dawned on Hitler that he had been fooled by a bookish man from Barcelona with a gift for verbal invention. On 29 July, 1944, Pujol learned he had been awarded the Iron Cross by the Führer for his "extraordinary services" to Germany. Pujol replied immediately, beseeching his handler to pass on his "humble thanks" to Hitler. What's more, he felt "unworthy" of such an honor.

American GIs prepare to hit the beaches of Normandy in the early dawn on June 6 1944. Though the Allies suffered heavy casualties on Omaha Beach, the losses would have been far greater had the Germans not kept thousands of troops and armor in the Calais region.

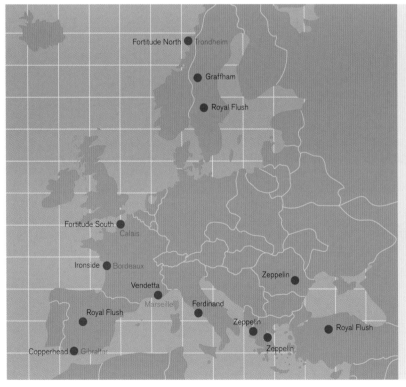

Fortitude North ● Trondheim

● Graffham

● Royal Flush

Fortitude South ●
Calais

Ironside ● Bordeaux

Vendetta ●

Royal Flush ●

Marseille ● Ferdinand

Zeppelin ●

Zeppelin ●

Royal Flush ●

Copperhead ● Gibraltar

Zeppelin ●

OPERATION BODYGUARD

The sites of all the subordinate deception plans encompassed by Operation Bodyguard. Planning for Bodyguard began in July 1943 and was definitely approved by the Allied leaders in December that year after the Tehran Conference. Though Fortitude North and South were the most important deceptions, the other operations all formed part of the overall strategy (entailing double agents, radio traffic and visual deception) to gradually dupe the Germans into believing the invasion would be launched in the Calais region.

THE SPECIAL AIR SERVICE IN FRANCE

"Who Dares Wins," the motto of the Special Air Service, which, as we saw in chapter 12, had been formed in 1941 by David Stirling to wage a guerrilla war against Rommel's Afrika Korps in North Africa. Though Stirling was captured in January 1943, by the spring of 1944 the SAS had achieved such success it was expanded into a 2500-strong brigade comprising two British regiments—1 and 2SAS, two French regiments 3 and 4SAS and a Belgian regiment, 5SAS.

Having taken part in the invasions of Sicily and Italy the two British regiments returned to the UK in early 1944 to begin preparing for the biggest invasion of them all: France.

Among those recruited to 1SAS were more than 130 men from the now redundant Auxiliary Units, the secret organization set up in the dark days of 1940 when a German invasion of Britain seemed imminent.

Appointed to overall command of the SAS Brigade was Roderick McLeod, an enthusiastic supporter of special forces but a man unsure how best to use the highly trained men at his disposal in the forthcoming invasion of France. In consultation with the Supreme Headquarters Allied Expeditionary Force (SHAEF), McLeod agreed that SAS Brigade should parachute into Normandy between the landing beaches and the German reserves (three panzer divisions) 36 hours in advance of the main invasion fleet. Once on the ground the SAS would deploy as a blocking line, preventing the German reserves from reinforcing their comrades at the landing beaches.

The SAS were furious when they learned of their role. Bill Stirling, David's elder brother and the commander of 2SAS, argued that the SAS should operate in France as they had in the desert, as a secret force operating in small units deep behind enemy lines. Stealth was their watchword, he reminded SHAEF. Though Stirling ultimately resigned in protest, his sacrifice wasn't in vain. At the end of May, just over a week before D-Day, an amended order was issued for the SAS Brigade for Operation Overlord, the codename for the invasion of France. Instead of the suicidal mission laid down by SHAEF in its original order, the SAS Brigade would carry out 43 missions in France involving the two British regiments, two French regiments and the squadron of Belgian troopers. With the exception of one mission—Operation Titanic (involving a six-man party dropping into Normandy a few hours ahead of the main invasion fleet to spread confusion with dummy parachutes)—all missions would occur deep behind enemy lines with the objective of harassing German forces heading north and attacking their lines of communication.

The honor of leading 1SAS into France went to A and B Squadrons. A Squadron's operation was codenamed Houndsworth and entailed dropping into the Massif du Morvan, west of Dijon, to cut railway lines between Lyon and Paris, arm and train the numerous local groups of Maquis, and generally make a nuisance of themselves from a base deep inside the wooded countryside.

B Squadron's operation was codenamed Bulbasket and would entail a party of around 35 men under the command of Captain John Tonkin parachuting into the Vienne region of France, between Poitiers and Châteauroux, and attacking the Germans whenever possible. Specific orders were flexible, with squadron commanders told to use their judgement in the selection of targets.

The advance parties of both operations parachuted into France in the early hours of June 6, just as the Allied invasion fleet crossed the Channel towards Normandy. Their task was to secure a drop zone for the main SAS parties to insert a few days later.

A Squadron were soon all safely hidden in the thick forests of the Morvan and on the afternoon of Saturday, June 24 they scored their first major success when they ambushed a detachment of Germans and White Russians (Soviet troops fighting for Germany) on a

An "Oscar" dummy in hessian cloth, one of hundreds dropped in the night of June 5, 1944, prior to the main Allied landing in Normandy. The dummies were designed to fool the Germans into believing they were being invaded by airborne troops but they were only partially successful.

quiet country lane. "We were spread over two hundred yards along the road and on a pre-arranged signal we opened up," wrote one of the SAS soldiers, John Noble, to his girlfriend, a few days after the attack. "Their order of march was a truck with a 20mm [cannon] on it, a private car, another truck with a 20mm, followed by a motorcycle. I had the first truck to deal with. As I opened fire with a bren, an ex-Russian POW (more anon) very thoughtfully chucked a grenade in the truck. The ambush was a complete success. Three prisoners were taken, the rest were killed. We destroyed the trucks and the car, and kept the motorcycle."

Soon the SAS received on the end of parachutes a small number of jeeps, enabling them to extend the range of their operations. In the most brazen strike they mortared a synthetic oil factory, 25 miles (40km) from the SAS camp, while the vehicles were also used to transport small sabotage teams to different sections of the railroad linking the region to Paris, thereby hampering the Germans as they endeavored to convey men and equipment north to where the Allies were gradually fighting their way inland from the Normandy beachhead. In addition, one ambush resulted in the discovery of some Gestapo mail and the SAS radioed their headquarters in England with "information about position and defence of Field Marshal Rommel's headquarters [and] details of flying bomb dumps and assemblies near Paris."

But while Houndsworth was a stunning success (in total they had killed or wounded more than 220 Germans and derailed six trains), Operation Bulbasket met with tragedy when their forest hideout was attacked by a force of some 500 Germans just after dawn on July 3.

Only seven SAS soldiers managed to evade the encirclement. Thirty of their comrades were caught and executed a few days later. A similar fate befell some of the men on Operation Gain, a 1SAS mission carried out by 58 members of D Squadron that commenced on the

A flight of US Air Force A-20 light bombers on their way to France. One of the tasks of the SAS once they had parachuted into France following the D-Day landings was to identify targets for British and American bombers, particularly columns of German troops travelling north to reinforce the bridgehead.

night of June 13–14. Gain's objective was to cut the German lateral railway communications in the bottleneck area of Rambouillet–Provins–Gien–Orleans–Chartres, all towns south of Paris that took trains to Normandy. Under the command of Ian Fenwick, the SAS established camp in the Foret d'Orleans and for the first couple of weeks the operation was a great success. Several railway lines were blown, a railway locomotive and 30 wagons were destroyed in their sidings and a motorized patrol was ambushed. But a reinforcement party was ambushed on the drop zone by the Germans in early July and half a dozen men were caught, tortured, and executed.

Nonetheless, overall Operation Gain inflicted considerable damage on the Germans in the two and a half months of its existence, including the cutting of 16 railroads, the derailment of two trains, the destruction of two engines and the annihilation of nearly 50 enemy vehicles. In addition, they had provided invaluable information on the strength and movement of German forces south of Paris.

Another spectacular 1SAS success in the summer of 1944 was B Squadron's Operation Haggard. Dropped into France in August there orders were to sow "despondency" among the retreating German troops by hitting them hard wherever and whenever they could. B Squadron gleefully accepted the challenge and by the time Operation Haggard was wound up on September 9th, they had killed or wounded an estimated 233 Germans, destroyed 37 motorized vehicles and blown up two bridges.

The men of 2SAS were held in reserve for several weeks as SHAEF waited to see how the Normandy landings progressed. It wasn't until late July that they were deployed on Operation Rupert, with orders to sabotage the railroads in eastern France between Nancy and Chalons-sur-Marne as the Germans began to pull back towards the Fatherland. But by the time they were down on the ground the SAS troops found themselves overrun by the American Third Army, now sweeping through the countryside after breaking out from the Normandy hedgerows. That breakout had repercussions for B Squadron of 2SAS, who had parachuted into the Vosges, a wooded range of hills that run north to south on the French side of the River Rhine. Loyton's role was to drop into the Vosges and attack the retreating Germans, but unfortunately just as they inserted into the Vosges, the American advance ground to a halt west of the River Meurthe. The Germans stopped retreating and dug in, resulting in the SAS being trapped in the centre of a large mass of enemy soldiers in an area where many of the local population considered themselves more German than French. In the weeks that followed 31 soldiers were caught and murdered by the Germans.

▶ The SAS Brigade were estimated to have killed 7,733 German soldiers during operations in France in the summer of 1944. They had had their heavily armored jeeps parachuted into the French countryside so they could launch devastating hit-and-run raids against German columns.

In direct contrast to the misery endured by the men on Operation Loyton, Roy Farran's C Squadron enjoyed a rich harvest throughout the six weeks of Operations Hardy and Wallace. Dropping close to Auxerre at the end of July, the SAS attacked the enemy with singular ferocity, aided in his work by the fluidity of the Allied advance and the confusion of the enemy retreat. Unlike the Vosges, where the Germans were determined to dig in and defend, the countryside between Auxerre and Dijon was perfect for the SAS to launch hit-and-run raids against an already demoralized opponent. In his report Major Roy Farran, in command of Operations Wallace and Hardy, claimed that he and his men had killed or wounded 500 Germans, destroyed 59 motorized vehicles, plus a train, and blown up 100,000 gallons of enemy fuel. 2SAS casualties were seven dead and seven wounded.

Overall, the SAS Brigade were estimated to have killed 7,733 German soldiers during operations in France in the summer of 1944. Some 740 motorized vehicles were destroyed, as were seven trains, 89 wagons, and 29 locomotives. Thirty-three trains were derailed and railway lines were cut on 164 occasions. SAS troops also called in 400 air strikes on German targets and carried out countless valuable reconnaissance patrols for the advancing Allied forces. SAS Brigade's casualties were 330 killed, wounded, or missing.

General Dwight Eisenhower, Supreme Allied Commander in Europe, expressed his gratitude in a letter to Brigadier Roderick McLeod: "I wish to send my congratulations to all ranks of the Special Air Service Brigade on the contribution which they have made to the success of the Allied Expeditionary Force," wrote Eisenhower. "The ruthlessness with which the enemy have attacked Special Air Service troops has been an indication of the injury which you were able to cause to the German armed forces both by your own efforts and by the information which you gave of German disposition and movements."

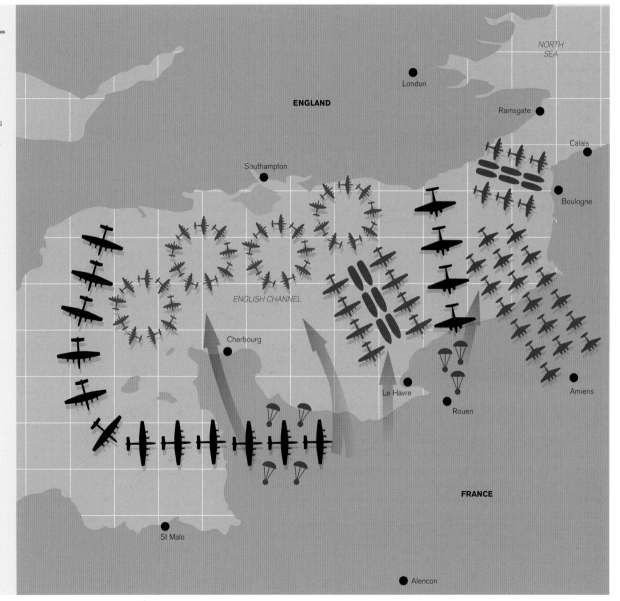

OPERATION OVERLORD

While Operation Titanic involved the dropping of dummy paratroopers, Mandrel, Taxable and Glimmer entailed the dropping of chaff over the English Channel in regular patterns to fool the German radar into believing a large invasion fleet was approaching France. Beneath the chaff, a fleet of small boats simulated the radio traffic expected of a large invasion fleet while towing radar reflective balloons.

Titanic

Mandrel

Taxable

Glimmer

ABC Patrol Area

SAS Parachute Landings

SAS Movements

ENGLAND

NORTH SEA

London

Ramsgate

Calais

Boulogne

Southampton

ENGLISH CHANNEL

Cherbourg

Le Havre

Amiens

Rouen

FRANCE

St Malo

Alencon

V-WEAPONS

As we saw in chapter four, the "battle of the beams" had been a secret war waged over British skies during the Luftwaffe Blitz of 1940–41. The last major air raid carried out by the German air force on the British people was on the night of May 10, 1941, when nearly 1,500 people were killed. Then the heavy bombardments ended, the Luftwaffe turning east towards Russia and the imminent German invasion.

Though there were sporadic, small air raids over the next three years the British people had come through the worst of the Luftwaffe's fury. Or so they thought.

At 0408 hours on Tuesday, June 13, 1944 two members of the Royal Observer Corps at their posts on the Kent coast saw a strange object streaking through the sky, flames shooting from its rear and making "a noise like a Model T-Ford going up a hill." Immediately they telephoned a warning to their command post at Maidstone: whatever it was, it was heading their way. At 0413 hours the object arrowed into the ground and exploded with appalling ferocity on heathland at Swanscombe, a couple of miles east of Dartford in Kent. The Vergeltungswaffen campaign had begun.

The object making the noise like a Model T-Ford was in fact a Vergeltungswaffe-1 (V-1) flying bomb. To some the cruise missile was known as a Buzz Bomb but the British came to call it a "Doodlebug"—because it doodled across the sky. From the ground it looked like a light aircraft with a wing span of nearly 18ft (5.5m) and measuring 25ft (7.6m) from top to tail. It was constructed from sheet steel and plywood, and was powered by a 600lb (272kg) jet engine giving it a cruising speed of around 400mph. When a V-1 hit the ground its 1,870lb (848kg) warhead detonated with devastating consequences for anyone in close proximity.

The British had been aware that Germany was producing a secret weapon, thanks to the courage of the Polish Resistance, who alerted them to tests being conducted on the Baltic coast. There was a meeting in Whitehall the day after the opening salvo in which

Lord Cherwell, the prime minister's scientific advisor, smugly declared: "The mountain hath roared and brought forth a mouse."

Five days later, at 0900 hours on Sunday June 18, the first V-1 bomb landed on Westminster, in Rutherford Street, killing 10 and injuring 62. Smoke from the incident was still visible two hours later as worshipers entered the Guards' Chapel attached to Wellington Barracks, in Birdcage Walk, just east of Buckingham Palace. Twenty minutes into the service a V-1 dived through the roof of the chapel and exploded. Auxiliary Fireman William Sansom recalled that when he arrived "the scene in its subsiding dust looked vast

A V-1 launched at the Belgian port of Antwerp in the fall of 1944. From the ground the rockets resembled an aircraft with a wingspan of nearly 18ft (5.5m) and measuring 25ft (7.6m) in length. They were constructed from sheet steel and plywood, and were powered by 600lb (272kg) jet engines.

◀ A close-up of a V-1 Flying Bomb in flight immediately after its release somewhere in France, on August 12, 1944. Though the Nazis' secret weapon—nicknamed the "Doodlebug"—was terrifying because of its noise it caused less damage than the Germans expected because of its indiscriminate nature.

and boxlike, impenetrable; sloping masses of the gray walls and roof shut in the wounded: the doors were blocked, the roof crammed down; it was difficult to find any entrance. But there was one—behind the altar." Of the 260-strong congregation, 119 were killed and 102 were seriously injured. Sansom thought it a miracle that anyone escaped.

In the first few days of the V-1s, people frequently mistook them for aircraft on fire. One child remembered looking up at one with his mother. "I hope the poor pilot gets down safely," she said; seconds later the bomb nosedived into London. Often the engine cut out before the V-1 began its descent. That was the moment people came to dread, what many described as the "deafening silence," as if the V-1 were pausing while searching for suitable prey. "The doodlebug was a terrible thing," remembered Una Quibell, a munitions worker in Hayes, Middlesex. "It looked like a dagger with flames coming out one end. While the engine was going you were OK, but when it stopped you had better take cover."

A disparity between the V-1 campaign and the Blitz of 1940–41 was the timing. The latter had been a nocturnal event for the most part, but the Germans liked to launch their Doodlebugs between 0800 hours and 0900 hours to catch the morning rush hour, and again around noon as office girls took an hour for lunch in the summer sun. One bomb came down on Aldwych at lunchtime on Friday, June 30, wreaking havoc among the office workers sunning themselves outside.

Another difference between the V-1s and the high-explosive bombs of the Luftwaffe was in the structural devastation caused. The blast damage of a V-1 was extensive, with flying glass being the greatest danger. On the other hand, unlike HE bombs, the Doodlebugs hardly ever penetrated the surface and so the broken water mains, ruptured gas, and severed electricity cables so prevalent during the Blitz were not a factor. However, the human damage was just as grave. Between June 13 and September 1, 1944

(when the V-1s launch pads in France were overrun by Allied forces advancing from Normandy), approximately 6,000 people in London and the surrounding counties were killed by Doodlebugs. The worst single incident was the destruction of the Guards' Chapel, but there were also horrific scenes at Sloane Court in Chelsea, where 74 people died, on Lewisham High Street, where 58 people died, and the carnage in Aldwych that resulted in the deaths of 48.

Three days before the last V-1 was fired at Britain, German leader Adolf Hitler ordered the launch of the Nazis' new and even more powerful secret weapon, the V-2 rocket. The offensive commenced on September 8, 1944 when a rocket was fired at Paris, exploding in the southeast of the city. On the same day a second rocket was fired from The Hague in Holland at Britain.

V-2 rockets began hitting Britain in September 1944 and caused extensive damage , such as the destruction wrought on the Chatsworth Baptist Church, in Norwood, London. Each rocket weighed 13 tons, a ton of which was high explosive, traveled at 3,000mph and descended from its ceiling of 328,000ft (11,582m) at four times the speed of sound.

"DOODLEBUGS"

Increasingly alarmed by the material and psychological threat posed by the "Doodlebug," the Ministry of Home Security issued instructions on how to guard against the new threat, advice that the London Evening Standard reproduced on its front page of June 16:

"When the engine of the pilotless engine stops, and the lights at the end of the machine are seen to go out, it may mean that the explosion will soon follow, perhaps in five to 15 seconds. So take refuge from blast."

By the middle of July 1944 some 3,000 V-1 rockets had been launched at London, causing a panic among the city's population. An estimated 360,000 women, children, and elderly people were evacuated to the surrounding countryside. Despite the panic, V-1s were susceptible to air defences with 924 shot down by RAF fighters en route to Britain and a further 261 blown out of the sky by ground fire.

The rocket that struck London did so in the evening, as Vere Hodgson noted in her diary: "At a quarter to seven a terrific explosion rent the air, followed by a low rumble. I nearly leapt out of my skin. No warning on, so it could not be the new secret weapon. Perhaps it was an explosion at a munitions factory, or a bomb of long delayed action."

The first V-2 that had fallen in London (in Chiswick) killed three people, all of whom died without terror, having not known what hit them. Immediately, Churchill ordered a news blackout, not to shield the truth from his people but to deny the rockets' range plotters from honing their aim. So Londoners were left to speculate whether the explosion was another of Hitler's secret weapons.

There were more mysterious explosions in the days that followed, but the only official proclamations on what they might be was an oblique reference to "gas mains explosions." Londoners laughed grimly. "We're being attacked by flying gas mains," remarked one.

The "gas main explosion" at Chiswick on September 8 was followed by similar incidents in Essex and Kent.

The government struggled to maintain the façade in the face of the gossip swirling around London that the Nazis had developed another secret weapon. It was called the Vergeltungswaffezwei (V-2) rocket and they were being fired from The Netherlands. Each rocket weighed 13 tons, a ton of which was high explosive, traveled at 3,000mph and descended from its ceiling of 328,000ft (11,582m) at four times the speed of sound. Work on the V-2s had started in the late 1930s although it wasn't until 1942 that Hitler came to see the potential impact the Vergeltungswaffe (reprisal) weapons might have. A new age of warfare had dawned.

It wasn't until November 10 that the British government finally conceded that the country was under attack from V-2 rockets, an announcement prompted by a German broadcast claiming that London had been "devastated" by the new weapon.

"For the last few weeks the enemy has been using his new weapon, the long-range rocket, and a number have landed at widely scattered points in this country," declared Churchill in a statement to the Commons. "In all, the casualties and damage have so far not been heavy, though I am sure the House will wish me to express my sympathy with the victims of this as with other attacks." The next day the prime minister's comments were reported in all the newspapers in more dramatic prose, the *Daily Herald* describing a "comet that dives from 70 miles … the most indiscriminate weapon of this or any other war. It is a sinister, eerie form of war."

▲ A total of 1,300 V-2s were launched at London from September 1944 to March 1945, although only 517 reached the capital. The Nazis' secret weapon had been a long time in development and they were tested at the Army Research Center in Peenemünde.

London started receiving more rockets, suffering more deaths as a result: nine at Peckham, 30 at Deptford, 33 at Wandsworth, 18 at Poplar, 25 at Greenwich, right up until the 251st V-2 hit the capital on Saturday, November 25. On that occasion 171 people were killed, including 11 who were liquidated, leaving no trace of their existence.

The rocket that destroyed a large part of New Cross was one of 1,300 V-2s launched at London from September 1944 to March 1945, although only 517 reached the capital.

London wasn't the only city to suffer. Around 1,600 rockets hit Antwerp while Paris, Lille, Liege, and several small towns and cities in western Europe were targeted. Yet despite the fact they killed several thousand people, the V-2s were never the terrifying secret weapon that the Nazis hoped would win them

the war. In London 2,754 civilians were killed by an estimated 1,402 rockets, meaning that on average each very expensive rocket accounted for just two deaths, hardly the casualty figures to bring a nation to its knees.

In truth the V-2s were less frightening than both the Doodlebugs and conventional bombs dropped from aircraft. After all, it's more natural to fear something you can see and hear rather than a rocket that travels so fast you're not aware of its presence until it explodes. "The V-2s were just a sort of bang and the floor rocked a bit," recalled Rosamond Boddy, a London office girl. "If you heard the bang you knew you were all right. You didn't hear anything before so you couldn't spend your whole life wondering if you were going to hear a bang, so one tried not to think about anything until they went off."

▼ Parts of the V-2 rocket were produced in the underground factory (**BELOW LEFT**) in the Kohnstein mountain near Nordhausen, Thuringia. An American soldier (**BELOW RIGHT**) inspects the propulsion unit of a Nazi V-2 rocket bomb that landed in Belgium in December, 1944.

JET WAR AND THE ME 262

The summer of 1944 was an extraordinary period in the history of warfare. Not only was the first cruise missile—the V-1—fired but the introduction of the V-2 rocket ushered in the era of ballistic missiles. But that wasn't all. In July 1944 both the British and Germans entered into operational service their jet fighter, the dawn of a new era in aerial warfare.

Both countries had been secretly working on the jet fighter for decades, as far back as the 1920s, and it was an incredible symmetry that both were ready in the same month.

Britain was first to propose a jet engine aircraft, a young engineer called Alan Arnold Griffith publishing a paper on jet turbines in the summer of 1926. The paper was devoured by Frank Whittle, then a teenage RAF recruit with a passion for jet engines who had written a thesis himself in which he propounded that aircraft must fly at higher altitudes, where air resistance is lower, if they were to achiever longer ranges and greater speeds. He tried to co-opt Griffith into working on developing a jet aircraft but the engineer believed a turbine lacked the power to generate flight.

Undeterred, Whittle pressed on alone and by the fall of 1929 had concluded that a fan enclosed in the fuselage would generate a flow of air fast enough to propel an aircraft to a high altitude. He dismissed the use of a piston engine, as they needed too much fuel, and was convinced the answer was a gas turbine. In 1930 he took out a patent for the world's inaugural jet engine but while he believed in his idea, few others did, not the RAF nor the companies whose financial backing he required if he was to turn his theory into reality.

For the next four years Whittle ploughed a lonely furrow, developing his skills as a conventional RAF pilot while also moonlighting as an innovator of jet engines. But everything remained on the drawing board and in 1934 he received permission from the RAF to enrol on a first-class honors degree in Mechanical Sciences Tripos at Peterhouse College in

THE SILVER BIRD

The Germans' dreams didn't just end with jet aircraft for there was also an ambition to build a top-secret "antipodal bomber"—a stratospheric aircraft capable of traveling around the world wreaking havoc as it went. The man behind the idea was Eugen Sanger, a Czech-born scientist and a pioneer in the study of rocket-powered weapons. Sanger was also a member of the Society for Space Travel and as early as 1933 he was writing papers on the possibilities of stratospheric warfare, which soon aroused the interest of the German Air Ministry. They were particularly interested in Sanger's idea of constructing a bomber that would have the capability to attack the United States of America from Germany. With the finances now at his disposal thanks to the Air Ministry, Sanger began work on his sub-orbital aircraft that he called Silbervogel (Silver Bird). For the rest of the 1930s Sanger developed his craft that would launched from a 2-mile (3.2km) track at a speed of approximately 1,200mph. Once airborne, the Silbervogel would climb to an altitude of 90 miles (145km), propelled by its rocket motors, reaching a velocity of nearly 14,000mph. It would then descend in a sub-orbital trajectory, re-entering the upper atmosphere at the opposite pole, before dropping a 4,000kg bomb on the USA. The craft would then continue across the Pacific and land in Japan after a flight of some 15,000 miles (2,414km). Unfortunately for Sanger, his faith in the project wasn't reciprocated by the Air Ministry and they shelved the Silbervogel in 1942.

Cambridge University. The following year the patent expired on his jet engine and Whittle lacked the small sum required for its renewal. But at his lowest ebb came salvation. Two bankers—Maurice Bonham-Carter and Lancelot Law Whyte—backed up their belief in the project with money and in January 1936 Power Jets Ltd became a registered company.

That same year in Germany a brilliant young engineer called Hans Joachim Pabst von Ohain obtained a patent for something similar to Whittle's jet engine. In 1933, while a 22-year-old student, von Ohain had come up with an idea of "an engine that did not require a propeller." After finishing his degree in 1935 he continued work on his project and a year later took out a patent on a "Process and Apparatus for Producing Airstreams for Propelling Airplanes." The biggest difference between Whittle's patent and von Ohain's design was that the German's creation used a centrifugal compressor *and* turbine installed side by side and back to back, with the flame cans secured around the outside of the apparatus.

Unlike Whittle, who still had not gained the confidence and belief of the aircraft industry, von Ohain's design impressed the Heinkel aircraft manufacturer and together they built the first prototype. Powered by hydrogen gas that burned rapidly through the components, the jet turbine was a success and plans were laid to implement them in aircraft.

Back in England, meanwhile, Whittle was also finally making progress now he had the financial backing of his two bankers. In April 1937 the first Whittle jet engine ran and the following year the Air Ministry finally agreed to fund further development. There was, of course, a proviso. As they were investing in the jet engine it was now a military project and so it came under the Official Secrets Act. Whittle was forbidden from openly discussing his jet engine, frustrating to a man who had devoted a decade of his life to getting his idea off the ground.

But the Air Ministry funding accelerated research and development into what the RAF believed would be the world's first jet aircraft. It was called the Gloster-Whittle E28/39 and in April 1941 it took to the air for the first time with Whittle at the controls. It wasn't until the following month that the Gloster-Whittle underwent its inaugural test flight proper (this time without Whittle, who was ordered by the RAF to remain on the ground). Flying for nearly 20 minutes, the jet aircraft reached a top speed of 340mph and reached an altitude of 25,000ft (7,620m).

The British were mightily encouraged although the smiles would have vanished from their faces if they had known of developments in Germany. Heinkel had employed Hans von Ohain as a designer following the success of the trials of his jet engine in 1937. By the end of August 1939—just days before the start of World War II—von Ohain's third design was ready to be tested. In utter secrecy the jet plane, an He 178, piloted by Erich Warsitz, was launched and the results were a total success. Described as a "small plane with a metal fuselage of conventional configuration and construction," the He 178's jet intake was in the nose and it had a tail-wheel undercarriage. There was, however, one glaring weakness: its combat duration was just ten minutes.

But Germany now clearly saw—more so than the British—the potential of jet aircraft as war machines. The He 178 was the inspiration behind the twin-jet He 280, the world's first prototype jet fighter. When this came off the production line Heinkel used it to impress upon the Luftwaffe the superiority of the jet fighter compared to the propeller-driven fighter aircraft. Over a set course, the lighter He 280 outperformed a Focke-Wulfe Fw 190 fighter. The Luftwaffe were won over but instead of commissioning the He 280 they

BELOW LEFT Hans Joachim Pabst von Ohain, the brilliant young engineer who was employed as an aircraft designer by Heinkel following the success of the trials of his jet engine in 1937.

BELOW RIGHT Britain's answer to von Ohain was Frank Whittle, who struggled for financial backing initially but who later designed the Gloster-Whittle jet engine, which made its first flight in May 1941.

The Gloster E28/39 **(ABOVE LEFT)** was the first Allied jet aircraft to fly thanks to years of research by British engineer Frank Whittle, whose preliminary drawing **(BELOW LEFT)** eventually led to the E28/39 and its jet engine cockpit **(BELOW RIGHT)**.

OPPOSITE A Gloster Meteor in full flight. Less powerful than its German jet engine rival, the Me 262, the Gloster Meteor had a maximum speed of 410mph and was used at the tail end of the war to shoot down German flying rockets headed towards Britain.

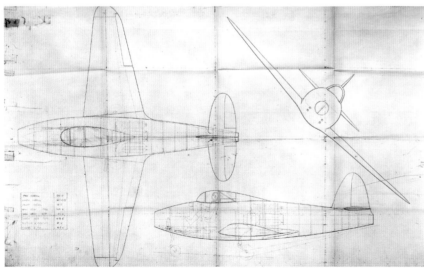

instead turned to Heinkel's great rival, the Messerschmitt company, to build the Me 262 Schwalbe (Swallow).

This entered operational service in July 1944, the same month as the RAF introduced their own jet fighter, the Gloster Meteor. Though they appeared in the sky at the same time there was no doubt that the Me 262 was the superior jet fighter. Faster than the Gloster Meteor (560mph to 410mph), the German fighter was also better armed and its pilots more willing to engage the enemy. In contrast the RAF were so concerned the Gloster Meteor might fall into enemy hands—and reveal secrets the Germans probably already knew—that they were ordered to fly over Allied territory and so spent the final months of the war shooting down German V-1 rockets as they were launched from across the Channel.

The Me 262 meanwhile were soon proving their worth against the British and American bombers conducting raids on German cities. Initially the Me 262s were hindered by their 30mm cannons that only became effective within 250 yards of an enemy aircraft—a serious problem given that the gunners on board American Flying Fortresses had a range of 800 yards. But this obstacle was soon overcome by the arrival of the R4M 5cm rocket. Fitted on wooden rails beneath the wings of an Me 262, the R4M fired 24 rockets with a cone of fire similar to that of a shotgun and from a range greater than that of the Flying Fortresses' guns.

Thus armed, the Me 262 became a deadly foe in the early spring of 1945. In the last week of February 1945 one fighter squadron of Me 262s—JG 7 "Hindenburg"—destroyed 45 four-engine bombers and 15 long-range fighters.

But despite the success of the German jet fighters, it was too little too late. The bomber stream over Germany by February 1945 was now as great as 2,000 at a time and there were too few Me 262s in service

ME 262

Type	Jet fighter aircraft
Crew	1
Length	34ft 9.5in (10.6m)
Wingspan	40ft 11.5in (12.4m)
Speed	541mph (870kmh)
Range	650 miles (1,046km)

The Messerschmitt company built its first jet engine, the Me 262 *Schwalbe* (Swallow), after seeing the success of von Ohain's designs with Heinkel. It entered operational service in July 1944 and caused great concern among Allied air crews. The Me 262 had the potential to inflict great damage on British and US aircraft had more of them been constructed before the end of the war. Nonetheless the appearance of the Me 262 ushered in a new era of aerial warfare—the jet age.

to pose a serious threat. Of the 1,294 built, only around a quarter ever flew combat missions. The fault for the shortage and, more significantly, their tardy introduction, lay with Hitler and the High Command. Air defense was always a low priority for Hitler, who liked to think only in terms of offensive action. Had he authorized—as his armament minister Albert Speer advised—the increased manufacture of more Me 262s earlier in the war who knows what might have been the outcome. But a glimpse was seen on April 7, 1945, when the JG7 squadron of Me 262s targeted the American bombers' fighter escorts, shooting down 28 Mustangs in one day with minimal losses themselves. In the same 24 hours 133 German propeller fighters—Me 109s and Fw 190s—were destroyed by American aircraft. So grave was the menace of the Me 262s that three days after their destruction of the 28 Mustangs, some 1,200 Allied bombers targeted their bases in and around Berlin. Never again would they pose the same level of threat to the American bombers.

Nonetheless in their brief operational life, the Me 262s had changed the face of aerial warfare. In its edition of February 1 the *New York Times* carried an article headlined "Jet Planes to play Bigger Role in War." The correspondent then predicted that the Me 262 had proved that "the jet-propelled fighter plane … will displace 'to a great degree' the standard type of fighter-escort craft" in future wars. He was right. The age of the jet fighter had arrived.

An Me 262 in production in 1944. Nazi armament minister Albert Speer had advised Hitler to authorize the increased manufacture of the Me-262 but the Fuhrer ignored his pleas.

THE MANHATTAN PROJECT AND THE ATOMIC AGE

On August 2 1939 Albert Einstein wrote a letter to Franklin D. Roosevelt, president of the United States, in which he began by outlining the latest research into harnessing the power of uranium conducted by Frederic Joliot in France and Leo Szilard in the USA. Einstein said a new era had dawned in warfare that would result in the construction of extremely powerful bombs. "A single bomb of this type, carried by boat and exploded in a port, might very well destroy the whole port together with some of the surrounding territory," wrote Einstein. The purpose of the letter wasn't just to keep the president informed of the latest developments in atomic research; Einstein was after increased government funding, particularly—as he pointed out to Roosevelt—since the Germans were starting to realize the important of atomic research and had halted the sale of uranium to America from Europe.

The letter had the desired effect. Roosevelt authorised the establishment of the "Advisory Uranium Committee," led by Lyman Briggs, to report back to him on the state of America's atomic research. The committee soon realized that fewer fissile materials were required to produce a

▲ The S-1 Uranium Committee at the Bohemian Grove, September 13, 1942. From left to right: Harold C. Urey, Ernest O. Lawrence, James B. Conant, Lyman J.Briggs, E. V. Murphree, and Arthur Compton.

bomb than originally thought and the committee reported back to Roosevelt in November 1939 that uranium "would provide a possible source of bombs with a destructiveness vastly greater than anything now known."

Roosevelt gave the go-ahead for scientists to start work on developing the world's first atomic bomb in October 1941, putting the army in charge of the overall running of the project. It was codenamed the "Manhattan Project because so many of the people involved were based in Manhattan in some of the ten research sites."

Work began in utter secrecy and although an estimated 5,000 people were involved in the Manhattan Project hardly any knew what the project's ultimate aim was: they worked only on their small area of expertise. At the heart of the research was the S-1 Uranium Committee although soon the word "uranium" was dropped for reasons of secrecy.

Money was no constraint to the Manhattan Project and the Committee applied for and received a budget totalling $54m. They also began recruiting some of the world's best scientists, including some from Britain and a theoretical physicist from California called Robert Oppenheimer. His task was to lead research into fast neutron calculations, critical to the understanding of critical mass and weapon detonation.

The day after the successful test Leo Szilard, one of the driving forces behind America's atomic program, drafted a petition—signed by 69 of his fellow scientists on the Manhattan Project—stating their opposition to the use of the bomb against civilian populations. Though the war with Germany was over President Harry Truman (who had succeeded Roosevelt following his death in April 1945) was already being advised by some of his military chiefs to use the bomb against Japan. Szilard and his cosignatories were horrified at the idea, writing:

"We, the undersigned, respectfully petition: first, that you exercise your power as Commander-in-Chief, to rule that the United States shall not resort to the use

THE ATOMIC TOOL

The first scientific research into the science that would lead eventually to the world's first atom bomb began in 1896 when a French scientist, Antoine Henri Becquerel, observed that uranium clouded a photographic plate even in a darkened room. He had inadvertently discovered radioactivity. Research progressed little in the three decades that followed but in 1932 two British scientists—Ernest Rutherford, often referred to as the "father of nuclear physics," and James Chadwick—made important discoveries, with the latter identifying the neutron and Rutherford observing the splitting of the nucleus. The crucial breakthrough, however, came in 1938 when two German scientists, Otto Hahn and Fritz Strassmann, split the atom. Hahn then passed on details to his Jewish friend and fellow scientist Lise Meitner, who fled Germany that same year, and began some research of her own in Sweden. In 1939 Meitner and her nephew, Otto Frisch, calculated the basic mathematics of nuclear fission and the huge amounts of energy that would be released in a nuclear explosion. The final scientific evidence of nuclear power came from a French physicist, Frederic Joliot, whose research demonstrated that "when the atomic nuclei were split in two, neutrons were ejected—and they would trigger a chain reaction."

of atomic bombs in this war unless the terms which will be imposed upon Japan have been made public in detail and Japan knowing these terms has refused to surrender; second, that in such an event the question whether or not to use atomic bombs be decided by you in the light of the considerations presented in this petition as well as all the other moral responsibilities which are involved."

Truman now faced an awful dilemma. As he confided to his diary on learning of the successful Trinity Test: "We have discovered the most terrible bomb in the history of the world. It may be the fire destruction prophesied in the Euphrates Valley Era, after Noah and his fabulous Ark." But to actually use it?

He asked General George Marshall, his chief of staff, what would it cost in lives if he ordered a land invasion of Japan. "It was his opinion that such an invasion would cost at a minimum a quarter of a million American casualties."

Truman warned Japan that he had a terrible new weapon and called on them to surrender. When they rejected his demands to sue for peace, Truman ordered the dropping of the first atomic bomb.

Where to drop it had been the subject of intense conversation for months. As early as April 1945 a long list of targets was drafted: Tokyo Bay, Kawasaki, Yokohama, Nagoya, Osaka, Kobe, Kyoto, Hiroshima, Kure, Yahata, Kokura, Shimonoseki, Yamaguchi, Kumamoto, Fukuoka, Nagasaki, Sasebo. By the end of July the list was narrowed down to Hiroshima, Kokura, Niigata, Nagasaki. On the 31st of the month Hiroshima was selected.

Situated in the southwest of Japan—approximately 500 miles (805km) from Tokyo—Hiroshima had a high concentration of troops and military installations and, unlike large swathes of Japan that had been heavily fire-bombed in recent months, it was relatively intact. This would make it easier for the Americans to assess the extent of the damage caused by their secret weapon.

MANHATTAN PROJECT SITES

In October 1942, as the S1 Committee began searching for a test site, Oppenheimer suggested Albuquerque in New Mexico where he owned a ranch. After several surveys a suitable site was found near the Los Alamos Ranch School and this was purchased by the federal government and codenamed "Site Y." Meanwhile research facilities were built at Oak Ridge, Tennessee (Site X) and all workers were subjected to tightest security imaginable on a daily basis.

There were three production facility sites at Oak Ridge, all located in valleys away from the nearby city of Knoxville, including a medium-sized reactor that produced uranium-235 and plutonium. This ensured the utmost secrecy but was also a caution against an accidental explosions. The residents of Knoxville—population 111,000—had no idea of course of the nature of the research at Oak Ridge, but they resented the fact that workers had unlimited ration stamps and the cash to buy what they wanted in the city.

But life at Oak Ridge had its drawbacks. Not only was the work demanding and relentless, but so was the security. Everyone and every vehicle was thoroughly searched leaving and entering the facilities and one worker later recalled that "if you got inquisitive, you were called on the carpet within two hours by government secret agents. Usually those summoned to explain were then escorted with bag and baggage to the gate and ordered to keep going."

By early 1945 the Manhattan Project scientists were ready to test a bomb. The site at New Mexico was Alamogordo and the date selected for the test (codenamed "Trinity") was July 16. Initially 0400 hours was the hour when the implosion plutonium bomb would be detonated but a thunderstorm delayed this by 90 minutes. The postponement only increased the tension among those present, including Enrico Fermi, director of the first nuclear chain reaction two and a half years earlier, Oppenheimer and several high-ranking military officers. Then at 0530 hours the bomb was exploded, detonating with 20 kilotons of force and disintegrating the 100ft (30m) metal tower beneath it. There was an intense blinding flash, a great blast of heat and a burst of sound reverberating through the valley. Witnesses estimated that the mushroom cloud caused by the explosion measured some 40,000ft (1,219m) across.

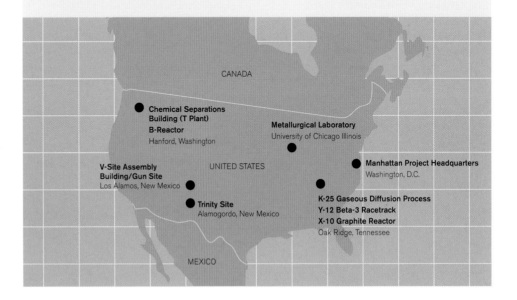

CANADA

Chemical Separations Building (T Plant)
B-Reactor
Hanford, Washington

Metallurgical Laboratory
University of Chicago Illinois

V-Site Assembly Building/Gun Site
Los Alamos, New Mexico

UNITED STATES

Manhattan Project Headquarters
Washington, D.C.

Trinity Site
Alamogordo, New Mexico

K-25 Gaseous Diffusion Process
Y-12 Beta-3 Racetrack
X-10 Graphite Reactor
Oak Ridge, Tennessee

MEXICO

OPPOSITE AND BELOW Scientists and workmen rig the world's first atomic bomb to raise it up onto a 100ft (30m) tower at the Trinity bomb test site near Alamogordo, New Mexico, July 6, 1945.

ABOVE RIGHT The blast that followed ten days later was captured on camera. The heat generated within the bomb's explosion was near 100 million degrees, more than 10 times the heat at the surface of the sun.

BELOW RIGHT An aerial view of the atomic bomb testing site shows the shallow crater dug by the blast 300ft (91m) around the tower from which the bomb hung. The area devastated by the bomb measured 4,800ft (1,463m) in diameter, and the steel tower that had been assembled 10 days earlier was entirely disintegrated.

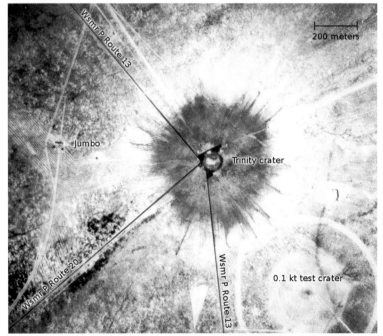

With the target selected, the crew was chosen to drop the bomb. The task fell to Colonel Paul W. Tibbets, a vastly experienced bomber pilot who commanded the 509th Composite Group. Flying a B-29, *Enola Gay*, Tibbets, took off from the island of Tinian in the North Pacific at 0245 hours on August 6. In the aircraft's bomb bay was "Little Boy," an atomic bomb measuring 28in (71cm) in diameter and 10ft (3m) in length. Only Tibbets of his crew of 12 knew the exact type of bomb they were carrying, a secret he revealed four hours into the flight. There was, however, another fact he failed to disclose: the dozen cyanide pills he had been given in the event they were shot down. He had also been told by his superiors that he was to shoot anyone who refused to take theirs lest the Japanese captured any of the crew alive.

Rendezvousing with two escorts over the Pacific island of Iwo Jima, the *Enola Gay* continued on towards Hiroshima, arriving just 17 seconds behind schedule. At 0815 hours local time the bomb was released. It took 43 seconds to fall from the *Enola Gay*'s altitude of 31,500ft (9,601m) to its detonation height of 1,900ft (179m).

The *Enola Gay* was 9 miles (14.5km) from Hiroshima when the bomb exploded, but the aircraft was buffeted by the force of the explosion, equivalent to 16 kilotons of TNT. "Fellows," said Tibbets over the aircraft's radio, "you have just dropped the first atomic bomb in history." Hiroshima was devastated by the explosion. Japanese officials estimated that nearly 70 per cent of the city's buildings were destroyed and another 6 to 7 per cent damaged. Between 70,000 and 80,000 people (30 per cent of the city's population) were killed by the blast and resultant firestorm. Thousands more would suffer for the rest of their lives from radiation.

Despite the appalling destruction Japan still refused to surrender. So Truman ordered the dropping of a second bomb, this one plutonium as opposed to the uranium-235 used at Hiroshima. Nicknamed "Fat Man," it weighed 4,670kg and it was dropped on the

DR. YOSHIO NISHINA

The rivalry that existed between decryption units in the Japanese army and navy (see page 72) also existed in their atomic research units, hindering the nation's development program. Both the Imperial Japanese Navy and the Imperial Japanese Army—the latter's, headed by Dr. Yoshio Nishina (who had known Albert Einstein)—made most progress in developing an atomic bomb. In 1931 Nishina established the Rikken Institute's Laboratory for Chemistry and Physics near Tokyo and throughout the 1930s he continued his civilian research until, in the summer of 1941, he began receiving funding from the army to work on what was codenamed the *Nichi* (Sun) project. In 1943 Japan approached Germany, requesting highly enriched uranium, a key component in an atomic bomb, but these communiqués were intercepted and read by Britain's Ultra codebreakers. Although a small quantity of uranium was shipped to Japan, the factories were it was stored were destroyed in Allied bombing raids. Eventually Nishina moved his project to northern Korea but he never succeeded in testing a bomb before America's attacks on Hiroshima and Nagasaki. The Japanese navy where similarly unsuccessful in their atomic research, known as the Kyoto Project and led by scientist Professor Bunsaku Arakatsu.

city of Nagasaki on August 9. Approximately 70,000 people died as a result of the bomb.

The dropping of a third bomb was planned but on August 14 Japan surrendered. Arguments over the bombing of Hiroshima and Nagasaki have raged ever since with some arguing it was the only way to defeat Japan and others saying it violated civilization.

One thing is certain. The destructive power of the atomic bombs shook the world so much that none has been used since, and nor hopefully will ever again.

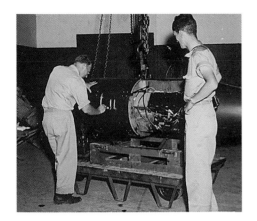

Commander A. F. Birch checks the "Little Boy" bomb **(ABOVE FAR LEFT)** before overseeing its loading onto a trailer ready to be transported to the *Enola Gay*. Three days after the first bomb, a second was dropped on Nagasaki. Called "Fat Man" it was similar to the one in the photograph **(ABOVE LEFT)** and differed from the Hiroshima bomb in that it was composed of plutonium and not uranium.

BELOW LEFT On August 6, 1945, the aircraft *Enola Gay* dropped the world's first atomic bomb on the Japanese city of Hiroshima. Dubbed "Little Boy," the bomb took 43 seconds to fall from the *Enola Gay*'s altitude of 31,500ft (9,601m) to its detonation height of 1,900ft (579m). In the resultant explosion between 70,000 and 80,000 people (30 per cent of the city's population) were killed.

EPILOGUE–THE SECRET COLD WAR

The end of World War II ushered in a new conflict—the Cold War, a decades-long stand-off between the "Eastern Bloc," those communist countries controlled by the Soviet Union, and the nations that comprised NATO (North Atlantic Treaty Organization), primarily the USA, Britain, and West Germany.

The British in particular struggled to adapt to a cold war as opposed to the "hot" war of 1939 to 1945. Within weeks of VJ Day, the War Office disbanded its Special Forces units—the SAS, SBS, and Long Range Desert Group—believing that there was no longer a need for such covert units. The attitude towards the Special Operations Executive was equally naïve and hostile, despite the protestations of Lord Roundell Selborne, the Minister of Economic Warfare, under whose auspices the SOE fell. He warned the government that an intelligence agency would be needed to counter "the Russian menace." But the new Labour government under Clement Attlee—who deposed Winston Churchill in the general election of July 1945—was blind to such entreaties. In January 1946 Attlee ordered the dissolution of the SOE and though a small number of personnel were subsumed into MI6, the majority returned to civilian life.

It was a terrible mistake on the part of the British Establishment, whose prevailing view was that intelligence work was the preserve of the well-connected and well-educated—men such as Kim Philby, the son of a distinguished civil servant and a graduate of Cambridge University in the 1930s. Philby was considered a rising star in MI6 as were the other members of the "Cambridge Five"—Donald Maclean, Anthony Blunt, Guy Burgess, and a fifth man who has never been publicly identified. All were highly regarded by British intelligence, but even more by Soviet intelligence, who had recruited the men as communist spies in the 1930s.

For years the men passed secrets to the Soviets before Burgess and Maclean defected in 1951. However, it was another five years before they were paraded by the Russians as double agents. According to the espionage historian Ben Macintyre, the exposure of Burgess and Maclean woke up British intelligence to the reality of Cold War espionage. "There was a feeling if you were the right sort, if you sounded right, if you'd been to the right schools, if you spoke with the right accent, then you could not be therefore anything other than what you seemed to be," said Macintyre. "[They] exposed one of the fault lines in British establishment life … making people realize people who look perfect on the outside may be far from perfect on the inside."

Whereas in World War II the Americans had leaned heavily on the British initially in the establishment of an intelligence service, in the Cold War it was vice versa. Initially, the American government was as short-sighted as the British vis-à-vis a future need for an intelligence agency. President Harry Truman disliked William "Wild Bill" Donovan, the man who had founded the Office of Strategic Services (OSS) and feared "that Donovan's proposed intelligence establishment might one day be used against Americans."

In September 1945 Truman signed the Executive Order that dissolved the OSS as of October 1, 1945 and Donovan had ten days to wind up his agency after four years of unstinting work on behalf of his country. In his address to his staff, Donovan told them: "You can go with the assurance that you have made a beginning in showing the people of America that only by decisions of national policy based upon accurate information can we have the chance of a peace that will endure."

Fortunately for the USA not everyone in authority regarded the OSS as a threat to the nation. Secretary of War Robert Patterson adopted a liberal interpretation of the presidential directive and ordered the military to "preserve as a unit such of these functions and facilities as are valuable for permanent peacetime purposes."

Two years later, as the threat posed by the Soviet Union became ever more alarming, the United States Congress passed the National Security Act of 1947, a component of which was the establishment of the Central Intelligence Agency (CIA).

For the next 43 years the CIA was at the forefront of the Cold War, implementing many of the lessons it had learned in the intelligence war against Germany's National Socialism in the struggle against Soviet communism.

In 1988, as communism entered its death throes, a service of dedication was held at CIA headquarters at the unveiling of a statue of General William J. Donovan, founder of the OSS nearly half a century earlier. In his address the then director of the CIA, William Webster, honored the work of his founder, declaring:

"To those of us here today, this is General Donovan's greatest legacy. He realized that a modern intelligence organization must not only provide today's tactical intelligence, it must provide tomorrow's long-term assessments. He recognized that an effective intelligence organization must not allow political pressures to influence its counsel. And, finally, he knew that no intelligence organization can succeed without recognizing the importance of people—people with discretion, ingenuity, loyalty, and a deep sense of responsibility to protect and promote American values."

▲ The Central Intelligence Agency (CIA) headquarters in Langley, Virginia, where, in 1988, a statue was unveiled of General William J. Donovan, founder of the OSS nearly half a century earlier. The statue is a permanent reminder of the fact that the CIA owes its existence to the vision of "Wild Bill" Donovan.

BIBLIOGRAPHY/FURTHER READING

Bagnold, Ralph
Sun, Sea, War & Wind
University of Arizona Press, 1991

Bekker, Cajus
The Luftwaffe War Diaries
Birlinn, 2001

Bierman, John & Smith, Colin
Alamein
Penguin, 2003

Borghese, Valerio J.
Sea Devils
Naval Institute Press, 1995

Breuer, William B.
Deceptions of World War II
John Wiley & Sons, 2001

Breuer, William B.
Secret Weapons of World War II
John Wiley, 2001

Cowles, Virginia
The Phantom Major
Collins, 1958

Dimbleby, Richard
The Frontiers Are Green
Hodder & Stoughton, 1943

Ford, Brian J.
Secret Weapons
Osprey 2011

Gilchrist, Donald
Castle Commando
Oliver & Boyd, 1960

James, Malcolm
Born of the Desert
Greenhill Books, 1991

Kelly, Saul
The Hunt for Zerzura
John Murray, 2003

Kurowski, Franz
Jump Into Hell
Stackpole, 2010

Lewin, Ronald
The Life & Death of the Afrika Korps
Pen & Sword, 2003

Liddell Hart, B.H
History of the Second World War
Cassell, 1970

Liddell Hart, Basil
The Rommel Papers
DaCapo Press, 1982

Linklater, Eric
The Campaign in Italy
Her Majesty's Stationary Office, 1951

Lloyd-Owen, David
The Desert My Dwelling Place
Cassell, 1957

Lloyd-Owen, David
The Long Range Desert Group
Pen & Sword, 2001

Maclean, Fitzroy
Eastern Approaches
Penguin, 1991

Moorehead, Alan
Desert War: The North African Campaign
H. Hamilton, 1965

Mortimer, Gavin
The Daring Dozen
Osprey, 2011

Mortimer, Gavin
The History of the Special Air Service in WW2
Osprey, 2012

Mortimer, Gavin
**Stirling's Men: the Inside History of
the SAS WW2**
Weidenfeld, 2004

Mortimer, Gavin
The Longest Night: Voices from the Blitz
Weidenfeld, 2005

Mortimer, Gavin
**The Men Who Made the SAS: History of the
Long Range Desert Group**
Constable, 2015

Mortimer, Gavin
Merrill's Marauders
Zenith Press, 2013

Peniakoff, Vladimir
Popski's Private Army
Harper & Collins, 1975

Pitt, Barrie
Special Boat Squadron
Corgi, 1985

Public Record Office
Special Forces in the Desert War 1940-1943
PRO Publications, 2001

Rankin, Nicholas
**Churchill's Wizards: The British Genius
for Deception**
Faber & Faber 2008

Saunders, H. St. G.
**The Green Beret: The Story of the
Commandos 1940-45**
Michael Joseph, 1949

Schmidt, Heinz W.
With Rommel in the Desert
Constable, 1998

Smith, Peter C.
Massacre at Tobruk
Stackpole Books, 2008

Smith, Peter C.
War in the Aegean
Stackpole Books, 2008

Timpson, Alistair
In Rommel's Backyard
Pen & Sword, 2010

Thompson, Julian
The War Behind Enemy Lines
Pan, 1999

Townsend, Peter
Duel in the Dark
Harrap, 1986

Von der Heydte, Baron
Return to Crete
WDL, 1959

Young, Martin & Stamp, Robbie
**Trojan Horses: Deception Operations
in Second World War**
Mandarin, 1989

INDEX

Ship names are shown in *italics*